Historic Ann Arbor:
An Architectural Guide

by Susan Wineberg and Patrick McCauley

First Edition

Historic Ann Arbor: An Architectural Guide

First Edition

Copyright © 2014 by the Ann Arbor Historical Foundation

Printed in the United States of America

Library of Congress Preassigned Control Number: 2014930254

ISBN: 978-0-9913466-0-8

Ann Arbor Historical Foundation
P. O. Box 7973
Ann Arbor, MI 48107

Table of Contents

Acknowledgements

W e would like to especially thank the board members of the Ann Arbor Historic Foundation—particularly Patricia Austin, Louisa Pieper, Pauline Walters, Ellen Ramsburgh, Mark Hildebrandt, Grace Shackman, Judy Chrisman, Ingrid Sheldon, Sabra Briere, Bev Willis, Carol Mull, Ed Rice, and Allison Poggi—for their efforts on behalf of this project. It has truly been a joint effort and we appreciate their editing expertise, their historical knowledge, and their enthusiasm for this project. It has been a labor of love for all of us.

Many others in the community have helped us with this book. Our thanks go to Fred Mayer, retired planner at the University of Michigan; Julie Truettner at the U-M Department of Architecture, Engineering and Construction; Karen Jania and the staff of the U-M Bentley Library; Amy Cantu and the helpful staff at the Ann Arbor District Library; Jill Thacher of the Ann Arbor Historic District Commission; Nancy Deromedi of A2 Modern; Wystan Stevens; Ray Detter; Terri Bartholomew, former president of the Ann Arbor Historic Foundation; and the staff at the Washtenaw County Register of Deeds. We are extremely grateful to our editor Peter Glaberman who was the first to labor over the text and Christine Victor, Jonathan Higgins, and Heather Galanty who designed, illustrated, and proofread the text. We'd also like to thank Jim Curtiss, who helped with our printing needs.

We also want to give a special thank you to our long-suffering spouses Andrea Kinney and Lars Bjorn.

—The Authors

"*We shape our buildings, and afterwards they shape us.*"

—Winston Churchill

Ann Arbor Historical Foundation
Board of Directors
2013–14

Preface

The Ann Arbor Historical Foundation has updated its previous guidebook to help educate the citizens of Ann Arbor about its great architectural heritage. This guide is a complete revision of a previous edition published in 1992 and slightly revised in 1998, entitled *Historic Buildings, Ann Arbor, Michigan*. It contains over 200 new entries, with a total of 375. This guide also includes 37 more University of Michigan buildings which were selected to represent important buildings on Central Campus, North Campus, and the Sports Campus. The Central Campus was declared the "Central Campus Historic District" and put on the National Register of Historic Places in 1978. Since the last edition, the city has added the Broadway Historic District to its roster of historic districts. We also have many new entries for modern architecture (post-World War II). However, the Individual Historic District was declared illegal in 2001 and no longer exists.

The guide has also added styles that were not in the previous edition, including Federal, Vernacular/Folk, Second Empire, Stick, Colonial/Georgian Revival, Spanish/Mission Revival, Arts and Crafts/Craftsman, Tudor Revival, Prairie, Collegiate Gothic, Art Moderne, Mid-Century Modern, and Brutalist.

We have divided the guide into neighborhoods, each with an accompanying map and explanatory text. All photographs were taken by the authors. Many of the buildings are in historic districts which are indicated at the end of the entry:

ASHB—Ann Street Historic Block (1979)

BHD—Broadway Historic District (2008)

CCHD—Central Campus Historic District (1978)

CFHD—Cobblestone Farm Historic District (1982)

DSHD—Division Street Historic District (1973)

ELHDB—East Liberty Street Historic Block (1992)

EWHD—East William Street Historic District (1989)

FAHD—Fourth/Ann Historic District (1989)

HABS—Historic American Buildings Survey

HDC—Historic District Commission

IHP—Individual Historic Properties

LSHD—Liberty Street Historic District (West) (1975)

MHPN—Michigan Historic Preservation Network

MSHD—Main Street Historic District (1989)

NBHD—Northern Brewery Historic District (1978)

NR—National Register of Historic Places

OFWHD—Old Fourth Ward Historic District (1983)

OWSHD—Old West Side Historic District (1978)

SR—State Register of Historic Places

SSHD—State Street Historic District (1992)

WHHD—Washtenaw/Hill Historic District I and II (1980 and 1986)

WSHD—William Street Historic District

Information about the historic districts is available through the City of Ann Arbor's website under Planning and Development: Historic Preservation:

http://www.a2gov.org/government/communityservices/planninganddevelopment/historicpreservation/Pages/Historic%20District%20Commission%20Main%20Page.aspx.

We have written this guide because we believe that an informed public is the best way to protect our local historic resources. Many of our historic buildings remain unprotected by local ordinances and we hope this guide will help preserve them for future generations.

About the Authors

Patrick McCauley is a lifelong resident of the Ann Arbor area, growing up in Salem and Superior Townships. He is a graduate of the University of Michigan (class of 2000) with a bachelor's degree in history. His love of historic architecture began during his 25 years of working on historic homes with his family's house painting and home restoration business. He has bought and restored three neglected historic homes in Ann Arbor since 2001, winning a Rehabilitation Award from the Ann Arbor Historic District Commission (HDC) in 2009 for his efforts. McCauley has volunteered at both the Kempf House Museum and Cobblestone Farm Museum, and served as Chair of the Germantown Historic District Study Committee. He currently serves on the Ann Arbor Historic District Commission, having held the positions of Chair and Vice Chair, and also on the board of the Ann Arbor Historical Foundation. He lives with his wife Andrea Kinney in a historic Greek Revival home on Ann Arbor's north side.

Susan Cee Wineberg was born and raised in Chicago, where she acquired her love of all things architectural, old and new. Her home was a Mid-Century Modern townhouse designed by a student of Mies van der Rohe. She came to Ann Arbor in 1964, worked as an archaeologist in Turkey, and obtained advanced degrees in Near Eastern Studies and Anthropology. The Ann Arbor Sesquicentennial and American Bicentennial fueled her interest in local history and in 1993 she obtained an MS in Historic Preservation at Eastern Michigan University.

Susan has served as President of the Washtenaw County Historical Society (1994–1999); on the Historic District Commission three times; as Chair of the Awards Committee of the HDC for 20 years; and on numerous committees, including the Downtown, Landmark, Individual Historic Properties, Lower Town, Old Fourth Ward, and Germantown Historic District Study Committees. She has written extensively on Ann Arbor and published *Lost Ann Arbor* in 2004, in addition to the second edition of this book, formerly entitled *Historic Buildings, Ann Arbor, Michigan*, in 1992. She lives with her husband Lars Bjorn in an 1850 Greek Revival house in the Old Fourth Ward Historic District.

Introduction

by Grace Shackman

I purchased the earlier version of this book (*Historic Buildings, Ann Arbor, Michigan*) in 1977 for $3.74 at the first Border's bookstore on State Street, where they put them on the checkout counter to encourage impulse buying. I remember being totally amazed that so much local history was retrievable. When I started writing about local history a few years later, I often referred to it and the second edition as a starting point for my research. This new edition will be even more valuable with more buildings, updates, and corrections.

In 1974, Ann Arbor was celebrating its 150th birthday with a number of events organized by a Sesquicentennial Commission. They appointed a Historic Marker Committee to select and research homes that merited special notice. The committee came up with a list of seventy-three buildings that needed recognition, and thus came the idea for the book. The first edition was written by Marjorie Reade, a member of this committee, with a few contributions from others. Frank Wilhelme, then-chair of the Historic District Commission, wrote in the introduction, "We hope to promote greater awareness of local history by calling attention to some of the city's outstanding buildings." The book sold well and was reprinted in 1986. Wilhelme's hope was realized in that none of the buildings in the first book have been torn down and quite a number have been restored.

In the late 1980s, Susan Wineberg was approached by Marjorie to help with an update. Susan had done the research on the Old Fourth Ward that qualified it to become an historic district and was in the process of earning a master's degree in historic preservation at Eastern Michigan University. Louisa Pieper, staff for the Ann Arbor Historic District Commission, secured several grants to help pay for labor and production. Marge reworked her original write-ups, adding new information and making corrections, while Susan wrote the new sections on about 100 buildings. When it was published in 1992 as the second edition, the book was well received and reprinted in 1998 with a few corrections. Used by teachers, librarians, researchers, homeowners—the list goes on—it made its way to countless bookshelves in the community.

After more than twenty years, the book clearly needed updating. Some of the buildings had been lost: the Freeman House at 1315 Hill, the Gaskell-Beakes House at 415 S. Fifth Avenue, the Art Deco Anberay Apartments at 619 East University, and the Spanish-style Planada Apartments at 1127 E. Ann. Others had reached the age of 50 and thus qualified for inclusion, especially our unique stock of Mid-Century Modern houses. Earlier editions had only three University of Michigan buildings (those on the National Register): the Detroit Observatory, the President's House, and Newberry Hall. This edition recognizes many more that are important parts of our community's architectural heritage.

For the new edition, *Historic Ann Arbor: An Architectural Guide*, Susan took her old mentor's role and re-worked her original entries. In the years since the book came out she had been keeping careful notes as new information surfaced or as errors were identified. The proliferation of historic websites and search engines like Google made new information available. Patrick McCauley, a U-M history graduate who has painted and done restoration work on many of Ann Arbor's historic homes, took Susan's old role of writing and researching the new sections. This edition has over 200 new entries, including almost 40 on campus. Keeping with the times, there will also be an e-Book version.

Patrick and Susan have produced a book that not only contains prodigious research about each building, but also puts them in context with the architectural styles explained in the front section and historic information included in overviews of each neighborhood. Susan and Patrick's love of Ann Arbor shines through every page.

—Grace Shackman

Architectural Styles of Ann Arbor, 1824–1971

The Federal Style (1780–1840)

Many of the city's earliest buildings were built in the Federal style, as can be seen in photographs of long-demolished structures. The Federal style is an American version of the English Adam style of the late 18th and early 19th centuries, and is characterized by elliptical or semicircular fanlights over the doors or windows, three-part Palladian windows, dentils in the cornice, and delicate, classically inspired exterior detailing. The form is also characterized by gables facing the sides of the houses, with a center entry in a symmetrical shoebox shape.

Perhaps the only remaining purely Federal-style building in Ann Arbor is the Exchange Block (see #3) built by Anson Brown in 1832. It features "blind arches" over the lower doors and windows and stepped parapet gables. The simple Mills-Corselius-Breed House (see #124) once contained elements of the Federal style that have since been removed in various renovations. The Federal style remains in some of the detailing of primarily Greek Revival buildings. Examples include the delicate gable returns of the Perry House (see #19), the fanlight in the north gable of the 1830s Kellogg-Warden House (see #190), and the stepped, parapeted gables of the Enoch James House (see #78). Palladian windows can be seen on the Reader Center at the U-M Arboretum (see #241). The more muscular and substantial classical detailing of the Greek Revival style quickly replaced the Federal style as the 1830s came to a close.

The Greek Revival Style (1820–1870)

The Greek Revival style dominated from the founding of Ann Arbor in 1824 through the end of the Civil War in 1865. With the end of the War of 1812, Americans sought a new national style and found inspiration from ancient Greece, whose democratic ideals matched their own. This peaked after the 1820s when Greece won its war of independence from the Turks. Greek temples, especially the Parthenon, were often the model. For less high-style buildings, several books were influential, especially Asher Benjamin's pattern books: *The American Builder's Companion* (1816) and *The Builder's Guide* (1838). Also important were pattern books by Minard Lefever: *The Modern Builder's Guide* (1833) and *The Beauties of Modern Architecture* (1835).

The style is characterized by a gable-front orientation, symmetrical and rectangular massing, low-pitched roofs, and heavy classical detailing: full or broken pediments in the gables, porches and porticoes, round or square columns, elaborate front door surrounds featuring classical pilasters, and sidelight and transom windows. One of the biggest transformations of the Greek Revival period is the orientation to the street, with the front door on the side rather than in the center.

Ann Arbor's Greek Revival buildings range from simple buildings with minor classical detailing, such as the c. 1850 Kuhn House (see #269), to elaborate temple-style buildings, such as the Wilson-Wahr House (see #144), which is considered to be one of the finest Greek Revival homes in the country. The more modest temple style is seen in the 1853 Bennett-Kempf House (#53). Buildings were either constructed with heavy timbers joined using the mortise and tenon system, or of solid masonry. They were either of wood clapboard siding, or of brick or adobe. The latter were often coated in stucco and scored to look like stone blocks to resemble ancient temples. Ann Arbor had so many of these stucco-over-brick houses in the 1840s that it was referred to as "a little stucco village."

The Vernacular or Folk Form (1840–1920)

Many of Ann Arbor's historic buildings were not built in any particular style and relied on traditional building forms decorated with minor detailing in the prevailing styles of the day. Often called Vernacular or Folk Houses, the three most dominant types built in Ann Arbor were the I-House, the Gabled Front or Homestead, and the Upright and Wing. These types are based on floor plans and massing rather than on exterior detailing, and therefore are not considered "styles."

The I-House (1830–1870)

The I-House is a traditional British Folk form that was used throughout the U.S. but was most popular in the South and Midwest, deriving its name from its appearance in states beginning with "I" (Illinois, Indiana, Iowa). An I-House has a central entry door, is two stories tall and one room deep, and has the long side of the house facing the street (i.e., side gabled). Examples include the 1847 Jackson-Weitbrecht House (see #268) and the 1837 Doty-Pulcipher House (see #6), both of which are embellished with some classical detailing.

Gable Front or Homestead (1860–1920)

Gable Front or Homestead buildings are an offshoot of the popular Greek Revival style. Post-Civil War urbanism and narrow city lots made this the dominant form of "Folk" building in late 19th-century Ann Arbor. They are usually two stories tall with the gable end facing the street. Many feature full-width front porches with Victorian, Colonial Revival, or Craftsman-style detailing. The Old West Side contains hundreds of great examples of this form, including the c. 1885 Wiegant-Hochrein House (see #282) and the 1910s homes of Mulholland and Murray Streets (see #277).

Upright and Wing Form (1850–1890)

Upright and Wing homes (sometimes called Gable Front and Wing) were another popular Vernacular building form that began during the Greek Revival era but really flourished following the Civil War. The

homes consist of a front gable portion with a side wing projecting out at a right angle, creating a T or L-shaped building. Usually the gable portion has no porch and the side wing has a porch spanning its width. A great example of this style is the 1885 Roth House (see #287). Often these began as Gable Front or Side Gable buildings and were added onto later as a family grew or increased its income. In the Hirth-Jenter House (see #266) and the Keating House (see #128), the architectural detailing makes it clear that the gable front and wing portions of the buildings were built in different periods.

The Italianate Style (1850–1880)

The Italianate style was a reaction to the rigidly formal, classical architecture that had dominated American buildings since the early 18th century. It combined the English picturesque with the buildings of Renaissance Italy, though American architects and builders ended up creating a truly unique architectural style. Several books were influential, including Palladio's *Four Books of Architecture* (1570), Andrew Jackson Downing's *Cottage Residences* (1842), and Alexander Jackson Davis' *Rural Residences* (1835).

Italianate buildings have low-pitched roofs that are either hipped or gabled with carved paired brackets in the eaves. Tall and narrow round-topped windows with large panes of glass are a hallmark of the style, as are bay windows and belvederes. Elaborate pediments above the windows are also common in

both domestic and commercial buildings. Quite often the cube shape is dominant for residences and are referred to as "Italianate Cubes" (see #123). High-style Italianate homes often featured towers or cupolas (see #325 and #353). Porches often have sawn decoration ("gingerbread") with thin, chamfered posts and no balustrade.

The Italianate style dominated Ann Arbor's downtown commercial district from 1860–1890, with many of the three-story brick business blocks built during this era. These buildings still define the character of downtown today, especially along Main Street, West Liberty, and Washington. The Walz Grocery Building (see #80) and Wagner Blacksmith Shop (see #117) are great and intact examples. Residential examples were executed in both solid masonry (see #56 and #161) and in wood (see #143), and were built almost exclusively by the city's wealthier residents.

The Gothic Revival Style (1845–1885)

The Gothic Revival style was also a reaction against the classicism that preceded it in the Georgian, Federal, and Greek Revival styles. It looked back to medieval architecture for its inspiration. Originating in Europe in the 18th century, Gothic Revival began to make an appearance in America by the 1830s, and proliferated thanks to the pattern books of architects like Alexander Jackson Davis and Andrew Jackson Downing.

Identifying features include asymmetrical facades, steeply pitched rooflines, tall and narrow windows, often with pointed (Gothic) arches, heavily decorated bargeboards with elaborate sawn trim, and large porches featuring Gothic-inspired gingerbread, including trefoils and quatrefoils. Many were brick covered in stucco.

Never a common style, Ann Arbor's earliest remaining Gothic Revival building is the stucco-covered, 1845 Silas Douglas House (see #173), which is also the first home in the city designed by an architect. Others were built in wood (see #256) or brick (see #145). A handful of beautiful fieldstone buildings and churches were built in the style during the 1860s and 1870s, all designed by the great British-trained Detroit architect Gordon Lloyd (see #149, #118, and #343).

The Second Empire Style (1855–1885)

There are only a handful of Second Empire buildings remaining in Ann Arbor. Along with Gothic Revival and Italianate, Second Empire was part of the Picturesque Movement that swept the country in the middle of the 19th century. Second Empire style was inspired by the French architecture popular under the reign of Napoleon III (itself a revival of an older style by the 17th-century Baroque architect Francois Mansart—hence the name Mansard for the signature roofs).

Second Empire buildings are distinguished by their distinctive dual-pitched, hipped Mansard roofs, Italianate-style arched windows with decorative hoods or pediments, and heavily carved brackets in the eaves. The only important examples remaining in the city are the Peter Brehm House built in 1870 (see #263) and the 1860 Peleg Marshall House at 400 S. Division, which has been significantly altered.

The Stick Style (1865–1890)

The style is characterized by large amounts of vertical, diagonal, and horizontal exterior carpentry or "stickwork." Buildings also have interlocking horizontal and vertical trim bands, decorative trusses in the gables, and steeply pitched rooflines. As such, the Stick style was a bridge between the Gothic Revival and Queen Anne, which quickly supplanted it while adopting many of its characteristics, including the wraparound porch, spindle detailing, stylized chimneys, and intersecting roof planes.

There are few, if any, purely Stick-style buildings in Ann Arbor, though many have Stick-style trim along with elements of the Gothic Revival and Queen Anne styles (see #25 and #126).

The Queen Anne Style (1875–1910)

The name is not technically correct since Queen Anne buildings were a revival of the architecture of Elizabethan and Jacobean England from the 16th and 17th centuries, not the English Baroque style of the 18th century during the reign of Queen Anne. In America, mass production and the availability of large amounts of wood and other materials led to a completely original American version of the style.

Technological advances of the post-Civil War era allowed the Queen Anne style to become the quintessential "Victorian" home (Victorian refers to the reign of Queen Victoria in England, which lasted from 1837–1901). Lighter "balloon" framing allowed homes to be larger, less boxy, and more asymmetrical, with more complicated rooflines with multiple hipped and/or gabled roofs, cross gables, and turrets. Mass production allowed affordable sawn trim, shingles, and turned spindle work, which were used extensively. Leaded and colored glass windows were also common.

A majority of Ann Arbor's Queen Anne homes are executed in wood. The popularity of the style coincided with the boom in the Michigan lumber industry. Smaller, more modest structures were built by the hundreds, as were many larger, more elaborate examples of the style (see #69, #142, and #302). Though Michigan white pine was the dominant building material, a number of landmark masonry examples were constructed in the city as well (see #112, #264, #286, and #309).

The Richardsonian Romanesque Style (1880–1900)

This heavy and substantial architectural style was developed in the United States by Boston architect Henry Hobson Richardson (hence the name "Richardsonian"), and drew its influence from European Romanesque buildings of the 11th and 12th century. It has French, Spanish, and Italian influences. Because these buildings were expensive to construct, the Richardsonian Romanesque style was used primarily in public buildings, train stations, churches, and the homes of the very wealthy.

The style is characterized by solid brick construction featuring rusticated and polychromed stonework, massive round-headed arches over recessed doors and windows, and large stone towers. Cut fieldstone examples in Ann Arbor include Newberry Hall/Kelsey Museum (see #219), the Michigan Central Railroad Depot (see #137), and the First Unitarian Church/Hobbs & Black (see #192). Harris Hall (see #175) is a good example in brick.

The Shingle Style (1890–1910)

The Shingle style was never as popular as the contemporaneous Queen Anne, Richardsonian Romanesque, or the later Colonial Revival style, but it borrowed from all three. It features Queen Anne asymmetry, textured shingled surfaces, and large porches; Richardsonian Romanesque arches, usually executed in wood; and Colonial Revival-style gambrel roofs, classical columns, and windows.

The style represents a shift in the late 19th century toward the more simplified and "authentic" architecture, hence the interest in Colonial Revival and Craftsman styles. This was influenced by the American Centennial celebration in 1876 in Philadelphia, when "colonial" was rediscovered in New England and especially Massachusetts. As the name "Shingle" indicates, buildings were sided with wood shingles on second stories and masonry and stonework on the first (see #178).

The Renaissance Revival Styles: Beaux Arts and Italian Renaissance (1900–1930)

Beaux Arts, Renaissance Revival, and Italian Renaissance buildings share a common inspiration—the buildings and detailing of Renaissance Italy, especially the 16th-century buildings of Andrea Palladio. In reaction to the Victorian rejection of classical architectural ideas, architects returned to classical detailing and form in efforts to simplify buildings and leave the fussiness of the Queen Anne style behind.

Beaux Arts buildings were usually constructed of large blocks of smooth, light-colored stone (primarily limestone), and were often embellished with garlands, swags, window crowns, pediments or keystones, quoins, modillions, and dentils. Paired columns with Corinthian capitals are a distinctive feature of the style. They are very busy buildings.

The cost of such ornamentation meant most Beaux Arts buildings were public or commercial buildings. The 1906 Glazier Building, which was built as a bank, is a good example of this style (see #91). Another good example is the 1909 U-M Museum of Art, built as Alumni Memorial Hall (see #222). The Clements Library (see #238) is a wonderful example of the Italian Renaissance Revival style.

The Colonial Revival/Georgian Revival Styles (1890–Present)

The American Centennial celebrations of 1876 sparked a new interest in America's architectural heritage, giving rise to the Colonial Revival style. The style drew from a diverse array of early influences, from Dutch Colonial (gambrel roofs), Post-Medieval English, Federal style, and even the Greek Revival style, though the 18th-century British Georgian style was the main architectural influence.

Identifying features include multi-paned, double-hung windows, often with keystones, symmetrical facades with side gables, and a central front doorway featuring sidelights or a semicircular fanlight above the door. Front doors are often sheltered by a small portico with classical columns. Three-part Palladian windows, decorative shutters, dentils or modillions, and dormer windows are also common in the style.

In the period between the early 1890s and 1905, some of the grand houses of the city were constructed in the Georgian style (see #300 and #354), though many still continued to be built in earlier styles like Queen Anne with some Colonial Revival detailing (#60 and #291). But after that, Colonial and Georgian Revival became the predominant styles in the first half of the 20th century, which was its heyday in Ann Arbor and the nation as a whole. Many featured authentic proportions and detailing (see #296 and #320). Although the post-World War II years were dominated by Mid-Century Modern, these "colonial" styles have remained popular and were revived again in the late 1970s after America celebrated its bicentennial in 1976.

The Spanish/Mission Styles (1905–1940)

Rare in Ann Arbor, the Mission and Spanish styles were part of another type of "Revival" architecture that looked to the past for inspiration, only this time it was Spain and the American Southwest. The style is distinguished by red tile roofs, stucco on exterior walls, Spanish-style parapets or dormers, large overhangs, arched windows, twisted metal or tile columns, shields, and arched porch supports. The term "mission" refers to the Catholic Missions along the California coast built over the centuries by Spanish priests.

The 1909 Malcolm House (see #294) is one of Ann Arbor's high-style examples. A few smaller examples were built around town (see #15). Many wonderful examples were demolished recently, including the Planada Apartments (1929) on East Ann and 1315 Hill (1908).

The Tudor Revival Style (1910–1940)

The Tudor Revival style is distinguished by steeply pitched rooflines and asymmetrical facades, narrow casement windows often with leaded and stained glass, oriel or bay windows, false half-timbering in the upper stories, and large decorated chimneys. Tudor Revival buildings frequently feature round-topped entry doors and are usually clad in at least two or three different materials, including brick, wood, stone, and stucco. This style was used primarily for residences.

The Tudor Revival style trailed only Colonial Revival and Craftsman style in popularity for residences. It proved remarkably flexible, and was common in both small (see #310) and large homes (see #359) in the first half of the 20th century. Many houses in Burns Park and Ives Woods were built in the style. In addition, the style was used for fraternities and sororities (see #318), apartment buildings (see #240 and #321), and the charming Tuomy Hills Gas Station (see #322).

The Prairie Style (1895–1925)

The Prairie style is associated primarily with Frank Lloyd Wright and other architects based in Chicago. It was a rejection of the "Revival" architecture popular in the late 19th and early 20th centuries, and was considered very modern and original. Louis Sullivan was prominent in Chicago during the 1890s and one of his students was Frank Lloyd Wright, who developed the Prairie style.

The style is mostly in the Midwest, and is distinguished by an emphasis on the horizontal, with low-pitched hipped rooflines, large overhangs, porches supported by short and bulky square columns, and horizontal bands of wood or masonry. The ideal was a building that harmonized with the surrounding natural landscape and was "one with nature."

In Ann Arbor, only Albert J.J. Rousseau, a local architect and U-M Professor of Architecture, embraced the style. His designs for Phi Kappa Sigma fraternity (see #352) in 1924 and for his own residence in 1928 (see #350) are among the few Prairie-style buildings in the city.

The Craftsman/Arts and Crafts Styles (1895–1935)

Craftsman and Arts and Crafts buildings are characterized by low-pitched roofs with large overhangs, decorative braces, exposed eaves, and rafter tails. Full-width porches were very common, often supported by square or tapered columns of wood, brick, or stone. In addition, a wide variety of siding materials were used, including wood shingle, stucco, brick, stone, and wood clapboards. Most houses were usually brick or clapboard on the first story, and stucco or shingles on the second. Many are bungalows.

The "Arts and Crafts" name came from California, where the architectural firm Greene and Greene designed a number of large "bungalows" in the 1890s and early 1900s, heavily influenced by Asian art and the British Arts and Crafts Movement at the 1893 Columbian Exposition. The "Craftsman" name came from Gustav Stickley, a furniture maker originally from Grand Rapids, Michigan. By 1903, Stickley was designing homes and products in addition to furniture, and popularized the style through his *Craftsman Magazine* which was published in the Craftsman Building in New York City. He built the designs and showcased them and their associated lifestyle at his Craftsman Farms in New Jersey. He too was reacting against the ostentation of the Victorian era and the mechanization of work resulting in factory-produced products—ideas championed by British Arts and Crafts proponents. His furniture and buildings emphasized the honest, the simple, and the true. By the end of World War I, this style was passé and the "colonial" was once again in fashion.

Kit houses from Sears, Aladdin Homes, Montgomery Ward, Gordon-Van Tine, and J.D. Loizeaux helped to spread the popularity of the style. The neighborhoods that sprang up during the 1910s and 1920s in all parts of Ann Arbor are filled with large quantities of Craftsman-style homes both small and large (see #151, #295, and #334).

The Collegiate Gothic Style (1900–1940)

This style is similar to the Gothic and Tudor Revival and was also inspired by buildings of Medieval England and Europe. The style was predominantly used in religious, academic, and other public buildings. Hallmarks of the style include brick or stone facades trimmed out in stone. "Medieval" details such as Gothic arches, oriel windows, castellated parapets, towers, gargoyles and other stone carvings, and stone window tracery were common elements.

The popularity of Collegiate Gothic in Ann Arbor stems from the presence of the University of Michigan, especially the Law Quadrangle (see #224). A number of public schools (see #40), Angell School (see #349), and the former University High School (see #227) were designed in the style. Public buildings (see #122) and places of worship (see #265) also used it. The style was very popular on the University of Michigan's campus, with a number of buildings by the Chicago architects Pond and Pond (see #212 and #223).

The Art Deco Style (1920–1950)

The forward-looking era of the 1920s sparked many architects to build in the streamlined styles of Art Deco and Art Moderne. The name was coined from the 1925 Exposition Internationale des Arts Décoratifs et Industriels Modernes in Paris and was heavily influenced by French art and design. The name doesn't appear until much later and was popularized in the 1960s by Bevis Hillier.

It emphasized sleekness and verticality, and is characterized by steel casement windows, smooth stone or stucco exteriors, and concentrated areas of geometric and flattened decoration and sculpture. Excavations in Egypt and Mesoamerica exposed exotic new designs that also contributed to the look. Curving forms were quite popular and this was also the era of the American skyscraper. Regional varieties can be found in Miami, Florida; Los Angeles, California; and the American Southwest.

Unlike the similar Art Moderne style, Art Deco was rarely used in private homes. It is illustrated in a handful of commercial buildings such as the Bus Depot (see #75), the Kleinschmidt facade (see #72), State Theater (see #101), and the Land Title Building (see #163); industrial buildings such as the Detroit Edison Warehouse (see #1); apartment buildings such as the Kingsley-Post (see #185); campus buildings such as the Victor Vaughan Building (see #207) and the Rackham Building (see #242); and churches like St. Mary's Church (see #106).

The Art Moderne Style (1930–1950)

The Art Moderne style is similar to Art Deco and emerged in the 1930s. It is also characterized by a low, horizontal appearance with a flat roof, and walls often of stone or covered in smooth stucco. Bands of contrasting materials are often used to enhance the horizontal and sleek nature of the buildings. Curved corners and upper-story porches and balustrades are common features, as are corner windows with horizontal steel muntins and windows made of glass block. The style was mostly used for nonresidential buildings.

Ann Arbor is lucky to have a number of fine Art Moderne homes (see #278 and #345). Many were designed by modernist architects like George Brigham who was also a professor at the University of Michigan. The sleek modern style was more common in commercial buildings such as the S.W. Trick Building (see #103) and the Argus II Building (see #249), public buildings such as the West Park Band Shell (see #34), and University buildings such as the LS&A Building (see #221).

Mid-Century Modern (1940–1970)

Many architectural historians consider Ann Arbor to have one of the best collections of Mid-Century Modern homes in the Midwest. This exceptional collection can be attributed to the progressive and forward-looking U-M School of Architecture and the large number of architects hired by them after World War II. They include: Eero Saarinen (see #369), George Brigham (see #18 and #346), Walter Sanders (see #358), Theodore Larsen (see #375), William Muschenheim (see #363), Alden Dow (see #226, #333, and #348), Robert Metcalf (see #332 and #356), David Osler (see #365 and #373), and the team of Edward Olencki and Joseph Albano (see #42 and #43). Frank Lloyd Wright's only house in Ann Arbor is from 1952 and is in this style (see #344).

Identifying features of the style are flat or nearly flat rooflines and horizontal massing, large expanses of glass allowing more natural light, functional and open floor plans, recessed entryways, and the setting of the houses into the landscape, often on hilly or uneven terrain. Many of these houses have fantastic views of nature. A large cluster can be found in the neighborhoods east of Washtenaw (collective-

ly known as Ann Arbor Hills), and off Geddes Road. Another cluster is on the north side (see #11 and neighbors).

Brutalist Style (1955–1975)

The term Brutalist originates from the French words "béton brut," or "raw concrete." The look and style began as a derivative of the poured and reinforced concrete that was being used in industrial architecture. It began to be used on non-commercial buildings in the early 1950s. In addition to the use of poured concrete, Brutalist buildings are characterized by large banks of glass, sharp angular and geometric lines, and a monolithic and fortress-like appearance from the street.

The style is often criticized for being cold and unwelcoming, but it is dramatic and eye-catching. Two Ann Arbor buildings are good examples of the style. One is the University Reformed Church (see #177) designed by Latvian-American architect Gunnar Birkerts. The other is the critically acclaimed Power Center (see #209) designed by the world-famous architectural firm Kevin Roche, John Dinkeloo and Associates.

THE NEIGHBORHOODS

THE NEIGHBORHOODS

1 LOWER TOWN/NORTHSIDE

2 MILLER ROAD/WATER HILL/SUNSET

3 DOWNTOWN/STATE STREET/
  GERMANTOWN

4 OLD FOURTH WARD/KERRYTOWN/
  NORTH MAIN

5 CENTRAL CAMPUS/MEDICAL CENTER

6 OLD WEST SIDE/FAR WEST

7 BURNS PARK/WASHTENAW/HILL/
  IVES WOODS/SCOTTWOOD

8 FAR SOUTH SIDE

9 GEDDES/OXBRIDGE/ORCHARD
  HILLS

10 ANN ARBOR HILLS

11 NORTH CAMPUS/FAR EAST SIDE

LOWER TOWN/ NORTHSIDE

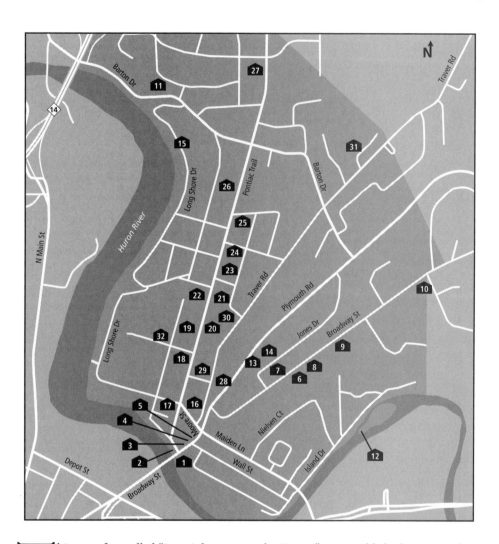

This area, first called "Ann Arbour upon the Huron," was established in 1832 where the Potawatomi Trail crosses the Huron River. Many roads come together here today, including Broadway, Wall, Maiden Lane, Plymouth Road, and Pontiac Trail. Renamed "Lower Town" not long afterward, it retains one of the highest concentrations of Greek Revival architecture in the state of Michigan, as well as some of the city's oldest buildings. It was platted in 1832 by Anson Brown (see #17) and his brother-in-law Edward Fuller as "Brown and Fuller's Addition." They even named the streets Broadway, Wall, and Maiden Lane after streets in New York City in the hopes that they would be a commercial success. They sought to make their settlement the center of town and built a grist mill and two commercial buildings: the Exchange Block, also known as the Anson Brown building (see #3), and the Washtenaw House. The Huron Block was built across the street in 1831–1835. Because of Brown's political influence, President Andrew Jackson appointed him postmaster and the post office was located in his building. This meant that business would boom because everyone had to come to the post office to get their mail.

The boom times were short-lived. Anson Brown died in the cholera epidemic of 1834. The year 1837 brought more crippling blows. First, the University of Michigan decided to locate on the other side of the river. The railroad, which came through in 1839, also located on the other side of the river. Most importantly, the entire country suffered through a depression known as the "Panic of 1837," which crushed real estate prices as "wildcat banks" were forced to close. The post office moved back to the "Upper Village" as well.

More than a century of stagnation followed, though a number of significant residences continued to be built until the Civil War, including the Jonathan H. Lund house (see #20), the Jay C. Taylor house (see #9), and the Reverend Guy Beckley house (see #22). Lower Town was a hotbed of anti-slavery activity in the 1840s and '50s, and Reverend Beckley was one of the most prominent abolitionists in Michigan, publishing the influential abolitionist newspaper *The Signal of Liberty*. His home was a known stop on the Underground Railroad, which helped self-emancipated African-Americans who were fleeing slavery to Canada. Along with Kerrytown, Lower Town was the first integrated neighborhood in Ann Arbor and maintains that tradition today. It remains the best place in the city to see pioneer architecture, with many pre-Civil War historic resources. Houses on Broadway, Traver, and Moore are now under the protection of the Broadway Historic District.

In addition to pre-Civil War buildings, the area boasts a number of Mid-Century Modern buildings from the 1950s and '60s on Laird Drive, Pontiac Trail (see #18), Hilldale (see #11), and Delafield. The commercial core at Broadway, Wall, and Maiden Lane, however, is still stagnant with many empty lots and few active businesses.

The University of Michigan built a parking structure and the Kellogg Eye Center on Wall and Maiden Lane and many houses were demolished. A few of the finest historic buildings were saved by moving them to new locations. The Burnham house (see #241) was moved to the Nichols Arboretum, the Kellogg-Warden house is now the WCHS Museum on Main Street (see #190), and the Sumner Hicks house (see #30) was moved to Traver Road.

982 Broadway
Edison Warehouse
1928

This building was built by Detroit Edison in 1928 for general storage and locker room use and was designed by Emil Lorch, Professor of Architecture at U-M. From the earliest days of Lower Town, this site had been used for water-powered industries which included a foundry, flour mills, paper and wool mills, and the Ann Arbor Agricultural Works until Edison purchased the site in 1925.

Built with a low-hipped, standing-seam metal roof, the building's beauty is in the pleasing contrasts of the reddish brick and the blonde terra-cotta cornice and bands. Behind the cornice is a large built-in copper gutter system. Though decorative elements have been stripped down to a minimum, the building exhibits some Art Deco detailing in the cornice and in the classically inspired Deco front entry.

In front of the building, at the foot of the Broadway Bridge, is a boulder with a bronze plate commemorating the spot where the Potawatomi and other Native American trails crossed the Huron River prior to the settlement of Ann Arbor. The marker was placed here in 1924 by the Sons of the American Revolution.

Former IHP

987 Broadway
Edison Power Station

1914

2

Anson Brown built the first flour mill on this site in 1831, which was replaced by William Sinclair's mill in 1860. This mill burned in a spectacular fire in the winter of 1904 and was replaced by a small hydroelectric plant in 1905. Detroit Edison built this building to replace that plant in 1914.

Designed by U-M Architecture Professor Emil Lorch, the building is of cinder block with a veneer of glazed red brick (actually street-paving blocks) set on a high, poured-cement foundation. Lorch's design shows the influence of Detroit architect Albert Kahn's factories for Ford Motor Company and his buildings for the University. The building originally featured large banks of steel, divided-light windows, which have since been replaced with sympathetic reproductions. Another Kahn influence can be seen in the building's decorative brick pilasters and their cast-cement capitals and bases, and the decorative brickwork with cement-block detailing around the windows. Now one hundred years old, the building is a great example of both functional and aesthetically pleasing buildings that architects designed in the early 20th century.

Former IHP

3

1001 Broadway
Exchange Block/Anson Brown Building 1832

This brick building, known as the Exchange Block when it was built in 1832 by Anson Brown, has distinctive "Dutch" stepped gables along its parapets. It is the oldest remaining commercial building in Ann Arbor, and is one of the few buildings in the Federal style. The builder, Anson Brown, was an immigrant from upstate New York where such Dutch-inspired buildings were popular. Hand-hewn timbers of oak are visible in the attic. The simple symmetrical facade is characteristic of the style, and the bracketed eaves were probably added in the 1860s. Graceful swan brackets once supported a fire escape on the south side.

Brown was part of a wave of immigrants who worked on the Erie Canal and then settled in Michigan. The canal connected Albany with Buffalo in 1825 and opened up the way to Michigan, as one could then take a steamer from Buffalo to Detroit. Anson joined his brother Daniel who was already in Ann Arbor running a business on Main Street. After Brown died in the cholera epidemic of 1834, he left behind this building, his home at 1029 Pontiac Trail, and much undeveloped property. His wife Desire, sister of his partner Fuller, inherited much of this property. She married Dr. Caleb Ormsby and continued to live in her Pontiac Trail house. Brown's building, and the connected Ingalls Block, are the only survivors of the Lower Town commercial district that prospered here until the Civil War.

After Brown's death this area became a backwater. Many businesses have occupied this space, including a sign company, a mattress company, and for many years the St. Vincent de Paul store. It was owned by the Colvin family for over 60 years.

Former IHP

1011 Broadway
Ingalls Block/Dr. Kellogg's Medical Works   1837/1937

4

1011 Broadway is the second oldest commercial building remaining in Ann Arbor, after 1001 Broadway to which it is attached. It was built in 1837 for pioneer Chester Ingalls and Dwight Kellogg. Ingalls was a member of the Ann Arbor Land Company, which platted the Eastern Addition to the city in 1839 and donated part of it as the original 40 acres of U-M. Ingalls Street is named after him. Ingalls was also a village trustee in 1836 and 1843 and the assessor in 1838. He and Caleb Ormsby (see #17) often served together.

In 1865, the building became the office of Dr. Kellogg's Medical Works. It was run by Dr. Daniel B. Kellogg (see #16), a renowned "clairvoyant physician" and healer, who along with his brother Leverette marketed patent medicines sold throughout Michigan as "Dr. Kellogg's Family Medicines." Daniel Kellogg died in 1876, and his brother and son Albert C. (also a clairvoyant physician) continued the business here until 1886, then working from home into the 1890s. It later served as a hardware store, barber shop, and rug making establishment.

An old lithograph of the building shows that it resembled the Exchange Block next door, though it was a story taller. It was built of solid masonry with Federal-style, parapeted gables. The building was originally four stories high, but in 1937 the top two floors were removed under the supervision of U-M Professor of Architecture Ralph Hammett. He significantly altered and "modernized" the building into what we see today with the help of contractors Pielemeir and Hilbert. A large plate-glass window was installed, flanked by two arched, inset doorways. Though the original architecture of the building has been significantly diminished, the building remains one of Ann Arbor's oldest.

1027 Broadway
August Herz Building   1874

The August Herz building is a fine example of a post-Civil War Italianate business block and is the only example of the commercial Italianate style in Lower Town. Though the building has been sadly neglected, it still retains many original features including a bracketed cornice, hooded Italianate windows, and much of its original store-front. The storefront is a rare survivor and still retains the original cast-iron decorative pilasters that flank the double front doors. The two-story height is unusual, as commercial buildings were usually three stories. When first built, there were two buildings side by side.

Herz was a native of Germany who came to Washtenaw County in 1856. During the 1860s he opened a grocery store and saloon here and became a successful wine merchant, also dealing in pelts, furs, and skins. He operated out of a different brick building that was destroyed in 1874 when a black powder keg exploded, destroying the masonry walls and injuring twenty-two people. Luckily, nobody was killed. Herz rebuilt following the devastating explosion and continued in business into the late 1890s.

Later there were other grocery stores housed in this building, including the Brousalis Grocery (1937), Broadway Market (1947), and the Broadway Party Store, which opened in 1958 and has been operated by the Hisok family since 1992.

Former IHP

1324 Broadway
Doty-Pulcipher House

6

1837

This wooden clapboard house was built in the simple Folk form known as an I-House (two stories high, one room deep) with hints of architectural detail in the Greek Revival door surround, entablature, simple gable returns, and end chimneys. It was built by Samuel Doty, an early pioneer of Ann Arbor from Stephentown, New York (by way of Connecticut). He purchased land on Broadway from Absalom Traver in 1837 and built this New England-style house that same year, with the help of his future son-in-law, carpenter Zerah Pulcipher. Doty served Ann Arbor in the first session of the State House of Representatives in 1837 but moved to Manchester in 1839.

In 1839, Pulcipher married Samuel Doty's daughter Caroline and the young couple moved into the house. During the next 55 years they had 8 children, and Zerah continued to work as a carpenter and cabinet maker. During the early years in the house he had a business manufacturing linseed oil, and from 1856 until 1860 he operated a match factory. Zerah died on January 3, 1894, followed by Caroline on March 17, 1895. The house was sold out of the family in 1897. It was occupied by the Wint family for three decades. Though marred by asbestos siding (an old photo shows the clapboard underneath), the house remains very much intact and is a survivor from the pioneer days of the 1830s.

In 1985, Doty's great-great-grandson Milo Ryan wrote the book *View of a Universe*, which described life in Ann Arbor in the early 20th century. He wrote in the *Ann Arbor Observer* that he was the first of his family to "admire, respect, and revere the old house." In the book he says, "…it was a simple kind of farmhouse, Puritan plain: two stories, window above and below on each side, three front windows…no porch just a wooden landing…fieldstone foundation…little in the way of decoration…Simple as it was, it set comfortably and with some charm on its site mounded on a nice green sward…all around it were woods of oak and elm, with an occasional maple to heighten the tone of autumn color. The land stretched in a strip all the way eastward to the Huron River…"

BHD

1327 Broadway
John H. and Charlotte Taylor House   c. 1850

The Taylor house is a side-gabled house with an attached wing, which is quite unusual for the time period. This is no doubt due to the fact that the house was built on two and a half city lots when most houses in the 1850s were on single lots. In Lower Town, cheaper land prices allowed for the purchase of multiple lots. With its double gable-end chimneys, front door transom window, front eyebrow windows, and side kitchen wing, this house is reminiscent of older buildings in New York State and New England. The house was noticed by U-M Professor of Architecture Emil Lorch during his 1930s studies for the Historic American Buildings Survey. He noted that anthemion (palm leaf) grilles covered the eyebrow windows (they are stored in the basement), the shiplap siding under the porch, and the two-panel front door.

John H. Taylor was a native of Montgomery County, New York and came to Washtenaw County with his parents in 1832. He worked in neighborhood paper mills for 18 years and then began a successful career moving houses, which was common in the 19th century (see #23). The Taylors lived in the house until 1871 when they moved to the more fashionable Division Street.

In the early 1880s, this house became the home of Ernest Rehberg and his wife Sarah (Dahlinger). Rehberg had been a brewer in Detroit and came to Ann Arbor to be foreman of the nearby Northern Brewery (see #14). In 1892 he founded the Ann Arbor Brewing Company, later renamed the Ann Arbor City Brewery. The brewery closed in 1908, and Rehberg and his son Carl founded the Ann Arbor Artificial Ice Company. In 1922, Carl and his sister Elsa founded the Arbor Springs Water Company, which is still in business today on Plymouth Road. Local artist Laura Strowe and her husband, UM-Dearborn professor Andrew, have lived here since 1979 and won a Preservation Award from the Historic District Commission in 2008.

BHD

1418 Broadway
Absalom Traver/Appolos and
Mary Ann Tuttle House

8

c. 1837

This house may have been constructed by Absalom Traver even before his 1837 plat known as Traver's Addition, which subdivided Broadway and Jones Drive (see #13). Traver purchased the land in 1831 and came back from New York City with his family in 1833. This may have been their first house. For its age the house is remarkably intact and still retains its original six-over-six double-hung windows, simple classical entry with sidelights, and small frieze-band windows. The front portico is thought to date to the early years of the building. The house's early date is confirmed in the use of hand-split "accordion" lath, and an 1837 coin found in the walls of the basement during a renovation by the current owners.

The first known occupants were Traver's daughter Mary Ann Tuttle and her husband Appolos who moved into the house soon after their 1845 marriage. Appolos Tuttle was a cooper, farmer, and dealer in fruit trees, but it was Mary Ann who actually purchased the house from her father, Absalom Traver, in 1853. The Tuttles lived in the house until 1856 and then moved to Saline where they are buried.

In 1859, the house became the residence of Frederick and Hannah Alber who were German immigrants from Wurttemberg (Swabia), Germany. Frederick Alber worked as a blacksmith. The family remained in the house until the early 1890s, after which the Staeblers lived there until the 1920s. Around 1937 Leo O'Hara and nurse Eleanor O'Hara began their occupancy. Descendants of this family have recently provided old photographs to the current owners Sabra Briere and David Cahill. Traver descendants have also recently contacted the owners and provided much information about Absalom Traver. Briere and Cahill were instrumental in the creation of the Broadway Historic District in 2008, and received a Preservation Award from the Historic District Commission in 1997. Briere has served on the Ann Arbor City Council since 2007.

BHD

9 | 1510 Broadway
Jay C. and Harriet Taylor House   1862

This high-style, red brick Italianate house from 1862 is a rarity in Lower Town, as fortunes were declining by the mid-19th century. The Taylor house is the finest Italianate residence in Ann Arbor north of the Huron River. Built of solid brick with paired brackets and arched six-over-six windows on the second story, the house is a landmark in the Broadway Historic District. The small entry porch and vestibule date to the early 20th century when porches built with bases of irregular-patterned stonework were popular in Ann Arbor.

Jay C. Taylor was a wealthy physician, who for a brief time was the manufacturer of bed springs, and also had a large and successful fruit farm. He married Harriet McCollum in 1844. In 1880 the Taylors' large farm, which stretched across Traver Road, had 1,200 peach trees and two acres of grape vines, producing 10,000 pounds of fruit. Two of the Taylors' children were gifted musicians. Their daughter Emily Allen became a prominent teacher and performer in Michigan and their son Jay C. Taylor Jr. gained national fame as a tenor in the Carleton and Castle Square opera companies in the late 1800s.

Jay C. Taylor Jr. lived in the old family home after the death of his parents with his wife Selina, an opera singer. Divorced in 1905, Jay C. Taylor Jr. continued to live in the house on Broadway with his second wife Anna. He died in 1956 at the age of 95, but the home remained in the family until 1974.

BHD

1660 Broadway
Samuel and Ophelia House

10

1862

The muscular cornice and corner pilasters and the large classical entry with sidelights and transom give this 1862 Greek Revival house an imposing air. The gable-front portion was built by Reverend Samuel House, who came to Michigan in 1843 with his wife Ophelia (Mitchell) from Volney, New York. House worked as a fruit farmer and was a minister in the Methodist Episcopal Church. They had previously lived across the street.

Samuel House sold the property to his daughter Izora and her husband Charles H. Manly, who added the side wing with the large Queen Anne windows, with their beautiful panes of colored glass and tulip cut plank shutters. Behind the main house is a small stable or carriage house.

Charles H. Manly was a prominent figure in 19th-century Ann Arbor. He served in the Civil War and lost his left arm at the battle of Gettysburg in 1863. He was active in the Democratic Party and was elected city recorder, city collector, justice of the peace, register of deeds, city treasurer, and mayor from 1890–91. He ran the farm on Broadway and also had a successful career in real estate. He sold the house in 1899 and moved to Jackson. They are buried in the House/Manly plot at Forest Hill Cemetery.

In 1901, farmer William Beaubien was renting the property and in 1914 fruit farmer Edward Manwaring began his association with the site which lasted until 1927. In the 1930s, the fruit farm was run by Edward Greene and his wife who also ran a nursery school. Both were on the faculty of U-M. It has been owned by the Pointer family for almost 30 years.

BHD

356 Hilldale

Myron and Barbara Levine House 1962

The Levine home exhibits the clean lines and geometric forms of the Mid-Century Modern style, and has spectacular views of the Huron River from its hilltop perch above Barton Drive. The home was built by Myron and Barbara Levine in 1962, shortly after Myron became associate professor of Human Genetics at the U-M Medical School. He was an expert on prokaryotic genetics and researched viral infections in humans. The Levines received a Preservation Award in 2012 from the Historic District Commission.

The house is cube-shaped with unadorned roof/wall junctions, and no overhang. The geometric aspects of the design are expressed through the use of dark cedar siding and white spaces. The front is dominated by a flat-roofed carport and large stacked plate-glass windows that illuminate the interior staircase. Similar large windows on the back capture the views of the Huron River.

The house is an early work by Ann Arbor architect Donald Van Curler who graduated from the U-M School of Architecture in 1960. Van Curler went on to a fifty-year career in his own firm Van Curler and Associates and with Flying Dutchman Management and Construction. Other notable Van Curler designs include the 1970 Campus Inn at 615 E. Huron, and the 1974 addition to the 1957 Alden Dow Ann Arbor Public Library (see #58).

1450 Island Drive
Island Park Shelter

1914

12

This picturesque local landmark would look at home in Jane Austen's England as it is reminiscent of classical "follies" that were built on European estates in the 18th and early 19th centuries. Island Park (originally called Picnic Park) is on the Huron River and has play areas, picnic tables, grills, benches, paths through the island, and this Classical Revival picnic shelter (another shelter was built in 1962 in the Mid-Century Modern style by architect Robert Metcalf). Created in 1905, the park is one of Ann Arbor's earliest city parks, spurred by the City Beautiful Movement.

The functional Island Park Shelter was built in 1914 by John Koch at a cost of $859.64, and originally provided men's and women's restrooms. The ornate half-round south portico is supported by four Ionic columns, an elaborate dentiled cornice, and courses of delicate trim. The north side of the building is without a portico but retains the Ionic columns and decorative cornice. All corners of the stucco building feature classical pilasters.

13 | 1309 Jones Drive
David LeSeur House   c. 1837

The David LeSeur house is a remnant of Ann Arbor's early years and is believed to have been constructed by Absalom Traver around 1837—the same year he created Traver's Addition (see #8). Smaller eyebrow windows are on the second floor. The house is obscured by vinyl siding and new windows but it still retains its fine original classical entry.

What is certain about the history of the house is that it was purchased by David LeSeur in 1840. LeSeur and his brother Erastus came from Erie County, New York in the 1830s and went into business together with some of Ann Arbor's earliest merchants. In 1856, LeSeur sold the property and moved with his wife Betsey (Greene) to Rochester, Minnesota.

The house then became the home of Thomas and Sarah (Cleaver) Wilkinson. Wilkinson was a veteran of the War of 1812 and a physician in Ann Arbor for many years. His son William Cleaver Wilkinson was a renowned poet, minister, theologian, and professor at the University of Chicago in the late 19th century. Sarah died in 1885 and Thomas in 1894. Laborer William J. Dorow and his wife Bertha then lived here from 1898 until 1943.

In 1944, it became the home of William and Mary Grindstaff. William was a gardener at Nielsen Greenhouses nearby on Maiden Lane. He and Mary lived here until their deaths in 2000 and 2002. They were known among gardeners throughout the Detroit area for their spectacular spring garden with thousands of bulbs. Their daughter Mary Ann Dunn continues to own the property.

BHD

1327 Jones Drive
Northern Brewery

1886

Traver Creek and nearby springs provided water for a brewery here beginning in 1872, when George Krause opened his brewery at this site. In 1884 Herman Hardinghaus took over the operation then known as the Northern Brewery after running breweries in Cincinnati, St. Louis, and Ypsilanti. Hardinghaus was trained in Germany and came to the U.S. in 1864. In 1892 the Ann Arbor Brewing Company was organized with Ernest Rehberg (see #7) as president and Hardinghaus as vice president and secretary. Their product was lager beer manufactured and bottled for export. Hardinghaus made his home next door at 1317 Jones, and it became known as the "Brewmaster's House."

Hardinghaus built this simple industrial brick structure in 1886. It is characterized by small arched windows on the first floor and wide arched windows on the second floor. The only decoration is a band of brick corbelling at the cornice line. The basement has the traditional arched brick lagering vaults so common among the German breweries in Ann Arbor (see #64 and #162).

Prohibition (1919–1933) ended alcohol production. The building gained a new life when it became the Ann Arbor Foundry, which lasted from 1920–1972. The Foundry was a unique business—owned by African-American Tom Cook and Charles Baker, a Jewish immigrant from Russia. Their 50-year partnership provided work for minorities and preserved an unusual industrial operation. It flourished in the 1950s making sewer grates, manhole covers, and other iron products. Both men worked in the foundry themselves well into their eighties.

After the death of Cook in 1971 and a state citation for air pollution, the foundry closed and remained empty until 1978 when the architecture firm of Fry/Peters restored it for its offices. They sought to retain the historic flavor and kept the overhead cranes and painted the taller stack orange. It was the first project in Ann Arbor to use tax credits for historic preservation. Today it is owned by the Northern Brewery, LLC and with the aid of architect Gary Cooper the lagering vaults are now rentable space. It was designated an Ann Arbor single resource historic district in 1978 and placed on the National Register in 1979.

NR, NBHD

15 1902 Longshore
Roswell E. and Edna Franklin House   1923

This small home is unique in that it is built of compressed adobe or rammed earth (see #310) and is in the Spanish Revival style. Begun in 1923, the home was designed and constructed over a ten-year period by Roswell E. Franklin and his brother Wallace. The clay they used for construction was dug from the site, put into forms, and compressed using pneumatic tampers, which was thought to give the adobe the strength of concrete. The foundation is standard concrete block, the adobe is covered in stucco, and the roof still features its original red tiles. An underground tunnel leads from the basement to the garage which is also built of rammed earth.

The original casement windows are made of special automotive windshield glass, a result of Roswell Franklin's position on the Automotive Engineering faculty at the University of Michigan. Franklin and his brother built gliders and tested them near the home at Argo Pond and later formed the Ypsilanti Glider Company. It produced 53 gliders between 1930 and 1933. One of their PS-2 gliders is in the Smithsonian Museum in Washington, D.C.

Roswell's wife Edna May (Hartt) was a Native American from Naponee, Nebraska who earned a master's degree in Public Health Nursing. They lived in the house until their deaths in 1973 and today the home is still owned by Franklin descendants.

Former IHP

723 Moore
Ormsby-Waite-Kellogg House
1837/1865

16

Sitting on a high foundation and somewhat hidden behind a large wall, huge staircase, large trees, and porch railings, this house is a gem waiting to be restored. It was built around 1837 as a speculative venture by Caleb Ormsby (see #17). It has a highly detailed Classical Revival doorway with sidelights and a complete entablature. It was sold to Joseph Waite in 1838 for $1,500, which included 5 lots. The front portion of this clapboard house (now covered in vinyl siding) was an I-House—two stories high, one room deep, with a central hallway. It quickly became a rooming house for workers at the Jones and Foley Paper Mill nearby. Times were tough after the Panic of 1837, when the banks failed and real estate lost its value.

In 1865, Dr. Daniel B. Kellogg added the rear portion and the hipped roof, transforming the house into an Italianate-style building. Kellogg was a "clairvoyant physician" with offices nearby on Broadway (see #4), who claimed he had supernatural powers allowing him to link medical diagnoses with many of the nostrums he manufactured. A true quack, Dr. Kellogg had no formal medical training but made a tidy business of selling his Magic Red Drops, Family Cathartic Pills, and Lung Remedy with the aid of his brother Leverette.

Kellogg died unexpectedly in 1876 at the young age of 42, and brother Leverette continued to sell the patent medicines. Daniel's son Albert followed into his father's unusual profession. An 1891 biography noted that Dr. Kellogg's "Family Remedies" were prescribed by druggists throughout Michigan, and that his pleasant home in the old part of town [Lower Town] was where he and his wife "keep up the old homestead."

By the late 1890s the old homestead was again a rooming house. This part of Ann Arbor was in decline and the house suffered as a result, but it did not go unnoticed. Prof. Emil Lorch of the U-M School of Architecture noted the beautiful classical entry in 1936 and wrote "Plus or minus good stairs, interior doors and trim," implying that original stairs, trim, and door hardware were still in place then. At that time the house was owned by Louis Goffe, a tenant for over 25 years. It remains a rooming house today.

BHD

17 1029 Pontiac Trail
Anson and Desire Brown House   c. 1830

High on a hill overlooking Pontiac Trail and often hidden by trees, the house at 1029 Pontiac Trail was built by Anson Brown around 1830 and is one of the few remaining homes associated with Ann Arbor's early founders. It is also one of the oldest houses in the city (see #328 and #125). Solid and understated, the gable-front house originally faced Swift Street, overlooking the Huron River, and had a large side wing that housed the kitchen. It has a classical entry with sidelights and a symmetrical arrangement of three bays. The windows probably date to the 1880s. It was moved to this spot in the 1890s.

Brown joined his brother Daniel in Ann Arbor in 1826 and by 1830 had begun to create his own village north of the Huron River. Together with brother-in-law Edward Fuller, he subdivided the area as Brown and Fuller's Addition. In 1832 he built the Exchange Block at 1001 Broadway (see #3) and lured business away from Main and Huron by securing the appointment of postmaster through his political connections and moving the post office to what was then called the "Lower Village." Brown's competition with Huron and Main was short-lived, as he died in an 1834 cholera epidemic.

Brown's widow Desire married physician Caleb Ormsby in 1836 and they continued to live in the house for many years, though they never recovered from the financial panic of 1837. In 1849, Ormsby went to California and joined the 49ers Gold Rush where he prospered as a merchant. He was killed in the famed shipwreck of the *S.S. Central America* on September 3, 1857.

In the late 19th century, the house became the home of Eli Moore and his wife Elizabeth. Moore and his father Lewis founded the Ann Arbor Agricultural Works in 1866 (see #1) which manufactured a wide variety of agricultural implements. The side wing of the house was removed in the late 1890s when Moore moved the main house to its current location facing Pontiac Trail. In 1910, the property was purchased by Gottlieb Gutekunst who lived here until 1950. The house has been owned by Roger Manela since 1972 and rented to various tenants.

Former IHP

1223 Pontiac Trail
Jean Paul Slusser House   1938

18

A Greek Revival house c. 1843 known as the Thompson Sinclair/David T. McCollum home stood on this site until it was purchased by Henry Ford in 1936. It was drawn and measured in 1934 by the Historic American Buildings Survey and known as the Sinclair House. Ford moved it to Greenfield Village in Dearborn where it can still be seen today as "The Ann Arbor House." Robert Frost lived in the Sinclair-McCollum home in the 1920s.

In 1938, U-M Professor of Architecture George Brigham used the original foundations and the exact footprint of the old Sinclair-McCollum House to design this modern home for U-M Art Professor and painter Jean Paul Slusser. Today the home looks much as it did when it was built, with a nearly flat roof and naturally stained horizontal cedar siding. The main entry to the house is hidden on the south side of the building. The small garage was built at the same time and matches the architecture of the main house.

In the mid-1920s Slusser lived across the street in the Lund House (see #20) while his friend Robert Frost occupied the old Sinclair-McCollum House. Slusser graduated from the University of Michigan in 1909 and began teaching in 1921, becoming a full professor of art in 1944. From 1947 to 1957 he was director of the U-M Museum of Art. He was a renowned painter and received many prestigious awards for his work. He was also an accomplished art critic. World-famous writer and poet W.H. Auden lived in the house in 1940 with Charles Miller, who described their year there together in his book *Auden: An American Friendship*.

Jean Paul Slusser died in 1981, and the University of Michigan honored him by naming the Jean Paul Slusser Gallery at the School of Art and Design on North Campus in his honor. It has been the home of Kenneth and Elizabeth Baird since 1990.

1317 Pontiac Trail
William and Saphrona Perry House   1836

William R. Perry came to Ann Arbor from Rome, New York in 1833 and operated the largest bookstore in the state west of Detroit. Perry and his wife Saphrona built this house on Pontiac Trail in 1836. The front portion is an I-House—two stories tall, one room deep, with a center entry. The rear wing is a 1 and ½ story portion that may have been the original kitchen. Both retain their original six-over-six windows. The roof's delicate gable returns harken back to the lighter, less muscular, Federal style of many early Ann Arbor buildings. The barn behind the house is thought to date from the early years of the house, and is probably the oldest barn remaining in the city of Ann Arbor. The front porch is not original.

Inside, the house has two original back-to-back fireplaces, with a Dutch oven or "bake oven"—features that were disappearing as more efficient cast-iron stoves became popular. It is believed that Perry hid runaway slaves and participated in the Underground Railroad. Pontiac Trail was a hotbed of abolitionist and Underground Railroad activity (see #22). Adding weight to this speculation is that Perry was an advertiser in the abolitionist newspaper *The Signal of Liberty* and an early member of the anti-slavery Republican Party. The house was documented as part of the Historic American Buildings Survey and is on the National Register of Historic Places. The house is also featured on Underground Railroad tours.

Perry went bankrupt in 1842 and was forced to sell the house. He remained in town serving as a justice of the peace and associate judge before moving to Racine, Wisconsin in 1851. In 1852, the house was sold to basket maker William H. Kordes and his wife Louisa. William lived in the house for 39 years until his death in 1891. Daughter Mary and her husband Frederick W. Bowen, a house painter and decorator, lived here until 1936.

In the 1950s, U-M Professor of Art Catherine Heller converted it from a duplex back to a single-family house. She redid the fireplace with handmade tiles resembling butter molds and added the kitchen wing. It has been home to John Kenny for over 30 years, who is responsible for putting the house on the National Register.

Former IHP, NR

1324 Pontiac Trail
Jonathan and Almy Lund House

20

1847

Jonathan Lund and his wife Sarah Almy Richmond Lund (known as Almy) arrived in Ann Arbor in 1837 and built this house nine years later. They lived in a smaller house on the property which they built in 1845 (see #23). Two years later, Lund was prosperous enough to hire local builders Robert and John Davidson (who had built the first Washtenaw County Courthouse) to build this unusual Greek Revival house. The house is stucco over brick, with the stucco made with skim milk to give it a particularly adhesive quality. It was scored to resemble stone, but the massing of the house is more an Italianate than Greek Revival (it is a cube rather than a rectangle). There is also an 1857 springhouse in the rear that has been beautifully renovated with a metal "witch's hat" roof. A square cupola, with Greek cut-out designs called Vitruvian scrolls, tops the main house. All of this is on a huge lot, giving the passerby a sense of what rural Ann Arbor once looked like. The house also has its original six-over-six windows. The porch, with its chamfered columns, likely dates from the late 1860s. The double main door with sidelights also dates from this era.

The Lunds were famous for their entertaining. Peacocks roamed the property and white pillars stood at the entry from the road. Lund owned a paper mill in Lower Town and manufactured paper for books and smoking tobacco, as well as colored and wrapping papers that were sold as far away as Chicago. He later joined with Volney Chapin (see #121) and Charles Chapin who eventually bought the firm. All were active in local politics. Ill health forced Lund to retire in 1858 and he died that year. Almy's brother Charles Richmond and his wife Amy Howland Richmond came to the farm and helped her settle Jonathon's affairs. They later became active in local politics and St. Andrew's Episcopal Church.

Following the Lunds, the home passed through a number of owners, including Alfred and Eliza Partridge, who subdivided the farm in 1867 as Partridge's Addition. Alfred H. Partridge served as mayor of Ann Arbor from 1869–1870. A later owner was Fremont Ward, who came from Washington in 1908 to supervise the construction of the post office on Main Street (see #89). He and his wife Flora Ward fell in love with the house and stayed. In the 1930s they converted part of it to apartments without changing the exterior.

In 1987, Robert and Nancy Harrington purchased the house and for 18 years they rented out the five apartments. In 2001, they moved in and restored it to its former glory. The Historic District Commission gave them a Rehabilitation Award in 2004.

Former IHP

21 1416 Pontiac Trail
John Christian and Marie Schmid House   1870s

The Schmid house was built at 217 S. First Street in the 1870s and moved in 1947 to its present location on Pontiac Trail. This Vernacular building is of no particular style, but resembles early New England types with the long side facing the street. It still boasts an original door surround with transom and sidelights and small pediments above the original four-over-four windows. The current porch and back wing were added after the house was moved to its present location. The Schmids first lived in a small house on their lot that probably dated to the 1830s. This earlier building became the back wing of the 1870s house. It was also moved in 1947 to the corner of Argo and Pontiac Trail and is a single-family house.

John Christian Schmid came to Ann Arbor from Wurttemberg, Germany in 1851 and worked as a carpenter before opening a lumber yard in 1866 near the corner of Liberty and Fifth. Schmid also manufactured window sashes, blinds (shutters), doors, and shingles. He was active with the Republican Party and elected alderman of the second ward for many years. Marie (Teufel) Schmid passed away in 1892 and John Christian died in 1900. Daughter Elizabeth lived at the house for two more years until her death in 1902, when the house became the home of another daughter, Pauline Schmid, until 1916.

In 1917, George J. and Julia Hertler bought the house. With his brothers Gottlob and Herman, he owned Hertler Brothers (see #49), an agricultural implement and feed store around the corner from the house's original location. Hertler remained here until 1947 when he was forced out by the city for a municipal parking structure.

The Mackmiller family purchased it from the city in 1947 for $50 and moved it to its present location.

Former IHP

1425 Pontiac Trail
Guy and Phyla Beckley House   c. 1839

22

This house, long known as "the slave house," is one of two brick houses on Pontiac Trail built in a style reminiscent of Georgian and Federal-style homes in New England. They were built by two brothers, Josiah (see #26) and the Rev. Guy Beckley. Guy Beckley was a devout Methodist and abolitionist who came to Ann Arbor in 1839 from Vermont with his wife and eight children, and purchased 28 acres from his brother. The Beckley houses are remarkably similar. They have a central entry and a symmetrical alignment of windows and doors. On either side of the central entry are two rows of windows, still with their original six-over-six design. The front door has its original glass sidelights.

The walls of the house are sixteen inches thick and made of fieldstone veneered with handmade brick from Josiah's brickyard. The heavy oak timbers of the framing are carefully mortised and tenoned together. The trim is oak and black walnut. "Modern" Franklin stoves were used for heating and cooking instead of fireplaces. Like several other 1830s houses (see #241), it has a cobblestone smokehouse in the rear. In 1955, the house was studied by U-M architecture professor Emil Lorch for the Library of Congress.

Beckley was committed to the cause of ending slavery and became the publisher of the *Signal of Liberty*, the anti-slavery newspaper for the state of Michigan (this paper is digitized and is available through the Ann Arbor District Library). The paper was edited by Theodore Foster of Scio Township. Beckley's house was an important way station on the Underground Railroad and is showcased on tours.

Guy Beckley died in 1847 and his wife died in 1850. They had been saddled with debt and the house had to be sold. It was occupied by the Pascal Mason family from 1862 to 1915, who also sheltered runaway slaves during the Civil War.

U-M Professor of Architecture Ralph W. Hammett purchased the house in 1933 when it was quite run down. An authority on architectural history, he undertook its restoration and added the side porch, rebuilt the missing front porch with Ionic capitals, and modernized the interior. For many decades it was owned by the Bertoni family who lovingly maintained it. Current owners Bethany and David Steinberg received a Preservation Award from the Historic District Commission in 2013 for their many years of stewardship.

Former IHP

23 1526 Pontiac Trail
Lund-Richmond-Spathelf House 1845

This simple timber-framed, gable-front house was built in 1845 as the first farmhouse of Jonathan H. and Almy (Richmond) Lund. In 1847, they completed their much larger home at 1324 Pontiac Trail (see #20) but kept this house on the property. Lund was a prosperous dry goods merchant, gentleman farmer, and paper manufacturer. He was active in the Whig Party and held a number of local offices. He was also an active member of St. Andrew's Episcopal Church (see #149), and was an advertiser, subscriber, and financial backer of neighbor Guy Beckley's abolitionist newspaper, *The Signal of Liberty*.

Following Jonathan's death in 1858, the house was occupied by Mrs. Lund's brother, Charles H. Richmond, his wife Amy (Howland), and her brother Philip H. Howland. Richmond and Howland extensively remodeled the house into a more refined residence in 1861, the same year that Philip H. Howland carved his initials on a board in the basement. This was also the year the Richmonds permanently settled in Ann Arbor. The house is believed to be the first private residence in Michigan to be dated through dendrochronology, which examines the pattern of tree rings in the wood from the house.

An old tintype of the house shows long-gone Gothic Revival and Italianate gingerbread that was added by the Richmonds. Charles H. Richmond was a prominent figure in 19th-century Michigan. He served as clerk to the Superintendent and Chief Indian Agent of Michigan in the 1840s, co-founded and was later president of the First National Bank of Ann Arbor, was a delegate to Michigan's Second Constitutional Convention in 1867, was a member of the Ann Arbor School Board, served as state senator from Washtenaw County, and was a commissioner to the 1893 Chicago World's Fair. By 1863, the Richmonds and Almy Lund had moved to an elegant mansion on Huron Street.

In 1867, the Lund farm was subdivided by Alfred and Eliza Partridge and the house was moved north into the old Lund fruit orchard (thus the names of the surrounding streets: Pear, Apple, Peach, and Plum, which is now John A. Woods Street). In 1869, it became the home and workshop of carpet weaver John George Spathelf and his wife Catherena. The Spathelfs built the kitchen wing in the 1870s (which originally stood on the north side and is now in the back of the house) as well as the front porch in the early 1900s. Though the exterior has been significantly altered over the years, the interior is very much intact and features much of the original trim and doors, the very steep 1840s staircase, Colonial-style exposed corner posts, and the 1870s wall and ceiling beadboard in the kitchen. The Spathelfs continued to live here until 1908. They also ran a meat market on Broadway for many years.

In 1916, the house was purchased by Henry Z. Petrie and in 1953 it became the home of Thelma and Burton Crawford, who found it a "wreck" and fixed it up, despite the fact that they were renters until 1966. In 2006, they split off the side lot on the north and sold the house separately to Patrick McCauley, who restored it with wife Andrea Kinney, and received a Rehabilitation Award from the Historic District Commission in 2008.

1528 Pontiac Trail
Albert and Leah Polhemus House

24

1848

The Albert and Leah Polhemus House was moved by McKinley Inc. from 411 E. Washington in 2006, when it was threatened with demolition by a high-rise development. The property was purchased by philanthropists Peter and Rita Heydon, and will become the first permanent home of the Washtenaw County African-American Historical Society. Lower Town was one of the primary centers of Ann Arbor's African-American community, and Pontiac Trail was a center of abolitionism and one of the main stopping points on the Underground Railroad in the mid-19th century (see #3 and #22). Restoration of the building for its new use continues at the time of publication.

The simple gable-fronted, painted brick Greek Revival home was built in 1848 by Albert Polhemus and his wife Leah. The home's Greek Revival architecture is sturdy and restrained, doing without the characteristic classical gable returns and pediment. It retains a very nice classical entry with dentils and sidelights. A former side wing had a full-width Gothic Revival porch on the south side, but was demolished when the building was moved. The small Gothic Revival portico that shelters the front door has slender, clustered triple columns of wood and probably dates to the 1860s. Though the interior has been extensively remodeled, the home still features many of its original windows with hand-blown glass, as well as the original banister and Egyptian Revival window casings.

Polhemus was born in New York and came to Ann Arbor with his family in 1840, where he set up shop as a boot and shoe manufacturer, prospering enough to build this large home. The house then became the home of Reverend Maltby Gelston, Jr. and his wife Marcia (Merwin). In the 1860s, Gelston, a graduate of Yale and a native of Connecticut, began a 54-year career as a supply (temporary) minister of the Presbyterian Church throughout lower Michigan. He is reported to never have missed a Sunday sermon. He died in 1893 and the home was then converted into a rooming house for widowed or unmarried women by his daughter Sarah. Large homes such as this often became rooming houses to service the growing student population of the city.

Former IHP

25 1622 Pontiac Trail
Augustus and Caroline Fruhauf House   1890

August Fruhauf and his wife Caroline (Nichdir) built this finely detailed home shortly after he purchased an entire block of Partridge's Addition in 1889. The 1½-story clapboard home's elaborate details span a wide array of Victorian influences, from the Gothic Revival steeply pitched rooflines, pointed vertical siding in the gables and front facade, to the intricately carved ornamental trusses, and Eastlake-inspired window trim of the Stick style. The home also features Queen Anne-style sunbursts in three of the home's gables. The over-the-top detailing on such a small home can be attributed to Fruhauf's work as a carpenter. In addition to carpentry, Fruhauf also manufactured cider and distilled peppermint to supplement his income. Fruhauf died at his home in 1899 at age 70 and Caroline lived here until her death in 1909. Son Alfred Fruhauf lived here until 1930.

The home was unsympathetically remodeled in the 20th century, though the current owners have restored a majority of the exterior. It has been owned and lovingly maintained since 1991 by David Michener, who works at the Matthaei Botanical Gardens, and his partner Will Strickland. Their garden here is a showstopper and noticed by all who pass by.

1709 Pontiac Trail

26

Josiah and Minerva Beckley-Millard House   1834

Built in 1834, this center-entry brick "Colonial" Georgian house is one of the oldest houses in Ann Arbor. Josiah and his family came to Ann Arbor in 1827 from Vermont after the opening of the Erie Canal. Beckley ran a brickyard, owned a cloth factory, and owned large swaths of land north of the river, including 73 acres purchased from Isaac Hull. He built this brick house with his handmade bricks. It is two stories high, with a symmetrical arrangement of windows and doors, characteristic of Georgian houses. Black metal stars are attached to the ends of iron rods that hold the brick walls in place. The original windows were replaced in the 1980s.

Beckley built a commercial block known as the Huron Block which stood at 1000 Broadway (now gone) and housed Beckley's stores. The upper floors were rented to various enterprises, including his brother Guy's (see #22) abolitionist newspaper *The Signal of Liberty*. He died in 1843 and in 1845 his widow Minerva married Warren Millard. In 1847, Millard purchased the house from the estate and the family lived here for another 100 years. In 1995, the owners added a garage and two-story rear wing which does little to detract from the beauty of the original house.

Today the house remains on its large lot, surrounded by mature trees, and looking almost as it did when Ann Arbor was just emerging from the wilderness of the Michigan Territory.

Former IHP

27 2021 Pontiac Trail
Sumner and Wesley Hicks House   1859

Sumner and Olive Hicks, pioneers who arrived in the 1830s, spent many of their early years in their home on Wall Street (see #30). In 1858, Sumner and his son Wesley purchased a 53-acre farm on Pontiac Trail and in 1859 built this house there. In form, the house is an interesting variation of the Greek Revival style known as "hen and chicks" or "basilica" style, with a two-story gable-fronted central portion flanked by one-story wings and an umbra (recessed) porch. This style was strongly influenced by the 16th-century Italian architect Andrea Palladio. The central portion of the house once had an open second-floor porch under the pediment (it was enclosed in the 1920s). The house exhibits Greek Revival details in its classical pediment and pilasters, as well as "eared" window trim, but it also shows hints of the Italianate style in the small decorative brackets under the eaves and the paired narrow windows on the front facade.

The Hicks family lived in the house until 1863, when it was sold to Robert McCormick. McCormick was another early pioneer in Washtenaw County who lived in the house with his second wife, Ellen (Howard) McCormick, the widow of his brother George W. McCormick. He died in 1869, followed by Ellen in 1873. Beginning in 1925, the surrounding farmland was broken up into lots as the Huron River Hills Subdivision.

The house was meticulously restored and decorated in period style by U-M Professor of Psychology Kent Berridge, who purchased the house in 1993. In 2009, he received a Preservation Award from the Historic District Commission.

1202 Traver
Traver District School

28

1839

Built in 1839, the Traver District School is the oldest remaining school building in the city of Ann Arbor. It was a private school under the direction of Dr. Thomas Holmes and had room for 40 students. The early board of directors consisted of prominent citizens of Lower Town including William Perry (see #19), Robert Davidson, and Josiah Beckley (see #26). It is assumed that bricks for the school building came from Beckley's brickyard, which provided bricks for many of the early buildings in Lower Town. The association of Beckley and Perry with the school has led to speculation that it may have been a stop on the Underground Railroad, though no proof has been found. Lower Town schools were not consolidated with Ann Arbor Public Schools until 1861.

In 1857, a larger school was built on Wall Street and the building was sold to Jonathan H. Lund (see #20 and #23). It was converted into a residence and sold to cabinet maker John Beasley, whose family occupied the building from the late 1850s well into the 20th century. The building is of solid masonry in the Greek Revival style and still retains its original side entrance door and sidelights. A series of additions in the last 30 years detract somewhat from the original architecture of the building, but the original brick structure remains intact. It was associated with the Lahti family for many years, and has been well maintained for almost 20 years by Tom Stulberg.

BHD

29   1219–1223 Traver
Armstrong Brothers Houses   c. 1830s, 1851

This pair of charming, tiny Greek Revival wood houses have long caught the attention of the public. They were built by carpenters Solomon and John Armstrong who worked on many of Lower Town's early buildings, including both Lund houses (see #20 and #23) and the Kellogg Mill. They came to Ann Arbor in the 1830s from Ballston Spa, New York with their father Sylvester. In 1843, they built a house farther down the hill on Traver, and in 1851 purchased the two lots where 1219 and 1223 Traver were built.

The house at 1219 Traver was probably a small cabin already on the lot before the Armstrongs purchased the property. This portion of the building is currently the dining room and downstairs bedroom. It features log floor joists—still covered with bark—and the original windows, which have a different profile than the rest of the house. The side-gabled portion dates to 1851 and for its small size exhibits particularly nice detailing, including an intricate classical doorway with delicate sidelights and pilasters. The interior has Egyptian Revival trim and a fine walnut newel post and banister.

In 1861, the Armstrongs sold the house to carpenter Amos Corey who was related to the family and who lived with them as early as 1850. It is believed that Corey added the Italianate porch across the entire front facade and front door. Amos Corey lived in the house until his death in 1909 at the age of 85. The house was then occupied by members of the Schlemmer family for much of the 20th century. The long tenures of its past owners and the good stewardship of the current owner have left the house remarkably unaltered by time. In 2009, owner Mary Underwood received a Preservation Award from the Historic District Commission.

Like 1219, 1223 Traver was also built in 1851. It is uncertain which Armstrong lived here in the early days. Both brothers seemed to have moved around a lot—including stints in Ypsilanti, Detroit, and Canada—probably where they were building houses. By 1868, John and his wife Susan left Traver Street and 1223 became the full-time home of Solomon and Angeline Armstrong, who probably added the porch then.

The house is a rare example of the Greek Revival style known as "hen and chicks" (see #27) and features a one and one-half story gable-front portion flanked by two one-story wings (like a mother hen sheltering her chicks). This style of Greek Revival is common in southern Michigan but almost non-existent elsewhere. Solomon Armstrong lived in the home until his death in 1897 and his daughter Jennie Armstrong, a dressmaker, continued to occupy the residence until 1919. The family of Emily Hatch and later Adaline Barbieux lived in the home for much of the 20th century.

BHD

1335 Traver
Sumner and Olive Hicks House
30
1846

The 1846 Hicks House which stood at 936 Wall Street was threatened with demolition by a condo development in 2002 and was saved by moving it up the road to 1335 Traver. The north side of Ann Arbor has a long history of houses being moved due to its slow development and the availability of open lots. The house lost its original windows but still retains much of its original massing.

Sumner Hicks was born in Sutton, Massachusetts, but later moved to Weathersfield, Vermont, where he married Olive Beckley, the sister of Josiah Beckley (see #26) and abolitionist Rev. Guy Beckley (see #22). In 1839, the couple came to Ann Arbor and Hicks became a successful wool manufacturer. He purchased two acres on Wall Street in 1846, and built this gable-front Greek Revival home that year. The side wing is thought to be a later 19th-century addition and the front porch was added in the early 20th century. It is believed that Sumner and Olive Hicks sheltered slaves who were traveling on the Underground Railroad. In 1858, Hicks and his son Wesley purchased property in what was then Ann Arbor Township and built a larger house (see #27). After 1863, Wesley and Mary Hicks moved back to the old home on Wall Street and lived there into the 1870s. Hicks sold it to William Campbell of Storms and Campbell, a woolen factory on Mill Street (Jones), and in the 1890s the house was occupied by the Storms family.

In the 20th century, the house was occupied by the Barth family after 1900. Their daughter Alfrieda married U-M mechanical engineering professor Clarence Kessler and lived here the rest of her life. Kessler, who died in 2000, won a Preservation Award from the Historic District Commission in 1989. Doolin Properties received a Rehabilitation Award from the Historic District Commission in 2004 for moving the house and restoring it.

During the 2002 move and renovation of the house, an 1820s "friendship book" belonging to Phyla Baker Beckley, the wife of Rev. Guy Beckley, was found in one of the walls. It is believed that it was left there by one of Guy and Phyla Beckley's daughters, who lived in the house in 1850 following the deaths of her parents.

Former IHP

31 1831 Traver
Eugene and Emily Leslie House—
Leslie Science and Nature Center   1923

Eugene and Emily (Ebner) Leslie built this Craftsman bungalow in 1923. The house is stucco on the first story, shingle on the second, and has a full-width front porch and shed roof dormers—all common features of the Craftsman style.

Eugene Leslie was a brilliant man who came to Ann Arbor in 1919 to work in the Chemical Engineering Department at the University of Michigan. Leslie left the university in 1928 to work for the petroleum industry, where he gained fame for his innovations in the refining of gasoline. He later founded the Leslie Laboratories in Ann Arbor and experimented with synthetic rubber. Emily Leslie also had a strong intellect, and as an avid gardener was a member of the National Farm and Garden Association and the Ann Arbor Garden Club. The Leslies also owned 207 acres along Traver Road where they grew fruit and raised cattle and pigs. Many of Eugene Leslie's early experiments took place in the outbuildings on the property.

Not having heirs, the Leslies deeded the property to the City of Ann Arbor in 1963 for recreational use. They continued to live in the house until their deaths in 1976. Today the farm is the site of the Leslie Park Golf Course and the very popular Leslie Science and Nature Center, which has programs for young and old and a fascinating Raptor Center. The non-profit's mission is to provide environmental education programs to create awareness and respect for the natural world.

1401 Wright
Fifth Ward/Fairview Cemetery

32

1831

Fairview Cemetery is Ann Arbor's oldest cemetery and contains a number of beautiful monuments and grave markers from the 19th century. The cemetery was established in 1831 as the Fifth Ward Cemetery on a bluff overlooking the Huron River and what later became Argo Pond. It was renamed Fairview Cemetery in 1898.

As one approaches the cemetery through the surrounding neighborhood, one notices remnants of 19th- and early 20th-century life. Many historic homes line Wright and Kellogg Streets, which have many mature trees and charming cobblestone gutters and stone walls. Fairview Cemetery is the final resting place of many of the Lower Town's prominent citizens and founding fathers, including Absalom Traver (see #8 and #13), Anson Brown (see #17), the Hon. Dwight Kellogg and his family (see #190), and Reverend Guy Beckley (see #22). In 1874, the Ladies Decoration Society erected an elaborate monument honoring the forty men from the Fifth Ward who fought for the Union in the Civil War. This monument was the focal point of elaborate Memorial Day celebrations for many years.

From the beginning, Fairview Cemetery had no religious affiliation and was the first racially integrated cemetery in the city. A number of prominent African-Americans are interred here, including poet and U-M Professor of English Robert Hayden—the first African-American Poet Laureate of the United States. When Forest Hill Cemetery opened in 1859 (see #343), most citizens of means chose to bury their loved ones there. Some had their deceased relatives re-interred from Fairview Cemetery. In 1891, a large number of very old graves from the former city burying ground at Huron and Fletcher were moved to Fairview. That site was renamed Felch Park in 1894 and remains as the lawn of the nearby U-M Power Center for the Performing Arts (see #209). These are some of the oldest graves in the cemetery and are clustered at the western edge.

MILLER ROAD/ WATER HILL/ SUNSET

The neighborhoods west of Main along Miller Road have been overlooked by architectural historians even though the area has many historic buildings. However, unlike the nearby Old West Side Historic District (the northern boundary is at Huron), where the German identity and Vernacular architecture work hand-in-hand, the Miller Road area has only recently acquired an identity as the Water Hill Neighborhood. The name Water Hill comes from the street names Spring, Bath, and Fountain, which in turn derive from the large number of springs and creeks that once ran through the neighborhood. Also, the city's main water pumping plant is on Sunset—one of the highest points in the city.

On maps we note that Water Hill is actually broken down into three neighborhoods: Upper Water Hill, which extends west from Brooks to Newport and contains the youngest houses; Water Hill, which is north of Summit and features Hunt Park; and Lower Water Hill, which is the oldest neighborhood and is south of Summit between Main and Brooks and includes Belize Park.

The area was first settled by Yankees from New England and New York, with some Irish and Germans. Beginning in the 1930s, a large African-American community made the Water Hill neighborhood their home. Miller Road has always been a main east/west road, and was settled earlier than the rest of the neighborhood. This can be seen in a number of high-style buildings (see #37 and #38). There are also some smaller pioneer homes (see #39) that still survive.

The oldest subdivisions were platted in 1859 along Spring, Fountain, Hiscock, and Felch, a bit later than other near-downtown neighborhoods. The neighborhood has modest examples of the Greek Revival (see #47), Italianate (see #46), Vernacular (see #45), and Queen Anne styles (see #35). There are also some very nice examples of the Arts and Crafts style (see #37).

West Park, established in 1909 where a tributary of Allen Creek once flowed, was the site of a Native American trail. The Band Shell and Gateway (see #34) are focal points of this neighborhood park. Hunt Park along Spring Street offers spectacular views of downtown Ann Arbor.

The 1950s brought an explosion of growth beyond Miller and hundreds of ranch houses were built on Pomona and Red Oak (Upper Water Hill). A number of stunning Mid-Century Modern homes were also built in the neighborhood (see #42 and #43), and on Orkney and Miner. Some of these were designed by well-known architects at U-M.

33 | 115 Chapin
Sylvester Noble House c. 1846

The Sylvester Noble House was probably built by Noble and his wife Europa (Taylor) around 1846. It's possible the home could be even older, dating from the time that Sylvester's brother Samuel B. Noble owned the property. It is a simple Greek Revival gable-front and side-wing home with very little decoration. Asbestos siding covers the original clapboards, but the original door with classical trim still exists. The gable roof also has typical returns on the main portion. The side wing appears to be original. The two-over-two windows are probably from the 1880s. Somewhat hidden by vegetation and siding are frieze windows on the south side.

Sylvester D. Noble came to Ann Arbor from New York State in 1834 and worked as a carpenter and pattern maker for the Tripp, Ailes, and Price Machine Shop. Samuel B. Noble, who also lived on what is now Chapin Street, had a nursery that raised fruit and ornamental shrubbery as early as 1839. Various nurseries later occupied this property. Until about 1880, Chapin Street was just a footpath that led between Huron and Miller, and the Nobles are listed as living on Huron into the 1870s. The street, called Noble after Sylvester's death in 1878, was changed to Chapin around 1880. It was named after Volney Chapin (see #121), who platted the area as Chapin's Addition, and whose foundry was nearby. Chapin was a major business leader in the early days of Ann Arbor's history.

The house was one of the main stopping points on the Underground Railroad in Ann Arbor. Sylvester, along with his brothers Samuel B. and Sylvanus, was a fervent abolitionist. He served on the executive committee of the Michigan Anti-Slavery Society and sheltered fugitive slaves in his home. His daughter Pamela remembered their home was always open to runaway slaves and that her father took them away at night in the back of his wagon. Noble even allowed fugitive slaves George and Martha Washington, who worked for the Nobles, to live on his property during the late 1840s. With the passage of the Fugitive Slave Act of 1850, they were forced to flee to Canada when their former master discovered where they were hiding. The Act required slaves to be returned to their owners if they were caught.

Sylvester Noble died in 1878 and his daughter Pamela remained in the house until about 1890 when she went to live with her sister Adelia and brother-in-law Judge Noah Cheever on Madison Street. Pamela Noble and Adelia Noble Cheever were known for their kindness and advocacy for U-M students. They donated their home on Madison Street for use as a women's dormitory and it was known as the Adelia Cheever House. This house is long gone but her name is memorialized in the Adelia Cheever Program at U-M which prepares women for leadership roles.

The house became a rental throughout most of the 20th century and has in the past few decades returned to single-family use.

215 Chapin
West Park Band Shell and Gateway   1938/1927

34

West Park was created in 1908 by the recently created City Parks Commission on land that had been an old Indian trail and part of a tributary of Allen Creek. The first sport played there was baseball. After a bond issue was passed in 1915, more amenities for tennis and playgrounds were built. The Gateway was built on the site of the former Third Ward School in 1927 at the Miller Street entrance. The gateway has four Ionic columns with wisteria draped on two large trellises that shade two benches.

Down the hill from the Gateway is the West Park Band Shell. It was constructed in 1938 by the Works Progress Administration (WPA). The building features a wonderful Art Moderne arch under which performances are staged. The rear wing serves as a dressing room for musicians and performers. From the beginning, the West Park Band Shell has been home to the Ann Arbor Civic Band, and in the 1960s was the scene of legendary concerts by rock icons the Grateful Dead and the MC5. In 2010, West Park underwent a major overhaul to improve the band shell and drainage in the park.

Former IHP

35 627 Gott
George and Ella Clark House   1890

A wonderful and modest example of the Queen Anne style, 627 Gott was built by carpenter George W. Clark and his wife Ella in 1890 as an investment property. The Clarks never lived in the house but nearby on Hiscock Street. Early tenants included John Jenkins, a printer for the *Ann Arbor Argus*, and lather George Quintal and his wife Martha.

George Clark's talents as a carpenter are evident in many details of the building: the decorative bargeboards with recessed panels, the sunburst in the gable, and a band of decorative cut shingles that wraps around the entire middle of the house. The front facade and side wing both feature large Queen Anne windows with multi-colored glass panes. The porches are small and restrained, with the lower porch featuring simple turned columns and recessed paneling in the frieze. The upper porch features shingled posts and decorative shingle siding. In 1995, owners James and Renee Mitchell, who had owned it since 1976, received a Preservation Award from the Historic District Commission for their constant maintenance over the years and for converting it back to a single-family house.

The home has a more recent large addition, which was designed not to compete with or detract from the original architecture. It forms a studio for Kate Tremel, ceramic artist and lecturer at the U-M Penny Stamps School of Art and Design. Tremel has had studio sales from the house from time to time. Since 2004, it has been the home of Tremel and Joshua Cole, Professor of History at U-M and Director of the Center for East European Studies.

Former IHP

Huron River Drive and Bird Road

36

Barton Dam

1912–1913

Completed in 1913, Barton Dam was the first of six dams built on the Huron River by Detroit Edison to bring hydroelectric power to Ann Arbor and the surrounding region. The Huron River had been Ann Arbor's primary source of water power since the first sawmill was built on the river in 1825. By the early 1900s, with the increased use of electricity in homes and businesses, Edison sought to harness the river's power to generate electricity. Detroit Edison's dam building projects changed the face of the Huron River to what we see today, creating large ponds above Barton, Argo, and Geddes Dams.

Gardner Stuart Williams was the engineer of Detroit Edison's dam building projects on the Huron, and U-M Architecture Professor Emil Lorch worked with Williams to design the dam and powerhouse that we see today. The earthen portion of the dam is massive (over 1,700 feet long and 34 feet high), but it is the power plant that really stands out. The building is a wonderful example of Lorch's tasteful designs for industrial buildings (see #2) and shows that functional and industrial buildings can also be beautiful. It is built on a high poured-concrete base with yellow brick laid in decorative bands following the triangular outlines of the building's gables and windows. The building's Dutch-influenced parapet gables are topped with concrete trimmings. Detroit Edison sold the dam and power plant to the city in the 1960s. The building, though empty, still looks much as it did 100 years ago.

37 605 Miller
Samuel and Lillian Burchfield House   1907

Built in 1907, this home is a unique variation on the Arts and Crafts style that was just becoming popular. The early date of the building is seen in the orange common brick and rubble stone foundation (later Arts and Crafts buildings used hard-fired bricks and had cinder block foundations). The asymmetrical design with different-sized windows on the front facade is a holdover from the Queen Anne period. The most striking features of the building are the brick-faced dormer with flared front gable and the arched front entry with hints of the Mission style.

The home was built by Samuel and Lillian (Hobson) Burchfield. Samuel Burchfield was a merchant tailor who owned a shop at 106 E. Huron St. Burchfield was active in the Republican Party and served as county coroner for many years. He was an avid outdoorsman and a member of the American Iris Society, where he gained notice for his hybrid irises after he introduced new varieties during the 1920s. Samuel died on November 14, 1928 and Lillian continued to live in the home until 1942. It has remained a single-family home and has been restored, maintaining an interesting example of an early Arts and Crafts-style building in the city.

707 Miller
Frederick and Mary Brown House

38

1894

Frederick Brown was a saloon keeper who also dealt in wine and cigars. Born in Germany, Brown came to America around 1870 and by the 1880s had opened his business at 111 N. Main. Most saloons were owned by Germans (see #287) and often ran afoul of the local temperance movement which had a strong presence in Ann Arbor. Newspapers of the time report that temperance advocates with Kodak cameras (called "Kodakers") attempted to enter Brown's saloon to photograph minors being served (Brown was fined more than once for serving alcohol to minors). Despite this pressure, Brown was successful enough to build this handsome Queen Anne house in 1894, a year after he married. Prohibition put an end to Fred Brown's saloon, but the 1922 city directory lists him as still in business selling "soft drinks." Fred Brown died in 1946 and his widow Mary continued to live in the house until 1963, when she was 90 years old.

The highlights of this imposing home are the porches. The front porch features turned columns, spindle work, and a mansard roof with pediment over the entrance. A two-story side porch with the same turned columns and spindle work is sheltered under the cross eave. The side porch undoubtedly has spectacular views of West Park and downtown Ann Arbor. In 1994, the owner removed modern siding and repaired the elaborate upper and lower spindle work and brackets.

Former IHP

809–813 Miller
Jacob and Anna Shultz Houses   c. 1840s

Cooper Jacob F. Shultz (also spelled Shiltz, Schultz, Schlitz, Schoeltz, or Schiltz) and his wife Anna probably built these two houses sometime between their purchase of the property in 1842 and 1853, when both houses appear on a city map. However, some features imply an earlier date and we know that the property was sold to Abram B. Guiteau in 1835. He might have built one or both the houses. The house at 809 was built with a massive timber frame, bark-covered log floor joists, beaded exposed corner posts on the interior, with accordion lath and brick nogging in the walls (see #8, #22, and #190), all of which are features found only in very early buildings in the city.

The smaller house at 813 Miller—a mere 823 square feet—is assumed to be the earlier of the two buildings. It served as the Shultz's first home and is a 1½-story side-gabled house with a central door flanked by two long, narrow windows. These probably date to the 1880s. The shed roof dormer and portico are not original. By 1860, the house belonged to Jacob's brother John Shultz. It was occupied later by Jacob and Anna's son Charles Shultz and his wife Louisa.

The house at 809 Miller is 1½ stories with the long side of the house facing the road and two doorways that allowed for separate entrances into the formal and informal parlors—very unusual for Ann Arbor. It is almost 1,300 square feet. It has eyebrow windows under the eaves and very simple gable returns on the sides. The full-width porch is probably from the 1860s. The Shultz family owned the houses until the late 1890s. In 2008, the Historic District Commission awarded Jeffrey Lamb and Leyla-Lau Lamb a Preservation Award for their maintenance of this historic property.

809 was a former IHP

920 Miller
Christian Mack School

40

1921

Built in the Collegiate Gothic style, the Christian Mack School features a pleasing combination of red brick with limestone trim. Elements of Gothic influence abound, including the main entry block with a round arched door, a prominent tower with castellated parapet, and an oriel window. The primary entrances to the building feature Gothic-style arches and the corners of the building have diagonal or French buttresses of brick and limestone. Some of the windows have pointed Gothic arches. The building originally housed 450 students for elementary and junior high school.

The school was built in 1921, during an Ann Arbor public school building boom. It replaced the old Third Ward School, which stood further to the east across Miller (see #34). That school was built in 1866, and renamed Mack School in 1901 to honor school board member and businessman Christian Mack. In 1974, a large addition was added to the 1921 building which is now the primary classroom space of the Mack Open School. It also houses a swimming pool.

Former IHP

1884 Miller
John and Jane Bird House   1869

John C. Bird came to Ann Arbor Township from New Jersey with his parents in 1833 after his father Furman Bird bought this parcel of land. Following his parents' deaths in the 1850s, John and his wife Jane (Slatford) made the family homestead their home. In 1860, the Birds began establishing a large orchard that became the first commercial peach orchard in town. The farm became known as "Peach Hill" (although hundreds of apple trees were also planted). John Bird served Ann Arbor Township as justice of the peace for 25 years and was an avid abolitionist and early supporter of the Republican Party. In 1869, he built the house we see today.

The Birds' Italianate home was built during the height of the style's popularity and features an "Italianate Cube" shape with a shallow hipped roof, a double-bracketed cornice with dentils, a curved frieze board, and a large wraparound porch—features of this style (see #123). This original porch is supported by slender posts with traces of their former Gothic Revival style in the clusters at the top of the columns. There is no balustrade. The four-over-four windows on the front are paired, with the upper windows framed by eared trim and pediments with Gothic Revival detailing—a feature repeated on the side windows as well. The front entrance has original painted glass sidelights and transom and an arch-paneled Italianate front door. The interior once had a curving stairway and 14 large, airy rooms.

Mr. and Mrs. Earl Martin, Bird descendants, still owned the home in 1967. Mrs. Martin was the daughter of the original owner and was born in the house. Mr. Martin, together with George McCalla, held the first Farm Bureau fair on these grounds in 1938. In 1953, the area was partially subdivided as "Arbor Heights" and later in 1955 it was subdivided as "Martin Acres." By 1967, the Martins had added apartments in the back, but the house had not changed much since the 1860s. The house has been in the Birkle family now for many years.

Former IHP

1150 Mixtwood
Edward and Irene Olencki House

42

1954

Like his colleague, friend, and neighbor Joseph Albano (see #43), Edward Olencki (they formed a local firm Albano & Olencki) was born in Chicago and studied architecture at the Illinois Institute of Technology (IIT) under Mies van der Rohe, one of the 20th century's greatest architects. Olencki came to the University of Michigan School of Architecture in 1948 and became Dean in 1964. He spent 40 years teaching furniture design, construction methods, and architectural design—with a special interest in church architecture. Olencki designed at least four residences in the city of Ann Arbor (see #364), most of which were in collaboration with Albano. He retired in 1987 and this house remained his home until 2000.

The house is long and low with a prominent garage in the typical massing of the Mid-Century Modern style. Built into the hilly terrain of the Upper Water Hill Neighborhood, Olencki designed the house with the garage set into the hill, and a patio on top which can be accessed from the front steps and front door. Large eaves and a nearly flat roof are supported by large rafters with exposed ends. The exposed rafters frame the large plate-glass and smaller clerestory windows—design elements that are similar to Joseph Albano's house at 1158 Pomona (see #43), leading to the speculation that the homes may have been designed by both architects. Panels on stilts cover the front facade and replace the traditional "porch."

43 1158 Pomona
Joseph and Emma Albano House 1955

Born in Chicago in 1906, architect Joseph Albano studied at Northwestern University and later at the Illinois Institute of Technology under the modern architecture master Mies van der Rohe. Albano and his wife Emma (Krechefsky) arrived in Ann Arbor in 1947 when Joseph began teaching at the University of Michigan School of Architecture. Unlike other professors of the day who built homes in Ann Arbor Hills, the Albanos built theirs on the northwest side of town (now called Upper Water Hill). The previous year, Albano's friend, colleague, and design partner Edward Olencki (see #42) had built his house around the corner on Mixtwood.

Joseph Albano designed his own home, possibly with Olencki's help, and it stands in stark contrast to the more conventional mid-century ranches that surround it. The home features the characteristic blank front facade that offers privacy from the street, as does the brick wall that screens a side porch and patio. The carport is an extension of the exposed rafters, which also create very large overhangs. The window configuration is similar to Olencki's house, with large plate-glass windows topped with smaller clerestory ones between the rafters. The flat roof and vertical cedar siding are typical features of the modern homes of the era.

Emma Albano was an accomplished photographer who studied under the influential American photographer Edward Weston and sold many photographs over her lifetime. The Albanos continued to live here following Joseph's retirement in 1971 and left Ann Arbor in 1975. It has been owned by Steven Sivak since 1995.

427–433 Spring
Samuel Burchfield Row House

44

1911

This four-unit townhouse arrangement of shared walls was built in 1911 and is highly unusual for the city of Ann Arbor. The building is in wood rather than masonry (see #140). Few other examples exist in the area. It is an odd mix of architectural styles, with elements of the Colonial Revival style in the central pediment, symmetrical facade, and columns supporting the classical porticoes; the Craftsman style in the building's exterior knee braces and original front doors; and finally the very dated, but lingering appearance of the Queen Anne styling in the front bay windows, one-over-one windows, and cantilevered, corner bump-outs. As a whole the building is a fascinating example of a form that never quite caught on in Ann Arbor and the common mishmash of styles that often were used in buildings.

It was erected in 1911 by Samuel Burchfield who built his own house just around the corner (see #37). Burchfield was a merchant tailor and served as county coroner for many years. The building was owned by the Burchfield family until 1961, when Samuel Levy and P. Root bought it. Early tenants were members of Ann Arbor's working class, with tradesmen and their families making up the bulk of the residents.

45 618 Spring
Nehemiah and Sarah Parsons House   c. 1867

The Parsons House is an excellent example of the upright-and-wing style of Vernacular Folk house that was popular in the Midwest following the Civil War. The wooden house retains vestiges of the Greek Revival style in its six-over-six windows and window pediments, but the steeply pitched roofs speak more to the Gothic Revival style. There are large overhanging eaves with no decoration to speak of.

Nehemiah Parsons was an early pioneer of Washtenaw County, buying land in Pittsfield Township in 1825 and serving as the first postmaster of Mallet's Creek in 1834. During the 1860s, Parsons was in the wool business with his nephew Addison P. Mills (see #46) under the name of A.P. Mills and Co. He was also chief engineer of the Ann Arbor Fire Department. He built the house in either 1867 or 1868, possibly as a speculative venture. He sold the house in 1869 to Henry and Anna Neeb and moved west to Missouri where he died in 1882. The Gregory and Phelps family owned the house from 1872 to 1912. From 1912 to 1963, the house was owned by the family of George and Grace Efner, who was a painter. It has been owned since 1994 by Mike Gerdenich and Ina Hanel, who are in the process of restoring it as we write.

625 Spring
Mills-Paul House   c. 1865

Addison P. Mills was a native son of Ann Arbor, being the firstborn of early pioneers Lorrin Mills and Harriet Parsons in 1829. Harriet Parsons was the second person to teach school in Ann Arbor before a public system was set up in 1830. In the 1850s and 1860s, Addison Mills ran a dry goods store below his father's tailoring shop and later went on to deal in sheep and wool with his uncle Nehemiah Parsons (see #45) and George Cropsey. Mills built this solid masonry Greek Revival-Italianate house between 1864 and 1866 at the southwest corner of Spring and Hiscock after Hiscock's Addition was platted in 1859.

The house is somewhat quirky and original with its mix of Italianate-style segmented arches over the windows and Greek Revival details, including classical cornice returns, six-over-six windows, the triangular window in the attic, and a doorway with full transom and sidelight windows. Addison Mills may have built the house as an investment and lived here briefly. It is one of the original houses in the area and reflects the post-Civil War prosperity of Ann Arbor.

In December of 1866, the house was purchased by Henry and Catherine (Cook) Paul. Henry Paul grew up on a farm in Scio Township and moved to Ann Arbor in the 1860s because of ill health. Here he began to manufacture furniture under the name Paul and Bissinger. Later he was in the lime and marble business. The Pauls sold the house in the mid-1870s and bought a farm in Pittsfield Township. The current porch appears to have been built in the early 20th century and replaced an older one. From 1910–1930 it was occupied by the Bury family and from 1940–1960 it was occupied by the Starry family. It has been a rental for many years.

Former IHP

47 626 Spring
William H. and Sarah McIntyre House   c. 1863

This modest and well-preserved Greek Revival home appears to have been built by William H. McIntyre in about 1863, and remained in the McIntyre family well into the 20th century. The house began as a simple, gable-front Greek Revival, with the wing on the north side added after 1880. The beautiful Italianate front porch appears to have been added when the wing was built. Note the columns with decoration at the capital and the lack of a balustrade. McIntyre married Sarah Maloney in 1865, and the couple raised their five children in the house on Spring Street.

The son of Irish immigrants, William H. McIntyre was born in Northfield Township in 1835 and at age 21 became constable in the township. In 1863, he moved to Ann Arbor to become jailer at the Washtenaw County Jail on North Main Street. He served as jailer for four years and then operated a grocery store for the next 30 years under the name Wicks and McIntyre.

Always active in public affairs, William McIntyre served as a city alderman in the 1870s and on the Board of Public Works, including many years as president.

Following his parents' deaths, their son Donald owned the house until 1930, although it was already being used as a rental, which is still its use today. A picture and description in the Urban Renewal files of the city from 1958 indicate that it was a seven-room frame house with an old barn. There were four rooms on the first floor, three on the second, and two old-style baths. It was on a stone foundation and had a coal-fired gravity furnace. It sold in 1955 for $7,750.

Downtown/ State Street/ Germantown

The downtown area contains what was John Allen and Elisha Walker Rumsey's original plat of the city from 1824. This plat stretched from Division Street to First Street as the eastern/western boundary, with William Street and Catherine Street making the southern and northern borders. The core of the city developed around Courthouse Square (see #87) at Main and Huron. Main, Huron, Liberty, and surrounding streets were all lined with residences mixed in with early wood and brick commercial structures. Very little remains of the first generation of buildings in downtown (see #48 and #78), though many can still be found in the Old Fourth Ward and Kerrytown neighborhoods which were platted shortly thereafter.

During the 1860s and 1870s, many of the first-generation buildings were demolished to make way for larger, more substantial brick Italianate buildings, many of which can still be found today (see #90 and #115). The building boom continued through the late 19th and early 20th centuries, with many more landmark buildings being constructed, including the city's first high rises (see #91, #94, and #107), which permanently altered Ann Arbor's small-town skyline. Also during this era buildings began springing up along State and Liberty to cater to the ever-increasing student population following the Civil War and World War I, offering the first indications of the growing importance of the University of Michigan in the city's economy. Nickels Arcade (see #104) and the Michigan Theater (see #79) are two notable landmarks of this part of town.

Following the Great Depression in the 1930s, the post-war trend toward suburban development (1950s), and the growing importance of the automobile, the downtown area began a long and steady decline. Many historic buildings were demolished to make way for parking or new developments, while others were simply neglected or had their facades hidden or remodeled. In the late 1960s, concerned citizens and historic preservationists began advocating for the preservation of Ann Arbor's remaining historic architecture. The city's purchase of the Kempf House (see #53) in 1969 was one of the earliest efforts to protect this architectural heritage, followed by the creation of the Ann Arbor Historic District Commission in 1971. This led to the creation of several downtown districts in 1975, 1989, and 1992, protecting buildings on Main Street, Liberty, Washington, and State. Today downtown Ann Arbor is bustling and thriving, and is often ranked as one of the best downtowns in America. The preserved historic architecture is one of the big draws to the very walkable, human-scale urban core.

48 214 W. Ann
David A. and Sabrina McCollum House   1830s

This side-gabled I-House with Greek Revival details was built by David A. and Sabrina McCollum sometime in the 1830s. The house is reported to have bark-covered log floor joists, a feature common in many of Ann Arbor's earliest buildings. The McCollums came to Ann Arbor from New York State in the late 1820s and built this house shortly after. David A. McCollum was active in the Liberty Party, a short-lived abolitionist party, and ran unsuccessfully for Director of the Poor in 1842 and for assessor in 1843 and 1844. In 1852, the McCollums sold the property to John Rose and moved to Kalamazoo County.

John Rose was a native of Lincolnshire, England and came to Washtenaw County in 1845. Rose and his wife Eliza Jane (Virrill) lived in the house until the late 1860s when they purchased a farm in Pittsfield Township. They continued to rent the house at 214, and in the early 1890s, built the house next door at 220 W. Ann. The house became a duplex in the early 20th century, with a second front entrance added, the center second-story window being removed, and a smaller porch replacing a larger full-width front porch.

Former IHP

210–212–216 S. Ashley
Mann and Zeeb/Hertler Brothers
1899/1910

49

Two simple brick buildings, one a storefront with paired arched windows and the other a drive-thru warehouse, comprise what was the Hertler Brothers Agricultural Implements store, currently Downtown Home and Garden. When they were constructed, horses were still the main transport of the day and Ashley Street contained many stables, feed barns, agricultural implements, distributors, and blacksmithing operations. This is the only survivor.

Mann and Zeeb Agricultural Implements originally built the storefront at 210 in 1899. Hertler Brothers was organized in 1906, and after buying this building they built their warehouse next door in 1910. The old drive-thru barn was built of rock-faced cement and covered with a brick veneer in the 1920s. In the old store at 210 there are still creaky wooden floors, ladders sliding along the shelving, and barrels full of bird seed. Ann Arbor old-timers remember the potbellied stove that customers huddled around in the winter. It has the atmosphere of an old country store with modern sensibilities.

Mark Hodesh bought the operation from the last of the Hertler Brothers in 1974 and began its slow transformation from farm to garden and from rural to urban. He preserved many of the original interior features, including an elaborate system of chutes to the basement that allowed a simple way to bag grains. Today, seed takes precedence over feed, and the former horse barn now accom-

modates lawn furniture, wood stoves, and an impressive selection of flower bulbs and gardening supplies. Hodesh has been recognized with many awards for his work in the preservation of the buildings.

50 300 S. Ashley
Dag-Wood/Fleetwood Diner   1948–1949

The Dag-Wood Diner Inc. of Toledo, Ohio was a producer of diner kits that could be purchased and assembled on site, unlike many of its competitors who built prefabricated diners that were trucked in. The company was short-lived, and ceased operation in 1949. Completed in early 1949 by owner Donald Reid, the Dag-Wood Diner was built with a metal frame covered in enameled steel panels. Reid had to petition the city council to allow the construction of a steel building for restaurant use, a change that was granted in August of 1948. Renamed the Fleetwood Diner in 1971, it has become an Ann Arbor institution, serving up classic, greasy-spoon diner fare to generations of Ann Arborites. Though the original enameled panels have been removed and the building is now covered in new stainless steel, the Fleetwood Diner still retains much of its historic charm and patina. It is an Ann Arbor landmark.

Former IHP

310 S. Ashley
Second Ward Public Building

51

1901

Built in 1901, the Second Ward Public Building was a polling place and a meeting hall for the primarily German residents of the second ward of the city. The building was constructed by the Koch brothers, John and Christian, for $1,055. At the time, John Koch was city alderman from the second ward. The Koch brothers reportedly built the building from reclaimed brick taken from the old U-M Chemistry Building, which they were renovating at the time. Bricks on the interior of the building have initials and names scratched into them from the 1880s and 1890s.

The building is simple, built of reclaimed common brick with a pleasant orange color. Rusticated stone is used on the front facade, as well as for window sills and lintels. A stone tablet on the front is engraved with the words "Second Ward Public Building." In 1926, the second floor of the building was rented to Stanger Furniture, and by 1959, the entire building was leased to the Sears and Roebuck Company which used it to store tires. In 1969, the building was purchased by local preservationists John and Mary Hathaway who have used the building, now known to many as "Hathaway's Hideaway," for special events and gatherings. The interior contains many historic artifacts relating to Ann Arbor history.

MSHD

52 303 S. Division
Emanuel and Anna Mann House   1850

Emanuel E. Mann was 16 years old when he arrived in Ann Arbor from Germany in 1830 with his mother and two sisters, Sophia and Louisa, to join their father Henry. They were the first Germans to arrive in Ann Arbor. Mann's glowing letters encouraged others to come and settle and thus began the large immigration from the Wurttemberg area of Germany to Ann Arbor.

The Manns opened Ann Arbor's first tannery where young Emanuel learned the trade. After the tannery burned, Mann went into business with Christian Eberbach (see #325) in his pharmaceutical company. Mann's sister Louisa married Frederick Schmid, the first German Protestant minister in Michigan, who helped establish churches all over the state. Mann later purchased a drug store on Main Street and his sons Albert and Eugene ran the Mann Brothers Drug Store well into the 1900s. Mann was very active in local politics and was vice president of the organizational meeting of the Republican Party held "under the oaks" in Jackson, Michigan in July of 1854. This party was later to nominate Abraham Lincoln for president. Mann also served on the school board, as an alderman, and as a state senator.

The house is another Vernacular example of the Greek Revival with a pedimented front with returns, a side-entry door with sidelights and transom, and walls of stucco-over-brick scored to resemble stone. There were so many of these stucco-over-brick homes at one point that Ann Arbor was referred to as a "little stucco village." The windows have been changed and the porch is not original. Built in 1850 for himself and wife Anna (Niethammer) and their children, Mann sold it in 1868 and retired to a nearby farm.

The house became a rental as early as 1937 when osteopaths Bert and Beth Haberer rented space here as the commercial district of Liberty Street (starting with the Michigan Theater) began to encroach on the residential portions in the 1930s. It was converted to business use in the 1950s. Despite an appearance that has suffered from neglect, this home remains a very important historic building.

Former IHP

312 S. Division

Henry DeWitt Bennett/Kempf House   1853

53

This local landmark was saved from the wrecking ball in 1969 when the City of Ann Arbor purchased it and made it a museum as part of its parks department. It is a classic example of a Greek Revival gable-fronted temple, with a pedimented portico of square columns and anthemion designs on the frieze windows in the upper floor of the house. Long renowned for its graceful simplicity, the Kempf House has been described in books and numerous publications and was listed on the National Register of Historic Places in 1973. It is thought to have been designed by Arden Ballard of Ypsilanti.

The house was built in 1853 for Henry DeWitt Bennett, who was postmaster (appointed by the President of the United States) and later Secretary and Steward of the University of Michigan from 1869–1886. When he retired to California, the house was purchased by his neighbor A.L. Noble (see #54) and rented to Reuben and Pauline (Widenmann) Kempf who purchased the house in 1890.

Kempf was a native of Pittsfield Township, a son of German immigrants who sent their son back to Germany to study music at the Royal Conservatory in Stuttgart. He returned to Ann Arbor to pursue a career as a musician and teacher. One of his major accomplishments, begun at the behest of the U-M President, was to organize a singing society (Lyra Male Chorus) to unite town and gown. He was choir director of St. Andrew's Church from 1895–1928. His wife Pauline Kempf, also a graduate of a music conservatory (Cincinnati), taught voice in the front parlor using the magnificent Steinway case piano.

Upon her death in 1953, the house was purchased by neighbors (the Parkers) who sold it to the city in 1969. The museum interprets the life and work of a German-American family in c. 1890 Ann Arbor. It is run by a volunteer non-profit that holds fundraisers, noon lectures, gives tours on Sundays, and hosts special events including Valentine Teas.

The unusual boxed-in staircase, which is entered from the center of the house, leads to several bedrooms furnished with locally made antique furniture. In addition to an All-mendinger organ, the pièce de résistance is in the front parlor—an 1877 Steinway concert grand piano purchased by Prof. Kempf and borrowed on many occasions by the University for visiting musicians. It has been in this location for over 100 years.

EWHD, NR, SR

54 320 S. Division
A.L. Noble House and Carriage House 1884/1892

Albert L. Noble came to Ann Arbor in 1869 to study at the University, but his eyes were bad and he turned toward business instead of academia. He partnered with Joe T. Jacobs in a clothing store on Main Street. He eventually sold his interest and opened his own store, known as the Star Clothing Company, which outfitted many University of Michigan students and businessmen alike. By 1883 he was successful enough to buy this property from his neighbor Henry Bennett and build this magnificent, imposing brick structure, showing signs of both the Italianate and Queen Anne styles. The slate roof, decorative chimneys, pressed brick, arched windows, and carved wood details on the porches, gable corners, and brackets show the influence of both. The fine stonework over the windows illustrates the craftsmanship of Anton Eisele (see #132). *The Ann Arbor Courier* reported in January of 1884 that it was "to be finished in the fall, $10,000." Another newspaper, *The Ann Arbor Democrat*, noted in November of 1884 that it was built by William Briggs, contractor.

In 1892, Noble became the first president of the State Savings Bank. In that year he erected the carriage house, which, remarkably, still stands today in the rear of the property, a rare example of what a typical late 19th-century homestead in central Ann Arbor would have looked like.

After the death of Noble's wife in 1902, the house had a series of owners until 1920 when Dr. David M. Cowie purchased it for a private hospital. Cowie was a professor of pediatrics and infectious diseases at the University of Michigan and many babies were born here. His claim to fame was in getting the state to adopt the use of iodized salt to prevent goiter. After his death in 1940, the house was converted to apartments.

EWHD

409 S. Division
First Church of Christ, Scientist   1913

This Neoclassical building in the style of Jefferson's Monticello (but with some Prairie School features) was constructed as the home of the First Church of Christ, Scientist, a society organized in 1901. They demolished an older home on the site and laid the cornerstone in 1912. The first services were held in 1913. The architect was Spencer Solon Beman (1887–1952), the son of renowned Chicago architect Solon Spencer Beman. The latter's claim to fame was the town of Pullman, an early planned community in Chicago. The son was trained at Oxford and returned to Chicago, specializing in churches and residential buildings. During his lifetime he executed drawings for over 100 churches in the Georgian and Neoclassical styles. The Koch Brothers, a local firm, were the contractors.

The Neoclassical features include the use of stucco over brick, the colonnaded entry with full pediment, and the many-faceted cupola on the roof. The wings and high windows are influenced by Frank Lloyd Wright's work in the Unity Temple of Oak Park, Illinois, which Beman no doubt saw.

The Christian Scientist Church moved to Washtenaw in 1950, but this building continued as a church for over 75 years until it was converted into a residence over 20 years ago.

EWHD

56 530 S. Division
John George Koch House
1874

Showcased by its high visibility next to Hanover Square at the intersections of Division, Packard, and Madison streets, this brick Italianate cube was built in 1874 for John George Koch. Koch was a local furniture maker who had originally apprenticed in Germany. Like many other Germans in Ann Arbor, Koch came from the Wurttemberg area in 1866. Also like many of this era, he worked and traveled through many parts of the United States before settling in Ann Arbor in 1872. He was the assistant superintendent of the Keck Furniture Company for seven years before setting up his own furniture business with Jacob Haller in 1880, known as Koch and Haller.

Koch sold the house in the 1880s to Sarah and William Rice, wealthy farmers descended from another Washtenaw pioneer family. A 1906 biography states that "he removed to the city of Ann Arbor and there his wife purchased a residence which he made his home until his death, enjoying in well-earned ease the fruits of his former toil." The house remained in the Rice family until World War I and then was converted into apartments.

In the 1940s, it was purchased by Claris Brown who converted it back to single-family use. The original brackets and heavy brick arches over the windows remain. The woodwork in the parlors was refinished after removing seven layers of paint. Brown was presented with a restoration award in 1988 by the Historic District Commission. It is now a rental.

Former IHP

100 N. Fifth

57

Ann Arbor City Hall/
Guy C. Larcom Municipal Building

1963

When City Hall was dedicated in 1963, this unusual inverted pyramid design (a poor man's Guggenheim, as one architect called it), designed by famous Michigan architect Alden Dow, was a re-creation of a typical "courthouse" square: it had an important municipal building surrounded by open space (in this case parking), trees, and gardens. At the time, it was described as "crisp and dignified and a reflection of the rejuvenation of the Central Business district. The Promenade Deck…is the modern equivalent of the town square and to be used for a wide variety of civic functions, exhibits, ceremonies and casual gatherings." The extension of each floor 18 inches beyond the one below was meant to "provide sun and weather protection to the grey tinted window areas which provide natural light to the office areas."

With its white bands of stucco-on-metal alternating between the windows and the flattened U-shaped arch of brick from front to back containing the elevators and heating units, this building stood out. From the very beginning it was controversial. Many considered it the ugliest building in Ann Arbor. Others considered it a work of genius, with an open-space floor design for offices that let workers interact, and plazas onto which they could walk out for fresh air and a cigarette. It is a true city landmark and very unique in Michigan.

Dow was an organic architect and had a design philosophy similar to that of Frank Lloyd Wright in his interest to design a whole environment. That meant picking colors, furnishings, and window designs that were all designed by the architect. Dow designed buildings specifically for their site and always had structural integrity and quality in all aspects of the work. Ann Arbor has one of the largest concentrations of Alden Dow buildings in the state, second only to Midland.

Overcrowding by the 1980s led to dissatisfaction by workers as the interior spaces had to be altered to accommodate more employees than originally intended and the organic elements of the design were no longer appreciated. A bond issue in 1987 that would have built underground parking, renovated the building, and added additional space to the east, was defeated.

When overcrowding reached its peak and the court space being rented was no longer available, discussions for expansion began again in 2000. Much wrangling occurred over whether to demolish the building, move City Hall to another site, put an addition on the east side, or put one on the west side. By 2006, a scheme for a west-side addition was proposed, and ground was broken in 2009. The new addition, known as the Justice Center, provided new court and police space. It was designed by Quinn Evans and opened in 2011. Part of this addition compromised the stepped nature of the west elevation of the Dow building, but the original building design can be seen from Ann Street. Also lost with the new addition was the sense of the "courthouse square" idea, though it remains another good example of Mid-Century Modern design in Ann Arbor's public buildings.

58 343 S. Fifth
Ann Arbor Public Library/District Library 1957/1974/1991

When this library opened in 1957, a dream was finally fulfilled after years of planning and controversy. The historic Beal House had to be demolished, the Ann Arbor School Board (the library was a part of the public school system at the time) had to approve, and the voters had to approve a millage. The voters were adamant that they wanted their new library to be downtown, so this site was purchased and well-known Michigan architect Alden Dow (later the architect laureate of Michigan; see #57 and #226) was selected to design a library for the future.

When it opened it was a revelation to the town: it had a two-story high reading room with light pouring in from glass walls. It had a community meeting space, a special children's room, nearby public parking, flexible bookshelves, a lack of interior walls that made the space open, a central checkout desk, an art alcove, a typing and photocopying room—and it was attractive! As Howard Peckham noted at the dedication, the event was not only "...the creation of an attractive building, but it is a day of honor because it represents a renewal of the trust placed on this community...to provide a 'means of education'...as required in the Northwest Territory Ordinance of 1787." It was a hit from the beginning and within months the library had increased patronage over 110%.

Dow designed many buildings in Ann Arbor, mostly for the university, but it was his designs for the Public Library and City Hall that defined the two most important public buildings in Ann Arbor. The restrained red brick building with two blue porcelain-on-enamel ribbons around the front and sides (one large one for planters and a thin line at the roof edge) was fairly typical of Dow's buildings since many of them had planters. The lovely walled garden on the south side and planters at ground level on the front (west) side are also typical Dow features. Dow was very interested in the relationship between buildings and nature.

In 1974, Donald Van Curler designed the first of two additions required by the increasing numbers of patrons and new technologies. A third addition by Osler and Milling was done in 1991. Each addition doubled the size of the library. All the additions are in red brick and blend with the original building. A glass "lookout" peeks out from the top of the third addition. In 2012, voters rejected a proposal to tear down the building and replace it.

438 S. Fifth

59

Erwin and Flora Schmid House

1925

Erwin Schmid was the grandson of influential German pastor Frederick Schmid who was the founder of the German Lutheran Church in Michigan. The fine Italianate residence of Pastor Schmid's son Frederick Schmid Jr. stood on this site until 1925, when it was razed by Erwin to build his more "modern" home.

Schmid hired Ann Arbor architect Herman Pipp to design the new residence. Pipp designed many notable buildings in the city including Nickels Arcade (see #104), Yost Ice Arena (see #225), and the Marchese Brothers Building (see #97). For the Schmids, Pipp created a completely unique version of the Arts and Crafts/Colonial homes that are otherwise very common in the city. The side-gabled colonial with Arts and Crafts-style shed dormer features brick on the first story and clapboard and shingles on the upper stories. The entry is framed with a simple entablature and brick arch that shelters the front door with its fanlight window. In a detail that resembles classical pilasters, Pipp has the first-story brick extending into the second story only on the outside corners of the building. Another unique feature is the many original paired casements, each featuring multi-paned leaded glass windows.

Erwin Schmid was a banker and partner in Muehlig and Schmid Hardware. He was very active in local government, serving on the Ann Arbor City Council, the Board of Fire Commissioners, and the Board of Education. Following the deaths of her parents, daughter Emma Schmid lived in the home until 2003. Along with 444 S. Fifth (see #60), the home still exhibits the original wrought-iron fence of Frederick Schmid Jr.'s house that once stood on the site.

60 444 S. Fifth
Schmid-Walz House   1905

The Schmid-Walz House shows the transition from the Queen Anne style popular in the late 19th century to the Colonial Revival style that would become hugely popular in the first half of the 20th century. The overall design and layout of the house is pure Queen Anne, with multiple rooflines and gabled roofs that project from a central hipped roof, windows of various sizes, including three different bay windows, and an asymmetrical facade. Hints of the Colonial Revival style are revealed in Doric columns and the large Palladian-style window on the north elevation.

The home was built by Erwin and Flora Schmid. Erwin Schmid was a partner in the hardware business of Muehlig and Schmid, and grandson of the famed Rev. Frederick Schmid. In 1917, the Schmids moved next door (see #59) and sold the house to William Walz and his wife Clara. William Walz, a veteran of the Spanish-American War, was a prominent banker, serving as president of the Ann Arbor United Savings Bank, as well as the top elected official of the Michigan Banking Association. Walz was also active in the Democratic Party, serving as president of city council, as well as mayor from 1909–1913. He was also a delegate to the 1940 Democratic Party Convention. Walz died in 1942, and the house passed to son William and his wife Kay. Kay continued to live in the house until her death in 2008 at age 101.

450 S. Fifth
Bassett-Ditz House

1849

This small and well-preserved Greek Revival house was built by school teacher Uri Bassett and his wife Hannah in 1849. Bassett taught at a private academy located around the corner at Fourth and William, and at the Michigan Normal School (now Eastern Michigan University) during the 1850s. The Bassetts sold the house in 1856. In 1860, the house was purchased by tailor Joseph Ditz and his wife Fredericka, both of whom were immigrants from Germany. Following the deaths of Joseph in 1887 and Fredericka Ditz in 1902, their widowed daughter Fredericka Stampfler and her daughter Luella moved into the house. The house remained in the Stampfler family into the 1960s.

The building began as the tiny one and one-half story southern portion. The only hint at the Greek Revival style are the simple gable returns and the six-over-six windows. The hipped roof, side wing, and porch were added by the Ditz family during the 1860s when the Italianate style was fashionable. The Bassett-Ditz House is a very rare survivor of this type of building in the near-downtown area. Tiny houses like this, built between 1825 and 1850, were once common in the near-downtown neighborhoods of Ann Arbor but were replaced by much grander homes and commercial buildings during the later 19th and early 20th centuries, and later by parking lots.

Former IHP

62 205 N. First
John and Ann Flynn House   1854

Irishman John Flynn and his wife Ann (Ryan) built the original front-gabled portion of this Greek Revival house in 1854. Flynn came to America in 1848, where he joined Washtenaw County's fast-growing Irish community. Flynn prospered as a well digger and mason and later as the owner of a lumber yard. Flynn and his wife Ann raised seven children in the house, and as the family grew, so did the house.

Between 1866 and 1880, the side wing with a small Gothic peak on the front elevation was added. The fanciful Italianate-style porch with thin chamfered columns was also added during this time period. Porches like these were popular additions to many Greek Revival houses during the 1860s (see #29 and #156) when porches and verandas were very much in fashion, and steam-powered sawmills made elaborate "gingerbread" more affordable.

The Flynn family lived in the home until the early 1900s. For much of the early 20th century the house served as the home of Emil and Antonia Rahr. Though the original windows have been replaced, the house still retains its original shutters and looks much as it did over 100 years ago.

Former IHP

120–130 S. First

Allmendinger Organ Factory   1888/1895/1906/1911

63

This block-long group of brick buildings was built in four stages as a factory for the Allmendinger Organ Company. The company was founded in 1872 by David F. Allmendinger, who first worked on the site in a frame house (the home of the Weils, the first Jewish family in Ann Arbor). Allmendinger apprenticed to Gottlieb Gaertner in 1867 and later married Gaertner's daughter and inherited the business. Allmendinger began modestly, using soup bones for the keys in his earliest organs when ivory was in short supply. He personally pedaled his handiwork from a wagon and eventually gained a reputation for fine workmanship.

His first customers were churches, but later he specialized in affordable reed organs that many farmers displayed and played in their parlors. Examples of these organs can be seen at the Kempf House (#53), and in an exhibit in the entry of 130 S. First, along with a history of the company and the family.

In its heyday, the factory made 5,000 organs and 600 pianos a year and shipped them all over the globe. These simple brick buildings, imposing in size, remain a fine example of utilitarian factory design. Factories like these anchored the Old West Side neighborhood and remind us of the days when workers were able to walk to work.

Allmendinger formed a stock company in 1888 and built the first of the four brick factories. He expanded to build Henderson Pianos in 1895 and later Ann Arbor Pianos, eventually changing the name to the Ann Arbor Organ Company. They even had a retail store on Main Street. Competition from phonographs and large companies like Sears caused the company to fold. A series of other businesses occupied the buildings, including Motor Products Company which made windshields.

Local realtor Mr. Carroll Benz purchased the buildings in 1935 and since then they have been known collectively as the Benz Building (even after the University bought it in 1969). It was purchased by Bill Martin of First Martin Associates in 1984 and remodeled into modern office space.

Former IHP

64 206–210 S. First
City Brewery/Ann Arbor Central Mills   1853–1905

An 1853 map notes "brewery" on this site and we know that by 1860 this was the G.F. Hauser City Brewery. In 1868, it was John Reyer's City Brewery and by 1872 it was the Elkhardt Bros. Brewery. Then came the Panic of 1873 that bankrupted many breweries, including this one. Germans like their beer to "lager," or age at cooler temperatures. In the basement today, the large brick lagering vaults remain, and are vestiges of this style of beer making.

In 1882, the Ann Arbor Central Mills acquired the property and it served as the center of a major flour mill operation until the 20th century. The newly invented thresher allowed for more wheat growing and Washtenaw County was one of the largest producers in the state. The original building in the Greek Revival style was clapboard, but was veneered with brick around 1900. Today the side sports a huge restored sign from the era: "King and White Loaf Flour."

The northernmost section of brick was built in 1905 and housed the mill offices. In 1973 it became the Blind Pig Saloon, one of the pioneers in redeveloping the west side of town, serving wine and sponsoring musical events. The original safe still serves as the wine cooler.

The old mill buildings were purchased by Ernst Lohr in 1939, and became Ann Arbor Implement until 1999. The buildings now house a variety of entertainment venues, including the Cavern Club, the Millennium Club, Gotham City, and Circus Bar and Billiards.

MSHD

111 S. Fourth
Heinrich Building

65

1870

The restoration of this building in 1975 sparked a renewed interest in downtown living and historic preservation which has prompted many projects since. This Italianate brick structure built in 1870 continued the tradition of a saloon on the site. It has the typical segmental arched windows on the second floor with curved arched windows on the third. It has retained its original windows, crowned with keystones with a leaf etched in each. Remarkably it also has its original cornice, a rarity in Ann Arbor. There are pilasters both at the corners and between the window bays, with diamond blocks and rosettes midway up the facade. An original storefront with cast-iron columns and stone quoins at the corners completes this picture of an 1870s commercial structure.

It was built by John D. Heinrich, who also owned the Kossuth Saloon near the train depot. Heinrich operated the saloon and hotel with his son-in-law George Stein until 1890. The building continued to operate as a saloon under various names until Prohibition. After that it housed a series of small businesses. The building next door at 113 S. Fourth Avenue was a blacksmith shop, but it has been more altered at the street level than 111 and was built later in the early 20th century. All the upper units were residential at first and later housed businesses and the Knights of Pythias.

By the 1970s it had deteriorated badly and the upper floors were almost empty. It was purchased by Peter and Bonnie DeLoof and Estelle and Herb Schneider in 1975 and converted to five apartments, now condominiums. They were pioneers in the effort to restore residential living to downtown.

MSHD, Former IHP

66 402 S. Fourth
Ottmar Eberbach House   1884/1928

The *Ann Arbor Democrat* of July 11, 1884 announced that "O. Eberbach's new house will be ready for occupancy in about six weeks. When completed it will be one of the finest residences in the city, costing $9,000. Wm. Niethammer is the contractor."

Eberbach's brick Italianate/Queen Anne house was part of a housing boom in the 1880s that kept local contractors busy. An earlier article in the *Ann Arbor Courier* noted that "this will make four handsome brick residences at this corner...about all the law will allow at one crossing." Cherry panels were used for the interior and the house had six handsomely decorated fireplaces. On the exterior it displays tall, narrow windows, a symmetrical floor plan, stone window hoods, many rooflines and chimneys, decorative eave carvings, and dormers. Two iron hitching posts still delineate the extent of the property.

Eberbach, like his father, local pharmacist Christian Eberbach (see #325), received his professional education in Germany. When he returned to Ann Arbor he joined the firm of Eberbach and Sons, manufacturers of pharmaceuticals and scientific equipment. It is still in business today in Ann Arbor as Eberbach Corporation. The Eberbach family maintained ownership of the home until 1974.

By the early 20th century, these downtown mansions were being converted to businesses as the business districts expanded and cars made living further from downtown possible. In 1928, General Tire Company built an addition on the west side of the house designed by R. S. Gerganoff (see #87) for their business with a drive-thru feature. The house was converted later to apartments. The Harris Tire Company later owned it and it eventually became a drive-thru beer depot. It still serves as a grocery and liquor store today.

WSHD

403 S. Fourth
Joe T. Jacobs House (Muehlig Funeral Chapel) 1877/1928

67

Part of a group of four brick Italianate houses that once graced this corner at William Street, this house was constructed by John Gates for Joe T. Jacobs, a clothier whose shop was on Main Street. It displays typical Italianate features, including paired brackets under extensive eaves, tall narrow windows capped by delicately carved limestone arches with keystones, projecting bays, and an asymmetrical floor plan. The *Ann Arbor Courier* of February 1877 remarked that "the inside work that is being done on Joe T. Jacobs' new house is being very finely executed. When completed it will be second to none in the county for convenience and ventilation." Although partly obscured by 20th-century additions, it still offers a glimmer of the grandness that once stood at this intersection.

Jacobs came to Ann Arbor from Ohio in 1867 and opened his eponymous clothing business in 1880. He was active in many civic affairs, including the school board, the Board of Indian Commissioners, the Knights Templar, and the Grand Army of the Republic. He was also a major partner in the Toledo, Ann Arbor and Northern Michigan Railway (see #243). The house was sold around 1910 to Dr. J.G. Lynds, a former Professor of Obstetrics and Gynecology at the University of Michigan, who used it as a private hospital for women called the "Ann Arbor Sanitarium" until 1918. In 1928, Muehlig Funeral Chapel purchased it and added the *porte-cochére* along William and a large garage. More remodeling occurred in 1951 and again in 1964 when the front portion was added and the parking lot expanded. Today it serves both as funeral home and residence of the general manager.

"Muehlig's" began as the carpentry shop of Florian Muehlig in 1852 in the 200 block of S. Main Street. Today Muehlig Funeral Chapel is one of the longest surviving businesses in the state of Michigan and has been recognized by the state for this achievement. It is the oldest funeral parlor in Michigan and the oldest continuously operating business in Ann Arbor.

WSHD

68 423 S. Fourth
Bethlehem German Evangelical Church 1895/1932/1966

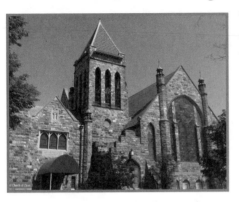

The history of Bethlehem Church is intimately tied to that of German immigration to Ann Arbor and Washtenaw County. Rev. Frederick Schmid arrived in 1833, responding to requests for services in German. What later became Bethlehem Church was the first German church in Michigan. A marker from the State of Michigan attests to this and to its importance in the development of other churches founded by Rev. Schmid.

In 1874, there was a split in the German community resulting in the creation of Bethlehem and Zion Lutheran. "For a time there were strong feelings between Bethlehem and Zion, not known as love," said Rev. Orval Willimann in a talk before the Washtenaw County Historic Society in 1983. Today both churches celebrate their common German ancestry.

By 1895, Bethlehem had enough money to hire German-American architect Richard Raseman from Detroit (also architect of the Harmonie Club) to build this fieldstone Gothic/Richardsonian Romanesque-style building— "Gothic with just enough variation to suit the modern eye" was noted at the dedication in 1896. It was built by Gladfied Contractors of Ypsilanti for $20,000. The interior features a beautiful chandelier, organ, gorgeous carved woodwork, and many German-made stained glass windows attributed to Glashuette Schonmunzach. The exterior features a pyramidal roof bell tower.

An addition designed by Ralph Hammett in a style similar to the original building was added in 1932–33. It featured a school, gymnasium, and a small auditorium. A more modern office addition was built in 1966. In 2009, the church celebrated its 175th anniversary. They received a Preservation Award from the Historic District Commission in 2011 for their over 100 years of maintenance and care.

SR

445 S. Fourth

George and Emma Wahr House

69

1890

This beautiful example of the exuberance of the Queen Anne style was built by John C. Walz (see #281) for local book dealer George Wahr and wife in 1890. It displays the woodworker's craft with its carved bargeboards, cutaway corners, decorative shingles, carved fretwork, sunbursts, dormers, bays, and gables, all blending in a marvelous totality. The current paint scheme enhances these various elements and brings joy to any passerby. Four years later, Wahr built a twin to this house at 120 N. Division (see #142) on the side lot of the property known as the Wilson-Wahr house (see #144), which he had purchased at a tax auction in 1893. The Division Street house still retains the original porch while this example shows the typical remodeling of porches to a simpler design in the early 20th century using stone wing walls.

Wahr was a successful book dealer and had stores on Main Street and State Street, the latter remaining open until the 1970s. It later housed one of the first Borders bookstores.

Following the Wahrs, the house was occupied by the Schaffer family for almost a century. George and Elizabeth Schaffer moved into the house in 1894 and by 1900 they had seven children living there with them. Several of the daughters remained with the parents until the 1930s. In 1935, the mother, now a widow, married Mr. Frank Ohlinger, who lived next door at 451 S. Fourth Ave. (see #71). In 1965, she was again widowed and her daughter Bertha moved into 451 and rented out 445. After Bertha's death the house was purchased by William Johnson who restored the building. He received a Preservation Award from the Historic District Commission in 1988. It is still well-maintained as a single-family residence.

Former IHP

70 442 S. Fourth
Gottlieb and Martha Wild House   1894

Built in 1894, this was the home of the Gottlieb Wild family for nearly one hundred years. Gottlieb Wild, a native of Stuttgart, Germany, came to America in 1882. Wild worked as a journeyman tailor before opening his own tailoring business, G.H. Wild and Co., in 1888. He married Martha Wurster of Dexter in 1891 and they had three children. Wild's tailoring business was very successful, and allowed him to build this fine home in 1894.

Having a central hipped roof and projecting front and cross gables, this textbook example of the Queen Anne style features varying textures, including "fish scale" shingles on the upper front and clapboards below. The home's front bay features horizontal and diagonal siding,

as well as smaller shingles. Multiple porches grace the home including a back and side porch that feature turned columns and spindlework. The two-tiered front porch is a hallmark of the Queen Anne style.

Gottlieb Wild died in the 1920s, and the home remained in the Wild family until 1988.

451 S. Fourth

Ward-Kerr House

71

1837/1887

This home appears to be a late 19th-century Queen Anne, but it started out decades earlier as an I-House, a Folk building form that is two rooms wide, one room deep, with two stories. The original home may have been built as early as 1837 by pioneer George Ward. Ward was a director of the Farmers and Mechanics Bank and owner of the Spring Mills with his old New York business associate Volney Chapin (see #121). Ward lived in the house until 1849. It changed hands a number of times before becoming the home of Sarah Brown, an older widow from New Jersey, who lived in the home for 30 years.

One of her boarders in later years was school teacher Ruthette Kerr. Ruthette's sister Cornelia Kerr, of Lodi Township, bought the house in 1887 and added on and remodeled the home into what we see today. Possibly because Kerr added on to an earlier house, the Ward-Kerr house is more restrained than some of its Queen Anne neighbors and features very little sawn millwork. The Queen Anne addition is thought to be the front part of the house, with its front gabled roof lower than the central hipped roof, which is topped with an additional gable. Complex roof forms were common in the style. The home features a small bay window. The front porch and entry with leaded glass sidelights are presumed to be later additions. Cornelia Kerr never married and lived in the house with her mother Harriet, father Alexander, and her sister Mary. Cornelia died in 1897 followed by her father in 1898. The home became a rental for many years and in 1920 it became the longtime home of Frank Ohlinger. Current owners Piotr Michalowski and Deanna Relyea received a Preservation Award in 2006.

Former IHP

72 206 E. Huron
Haller's Jewelry/Ann Arbor Tribune Building   1860/1931

The distinctive Art Deco facade was added to this brick building in 1931 when it was owned by the *Ann Arbor Tribune*, a formerly German language newspaper. The building may date back as far as 1860, when it would have been Haller's Jewelry. Later it was the bakery of Fred and Mary Heusel.

The *Ann Arbor Tribune* developed out of other German papers, including *Die Neue Post* published by Eugene Helber (see #312), who was very pro-German during World War I and felt the pressure to change the name of the paper and publish it in English.

The bowed-out facade with its pointed cap, bank of steel casement windows, and muscular limestone entry all say Art Deco. The Kleinschmidt name was added after the Springer-Kleinschmidt Insurance Company purchased the building in 1939, and is still engraved above the doorway. Remarkably, the interior with molded metal walls and ceilings remains. In 1987 the owners received a Preservation Award from the Historic District Commission.

Former IHP

219 E. Huron
Firemen's Hall

73

1882

This Italianate brick firehouse looks somewhat like a medieval church with a bell tower, or a modified Italian villa of the 1300s from Florence. It was designed by Detroit architect William Scott (after designs by local architects George Scott and Arthur Marshall were rejected) and was built in 1882–83. The contractors were local masons Tessmer and Ross, who met their budget of $10,000 under the watchful eye of the city council, still making this the most expensive structure the city owned at the time. The building has soaring arches, rows of brick corbelling, limestone caps with carved rosettes and lintels, and an 1882 date stone in the Huron Street lunette in the gable. These were typical features of the Italian villa style in America. One of the most distinctive elements is the sculpture of a fireman's cap in the window lintels. In those days, firemen were volunteers and rode wagons pulled by horses. It was a time when cities built fine municipal structures to express their civic pride.

By the mid-20th century, it had long been regarded as old fashioned. The building began to be appreciated again during the Sesquicentennial of Ann Arbor in 1974 and historic preservationists urged its protection. The red paint was removed and the stonework cleaned. The bays for the trucks were preserved and a weather vane was added to the tower (whose original purpose was to hold drying hoses and the alarm bell). A worthy gem, it became the symbol of the new historic preservation movement. It appeared on the covers of many books and magazines, including the first edition of *Historic Buildings, Ann Arbor, Michigan* in 1975.

In the late 1970s, a new station was built next door on Fifth, and a new use was needed. In 1978, Cynthia Yao stepped in and proposed what is now the Ann Arbor Hands-On Museum—a touch-and-tell type of museum that was gaining popularity for teaching science to children. It opened in 1982, with 25 exhibits on two floors. It eventually expanded to four floors and to other buildings nearby. Today this museum is a major tourist attraction with 250 interactive exhibits still maintained by a vast army of volunteers.

NR, SR, OFWHD

74 340 E. Huron
Ann Arbor News Building   1936

Built in 1936, this Art Deco building was the home of *The Ann Arbor Daily News* (later *Ann Arbor News*) for sixty-three years. It was designed by the famed Detroit architect Albert Kahn, who designed many of the printing and production buildings for *The Ann Arbor News'* parent company Booth Newspapers. While Kahn designed a number of distinguished residences and campus buildings in Ann Arbor, this is his only commercial building in the city. John Knight served as architectural engineer on the project and the construction was completed by the Esslinger-Misch Co. of Detroit, who also built the Michigan Theater Building (see #79).

Kahn's design (the portion at the corner of Division and Washington) is stripped down and modern for the time, clad in limestone, with black granite trimmings. Two aluminum bands wrap around the cornice of the building, and stylized aluminum bas-relief panels are set in the building's black granite, representing the subjects covered by the paper. The reliefs were done by the Italian-born sculptor Corrado Parducci, who often worked on Kahn-designed buildings, and were cast by C.W. Olson Inc. Parducci's work can also be seen in the Rackham Auditorium (see #242), as well as a number of Detroit landmarks including the Guardian Building, the Fischer Building, and the Masonic Temple lobby.

In 1962, a sympathetic addition was made to the building's west side and another large addition was added to the south side in 1967. With the decline of print media in the new millennium, *The Ann Arbor News* closed its doors for good in 2009, after being in almost continuous operation for 174 years. Recently this wonderful Art Deco building has become the home of the University of Michigan Credit Union.

116 W. Huron
Ann Arbor Bus Depot

75

1940

One of the few examples of an Art Deco building in Ann Arbor, the bus depot was built by the Greyhound Company in 1940, replacing an earlier building which had served the interurban railroads. It represents a simple yet eye-catching example of this style with its smooth-sawn Indiana limestone facade, curved windows, and stainless steel trim. The vertical blade sign plays off the horizontal curve of the window, which ends in a semicircle at the west end of the building.

The building was designed by the Cleveland, Ohio firm of Banfield and Cumming, with aid from local architect Douglas Loree. Shortly after it was completed it was highlighted in a book about bus depots entitled *Modern Bus Terminals and Post Houses*. The interior was very elegant, with stainless steel stairways and birch wood cabinetry. That disappeared long ago, but the exterior remains almost completely intact.

It was purchased by First Martin Corporation in 1998 and was proposed for demolition. First Martin has recently restored the building's facade, and it is still used as a bus depot. The stylish facade is a favorite subject for photographers, artists, and tourists. Plans in 2014 for a hotel at this site show only the facade being preserved.

Former IHP

76 213–241 E. Liberty
Zwerdling Block   1915

This example of the Beaux Arts style, popular for commercial buildings in the early 20th century, was built by Osias Zwerdling for his fur business in 1915, and originally was of patterned white brick. Typical of the style are classical elements, including a small central cornice, modillions, brackets, and a tin cornice made to resemble terracotta. Zwerdling arrived in Ann Arbor as an immigrant in 1903 and by 1915 he was successful enough to move the Koch House, which was on the site, to Fourth Avenue and build this three-bay building. Zwerdling was also a well-known philanthropist and leader of the Jewish community in Ann Arbor. He was an organizer of the Beth Israel Congregation and the Hillel Foundation for University of Michigan students (the second in

the U.S.). When interviewed in 1974 at the age of 96, he still maintained an active interest in the building and did his own accounts.

Supporters of Mr. Zwerdling and his family organized an effort in 1992 to restore the sign for his fur business on the wall in the alley, which was painted by a local artist in the 1920s in an Art Deco style. The sign was re-dedicated in 1997 with a ribbon cutting by the mayor and in 1998 it received a Special Merit Award from the Historic District Commission.

In 1978, this building was joined to the Darling block next door to create the East Liberty Plaza—a mini-mall that includes many types of businesses, using the lower levels as well as the street level for shopping. It was the brainchild of Estelle Schneider and Bonnie DeLoof who believed in recycling old downtown buildings. At the time quite revolutionary, it remains unique in its efforts to improve and enhance the downtown shopping experience.

MSHD

241–293 E. Liberty
Darling Block

77

1915

This brown brick Beaux Arts building was built for Dr. Cyrenus Darling and designed by Detroit architects Malcolmson and Higginbotham (more noted for their schools, like the former Ann Arbor High School). L.D. Wines supervised the construction of this fireproof building, and in 1917 Dr. Darling and Dr. Charles L. Washburne opened their offices on the second floor. Below them was the famed Fischer Pharmacy, at the corner until 1977, and the equally famed Goodhew Flowers, also an original tenant until 1977. Dr. Darling was an activist in local affairs, helping organize the first St. Joseph Mercy Hospital (he served as chief of staff), and serving on the Medical School faculty at the University of Michigan, as well as becoming the Dean of Dentistry. He also served one term as mayor of Ann Arbor. Osias Zwerdling (see #76) purchased the building in 1934 from the Darling estate. It was joined to Mr. Zwerdling's building in 1978 to form the East Liberty Plaza mini-mall.

The style features elements of a classical nature that characterize the Beaux Arts look, including formal symmetry, strong horizontal lines, and elaborately decorative details on a plain background. Roof forms are usually submerged behind the facades. Over the entry to the second level is a decorative terra-cotta frame embellished with curvilinear floral elements and the name "Darling" prominently inscribed in the stone above. It is a tour de force of the carver's art. The building houses Afternoon Delight and a number of other shops symbolic of the vitality of downtown Ann Arbor.

MSHD

78 321 E. Liberty
Enoch and Armanilla James House 1849

Emil Lorch, former Dean of the University of Michigan Architecture School, described this unpainted brick Federal-style building in 1936 as "a two and one half story Eastern City row type, rare in Michigan." In form it resembles what some would call a Philadelphia townhouse, being three bays wide with a tall, narrow facade and with stepped gables on the roof, similar to those found on the 1832 Anson Brown building (see #3). It has a simple yet elegant doorway with sidelights, topped by a transom window. The large residential area it was once part of has now been reduced to this one block, which is the East Liberty Street Historic District.

This pre-Civil War house was built by Enoch James and was part of a pair that were back to back between Washington and Liberty Streets. James was a mercantile man, originally from Massachusetts, and was the brother of Luther James (see #146). Cornelia Corselius describes the family in her 1909 manuscript on Ann Arbor's historic houses as being "prominent society people in the 1850s and 60s." Her friend Lucy Chapin's photograph in that manuscript shows the portico the same as the one there today (it probably dates to 1900). James lived in this house with his wife Armanilla until their deaths in the late 1860s.

Late in the 19th century, it was a boarding house with as many as seven renters. It was converted to a duplex in 1980 by owner David Copi.

ELHDB

521–609 E. Liberty
Michigan Theater Building

79

1927

Both the Michigan Theater and a number of shops operate from this brick building designed by Detroit architect Maurice Finkel in 1927. The theater entry is in a highly exuberant Lombard Romanesque style with blue and green tile work, glazed terra-cotta trim, grouped arched windows with medallions in colored tile within the arches, classical columns with Byzantine capitals, and two domes flanking the entry on the roof. The theater was built by local businessman Angelo Poulos and contained an 1,800-seat auditorium and an office block of seven

stores. When it opened in January of 1928, it was the finest theater in Ann Arbor, presenting live entertainment as well as movies.

The seven stores are in a more mundane portion of the building, constructed in light-colored brick with stone lintels above rectangular windows. Several projections from the roofline have "Michigan Theater Building" written on stone pediments. The original window transoms in most of this portion were covered in a 1956 modernization. Much of the commercial building remains in its 1956 condition. However, the theater portion and two stores flanking the theater were given a full-scale restoration in 2000. The John Leidy Shops occupied two of the storefronts for over 50 years and were almost as iconic as the theater!

In 1977, it was announced that the theater would close and become a mini-mall. Ann Arbor citizens, led by the Motor City Theater Organ Society, organized support to convince the city to buy the theater and run it as a non-profit. The city purchased the theater in 1979 and sold it back to the Michigan Theater Foundation in 2007. In those intervening years, fundraising campaigns raised millions of dollars to restore the interior lobbies and auditorium, and later the exterior and outer lobby. A new marquee was installed in 2000 as well as a new blade sign. In 1999, a second theater for 200 called the Screening Room was constructed in the back. In the hallway leading to the Screening Room is the Ford Gallery of Ann Arbor Founders, containing panels discussing various aspects of Ann Arbor history. Today the theater still presents movies and live events, and is the home of the Ann Arbor Symphony Orchestra. It remains a "Shrine to Art." It has won many awards from the Historic District Commission.

SSHD

80 111 W. Liberty
Ludwig Walz Grocery and Saloon   1880

This late-era brick Italianate building with its original rounded-arch windows, segmental and round arches and keystones, articulated brick columns between the windows, brick corbelling below the cornice, and paired brackets under the cornice, was constructed for grocer Ludwig Walz in 1880. It is one of the few Italianate buildings in Ann Arbor to have its original storefront. Born in Germany in 1843, Walz came to Ann Arbor when he was two and apprenticed to confectioner Herman Schlotterbeck in the German fashion for training students. Walz was able to open his own shop here and remained until 1892 when his son-in-law Sid Millard converted it to a printing shop.

Until the late 1970s, the Millard Press printed tickets and other items for the University of Michigan Athletic Department. A wall of autographed photos of the teams greeted visitors to the shop. When Millard retired, his neighbors at 113 W. Liberty (see #82), Carolyn and Joseph Arcure, bought the building and restored it using salvaged brackets from the former William Maynard house, which was demolished in 1990. On the upper floors are attractive condos, early examples of "loft living" in Ann Arbor when they were converted in the 1990s.

LSHD

112–122 W. Liberty
Adam and Anton Schaeberle Block

81

1866

This row of Italianate brick buildings, which have typical windows with segmental round-topped brick arches, is a simple version of this style, especially since it lacks its elaborate original cornice. In 1868, the Schaeberle brothers sold lots 114, 116, 120, and 122, retaining 118 for their harness shop. The new owners included George Huss, John Laubengayer, and Conrad Wetzel. In 1872, Jacob Binder had his meat market at 114, Huss' shop later became the Gauss Boot and Shoe Store, and Laubengayer's lot was a flour and feed store at 120 and

122. The upper floors were used as the residences for the store occupants and their families. By 1883 the building at 112 had been remodeled to conform to the others, and the former space between the buildings was filled by narrow windows on this section. The buildings have stone basements, exterior brick walls a foot thick, and pressed metal ceilings.

These five buildings have housed many of Ann Arbor's iconic businesses, including Ehnis and Sons, The Round Table, Mr. Flood's Party, The Old Town Bar, the West End Grill, and Bella Ciao restaurant. The renovation of these storefronts in the 1970s spurred renewed interest in preservation throughout the downtown and inspired efforts to create the Old West Side and Main Street Historic Districts. These buildings received Preservation Awards in 1984.

MSHD

82 113 W. Liberty
Haarer Building   1888

Many decorative touches embellish this handsome brick Richardsonian Romanesque building, including round-topped windows on the main floor and rectangular windows on the second, a strong corner emphasis ending in bulbous stones, and patterns of pressed brick. Fancy brass hardware and twisty numerals indicate the date of construction (see #137 and #219). The round-arched windows (grouped together as a unit) and rounded bricks are characteristic of the style. Original cast-iron pillars grace the entry to the store, and the plate-glass storefronts were some of the first in town. An impressive fireplace of marbleized slate graced the parlor of the spacious family apartment above. A metal weather vane with a pierced "H" tops the front gable, a design based on old photos commissioned by the couple who restored the building in the 1970s.

John Haarer, a local photographer, was the builder. He moved a frame structure off the site that had housed his "Photographic Art Gallery." Books, stationary, and insurance followed, and by 1940 descendant Julius Haarer owned the Haarer Book Company, Haarer Insurance, and managed Buhr Machine Tool Company.

In 1964, the City of Ann Arbor purchased this building with the intention of demolishing it for a parking lot. Citizen protest scotched this idea and in 1974 this building served as the headquarters of the Sesquicentennial Commission as the city celebrated its 150th birthday with events, exhibits, and a monthly newsletter. It became part of the Liberty Street Historic District in 1975.

Joseph and Carolyn Arcure purchased the building in 1975 and restored the upper floors for their own living space, marking the beginning of loft living in downtown. They received a Preservation Award in 1984, the first year awards were given. Jay Platt opened the West Side Book Shop in 1975.

LSHD

115 W. Liberty
Walker Brothers Building

83

1893

This building served until 1921 as the office and showroom for Walker Brothers Carriage Works which were originally next door. At one time it was Ray Fisher's Bike Shop. The police firing range was on the third floor. For many years it was the home of Rider's Hobby Shop and it is still referred to as the Rider's Building in some circles. It is an excellent example of a Richardsonian Romanesque brick building (like its neighbor to the east) with linked arched windows on the second floor and rectangular ones on the third. The cornice area contains interesting patterns of brickwork in three sections separated by protruding brick corbels. The building still has the original storefront with cast-iron columns topped by decorative iron moldings, the original kick plates, and large plate-glass windows that were the rage in the 1890s.

In 2000, after 54 years, Rider's moved out of downtown. Rehabilitation of the building was already underway in 1999 as local developers Allen and Kwan converted the upper floors to loft living. Today it contains two condos and retail on the ground floor and is part of the lively street scene on West Liberty that started in the late 1960s.

LSHD

84 117 W. Liberty
Christian Walker & Brother Building/
Ann Arbor Carriage Works   1886

Before cars became the preferred mode of travel, carriage building was one of the country's largest industries. Every town had its carriage works, which could be quite small affairs. A carriage trimmer and painter would work with woodworkers, upholsterers, and smiths. Christian Walker started small in 1867, and unlike most manufacturers, he made each carriage from scratch—from the springs and axles to the chassis, wheels, and bodies. C. Walker & Brother (which included his brother George) grew to become a real factory and built this elaborate building by 1886. Though he died in 1888, the firm continued, and in 1891, they employed some 20 workers and turned out "over 700 carriages, coaches and sleighs each year" according to the *Ann Arbor Register*. Never wanting to use the derogatory term "buggy," the store advertised "stylish carriages, dignified looking coaches, graceful phaetons, nobby surreys, and jaunty sleighs." A carriage made by the Walker brothers was recently installed at Downtown Home and Garden (see #49).

The building is a fine example of a late Italianate style, with a symmetrical front facade of tall, narrow windows topped by brick arches, with the addition of stones at the ends and centers of the arches giving a colorful effect. A small cornice on the roof announced the owner and the date in the ornate style of the late 1880s.

Despite building a showroom next door, in 1893 the business went under and in 1894 the building was sold to the Henne and Stanger Furniture Company, which remained until the 1950s (traces of their painted ad can still be seen on the west wall). Later it became a Sears catalogue store. It was saved from demolition in the 1970s under pressure from a renewed public interest in Ann Arbor's downtown architectural heritage, and a small historic district known as the West Liberty Historic District was established in 1973. In 1974 the Ann Arbor Art Center purchased the building and has done an award-winning job of restoration and preservation. They have a retail shop, art classes, and exhibits as well.

LSHD

213–215 W. Liberty
Schlenker Hardware Building

1906

The Schlenker Hardware Building shows the wonderful possibilities of adaptive reuse and restoration of historic buildings in Ann Arbor's downtown. In 2001 the building was extensively renovated and restored for office use by Liberty Land LLC, spearheaded by Janet Muhleman, with designs by Smith Group Architects and construction work done by J.C. Beal Construction. A large addition was added to the back, and the original building was stripped of its c. 1940s enameled steel panels and paint. The fine brickwork was restored and reconstructed, including the front parapet which had been removed in an earlier renovation. A tasteful early 20th-century style storefront was also installed. The Historic District Commission recognized their work with an award.

The building was built in 1906 by Christian Schlenker to house his hardware business which began on Main Street in 1886. Schlenker Hardware occupied the main floor of the building, selling stoves, furnaces, paints, and hardware. It was among the first in town to sell radios and refrigerators. The building's upper floor was used as a residence by the Schlenker family. Lasting longer than its 19th-century competitors, Schlenker Hardware stayed in the family and in business until 1995, when it closed its doors for good.

MSHD

86 308 E. Madison
Willey-Wallenberg House   1904

The last remaining residence of Raoul Wallenberg in Ann Arbor, this modest and unas-suming Dutch Colonial Revival home was built in 1904 by a professor in the University of Michigan's X-ray laboratory, Vernon J. Willey. Wallenberg was born in Sweden in 1912 to an elite family of bankers, military officers, and industrialists. He enjoyed his years in Ann Arbor (from 1931–1935) studying architecture and graduating with honors in three and a half years.

In the early 1940s, Wallenberg traveled extensively to Hungary as director and joint owner of the Mid-European Trading Company, eventually learning Hungarian. As the war ravaged Hungary in 1944 and Hungarian Jews began being deported to death camps, Wallenberg was appointed to lead the War Refugee Board's mission in Hungary. Along with Swedish diplomat Per Anger, Wallenberg began issuing Swedish protective passes to Hungarian Jews in Budapest. In addition, he sheltered Jews in houses owned by Sweden that were considered Swedish territory, and employed hundreds of Jews on his staff. Raoul Wallenberg charmed and bribed powerful members of the German regime in order to prevent deportations, and at great risk to his own personal safety, followed the trains and death marches in order to pass out the Swedish protective passes. Wallenberg's efforts led to the saving of as many as 100,000 Hungarian Jews before the Soviet forces liberated Hungary in 1945. He was arrested by the Soviets in January of 1945, possibly on suspicion of being a spy, and was never seen again. He is believed to have died in Soviet custody in 1947.

Around the world, Raoul Wallenberg is honored for his efforts to save the Jews of Hungary from the death camps. In 1981, he was made an honorary citizen of the United States and in 1990, the University of Michigan began awarding the Wallenberg Medal to outstanding humanitarians.

Former IHP

100 N. Main
Washtenaw County Courthouse

87

1954–1956

In 1824, John Allen donated an entire city block for a courthouse in the center of his new settlement, ensuring that Ann Arbor would become the Washtenaw County seat. The first courthouse, built in 1834, was designed by John Bryan. In 1878, the county built a grander Renaissance Revival-styled building designed by George W. Bunting.

The current court building was designed by Bulgarian-born architect Ralph S. Gerganoff (see #107 and #185) in 1954. It was built around the 1878 courthouse, which allowed for county business to continue while the new building was being completed. The steel-framed building stands four stories tall at its tallest point. The exterior is sleek and modern, sided in granite and limestone, with a flat roof and large banks of windows. The building's entrance is an understated and somewhat plain flat-roofed vestibule.

The two stone relief sculptures on the south-facing facade were carved by sculptor Carleton W. Angell of Ann Arbor. The four main classical figures represent peace, law, justice and learning, while the smaller figures represent Washtenaw County's history, including the interesting inclusion of a beer bottle, a nod to the brewing tradition of the area's German settlers. Other works done by Angell in Ann Arbor are found at the Arbor Crest Cemetery, where he designed the Four Chaplains Monument, and at the Washtenong Memorial Gardens, where Angell designed the Veterans Memorial. The interior of the courthouse still retains many of its original finishes, including marble walls, stainless steel doors. and terrazzo floors.

While members of the community still mourn the destruction of the county's 1878 courthouse and decry its modern replacement, Gerganoff's design for the third court building is slowly being recognized as a Mid-Century Modern classic.

88 219–223 N. Main
Pardon Block   1867/1894/1899

This tripartite grouping of Richardsonian Romanesque building facades was actually built in three stages, as indicated in the stone half-circles in the gables of the front facades. The first was 223 with its date stone "1894." 219 was built in 1899 according to the date stone and the central portion (221) reads "Pardon Block" in the gable. The 221 and 223 structures were built earlier as evidenced by the long narrow windows with arched tops on the north side. This was probably the Smith Block, built in 1867 by W.F. Mallory. Smith sold boots and shoes and later Hall and Smith ran a grocery here in the 1870s. In the 1880s, it was John Schneider's butcher shop.

The facades were constructed by Charles F. Pardon, a butcher and grocer. He had purchased the stock of J.H. Miller and created a combined grocery and meat market in the two storefronts. He also bought the stock of the Eberhart bakery and sold it to his youngest brother Frank who moved into the new space in 1899. They were born to immigrants from Germany—a family of 8 kids, 3 of whom became butchers. A series of other bakeries, butchers, and grocers have come and gone, but the Pardon Block name has remained. All three facades have the linked arched windows outlined in limestone on the first floor and rectangular windows on the second that are features of this style. Built of brick, they have emphasized corners topped by bulbous finials.

In 1988, the architectural preservation firm of Quinn Evans purchased the building and restored the 219 portion, demonstrating proper techniques of preservation to serve as a model for others. They received a Rehabilitation Award from the Historic District Commission in 1988. Duane Renken purchased and restored the other two sections and won a Rehabilitation Award in 1989. New storefronts in a more appropriate style were constructed using old photos as a guide, and paint was removed. This part of town saw a revival with the restoration of the former post office across the street and the Dr. Chase Building just to the north across Miller. Since then, other buildings have been restored as well.

Former IHP

220 N. Main
U.S. Post Office

89

1909/1932

Architect Fremont Ward was hired to help build a new post office in 1908 and supervised the construction work by C. Hoertz & Sons of Grand Rapids, which followed plans drawn by the architecture staff at the Treasury Department. They selected a classical design built of smooth-cut gray limestone with a central entry flanked by large windows outlined in garland window hoods and capped by decorative keystones. A Renaissance-style balustrade was built instead of a cornice. The center portion with a cartouche was added later.

The site had been the Polhemus Livery Stable from 1874–1908. The new post office opened in 1909. It was the ninth building to house a post office and the first architecturally significant federal building in Ann Arbor. Originally it was a square building with five large windows and entries on four sides. It was expanded in 1932 into a rectangular shape with seven windows and a single entry. The additions were so carefully done that it is hard to tell it was ever a smaller building. Many original features remain inside, including marble wainscoting, terrazzo floors in the lobby, ornate plaster moldings on the sixteen-foot ceilings, and wonderful wood trim.

The building served as the central post office until 1959. It became a downtown sub-station when the newer post office was built on Stadium Blvd. When the Federal Building on Liberty was completed in 1977, it was closed. Within a few years the building was sold to Washtenaw County which restored the building, maintaining both the exterior and interior features whenever possible. Today it houses the administrative offices of the Washtenaw County government. It was placed on the National Register of Historic Places in 1978 and received a Special Merit Award for Adaptive Reuse from the HDC in 1990. It maintains many of the former post office features, including old boxes and walk-up windows.

NR, Former IHP

90 301–305 N. Main
Dr. Chase's Steam Printing House   1864/1868

This commercial brick building in the Italianate style so popular in the 1860s has tall windows with triple-arched brick hoods and a four-over-four sash. It was built in two stages as confirmed by two date stones. It had a projecting cornice in the center section and a standard cornice with paired brackets under the eaves. These were later removed, and the building now lacks these distinctive features. It retains the corbeled arcading within which the windows are set, brick piers that divide the bays, and dentate brickwork over the third floor in the central unit.

Begun in 1864 by W.H. Mallory (see #253), and tripled in size in 1868, it served as the headquarters of the publishing phenomenon, *Dr. Chase's Recipes or Information for Everybody*. This book was a collection of advice on everything, from cancer cures, beekeeping, bread baking, fishing, women's problems, recipes, and medical remedies. It was the brainchild of Dr. Alvan Wood Chase, who received his medical degree from the Eclectic Medical Institute in Cincinnati after sixteen weeks of study. Despite his lack of credentials, this booklet was once said to have been second only to the Bible in sold copies. Dr. Chase also published a Republican newspaper known as the *Peninsular Courier and Family Visitant*, later shortened to *Courier*, and the building was known as the Courier Block for years.

Despite his successes, Chase sold the business to Rice A. Beal in 1869 and moved to Minnesota for his health. He returned a year later, fit and raring to get back his book and newspaper. Beal declined to sell and got rich selling *Dr. Chase's Recipes*. Beal died in 1883 and his son Junius, later a U-M Regent, continued to publish the *Courier* and the recipe book.

In the 20th century the building was used for a succession of businesses, including a rug factory, grocery, and warehouse. It was purchased and restored in 1969 by the planning firm of Johnson, Johnson and Roy. They received an award in 1976 from the Bicentennial

Commission and spearheaded the restoration of many buildings in this area. In 1993, the Dobson-McComber Insurance Agency purchased it for their 100th anniversary. They worked with Quinn Evans to restore the windows to their original appearance and to improve accessibility.

Former IHP

100 S. Main
Glazier Building

91

1906

Jackson architect Claire Allen designed this fine example of a Beaux Arts building in 1906 for Frank P. Glazier, a wealthy banker and stove factory owner from Chelsea, Michigan. It is constructed of red brick with fluted limestone columns, rosettes, and garlands over the windows. The elaborate cornice, which had been removed in the 1950s, was completely restored by owner Dennis Dahlman in 2008, who received an award from the Historic Distric Commission. The style had been made popular by the Columbian Exposition in 1893 in Chicago.

Frank Glazier was the State Treasurer in 1906, but was jailed over corruption charges for using state funds to build this building and pad his own bank. The Panic of 1907 caused the collapse of his financial empire and in 1910 he was convicted of embezzlement and sent to Jackson Prison.

The First National Bank then moved into the building and stayed until 1929. From 1930–1975 it was the home of the Ann Arbor Trust Company (run by Russell Dobson, Earl Cress, and William Brown), which dealt in securities, mortgages, insurance, real estate, and property management. It has held a series of banks since.

MSHD

92 120–124 S. Main
First National Bank Block   1867

Shortly after it opened as the "Bank Building" in 1867, this structure was described as having "a freestone front, in which are large and elegant stores and the First National Bank." This bank was the first federally chartered bank in Michigan and only the twenty-second such bank in the U.S.

The building is of solid brick, with various bays of arched windows on both floors, typical of the Italianate commercial style popular in the 1860s and '70s. The bank portion has a more Gothic front, with pointed arches and a cornice that rose above the others, fitted with higher brackets and pointed pinnacles which increased its visual domination.

For almost 100 years this building was known as "Goodyear's" because of the department store that over the 20th century eventually occupied the entire building. Goodyear's was the major retail anchor of downtown for almost a century. It closed in 1983.

Preservationists and business interests tried to find a suitable tenant, and in 1984, using newly created tax credits, a consortium restored the original facade of the building. The interior spaces were carved into smaller units that house a variety of businesses.

MSHD

126 S. Main
Philip Bach Building

93

1867

A photograph taken in 1867 shows this impressive Italianate brick block newly opened with the dry goods business of Philip Bach occupying the ground floor. The photo shows the original wide flat cornice supported by ornate brackets typical of the style. The name "Philip Bach" is over the awning and a large "Business College" sign sits atop the roof.

Bach formed partnerships, and the business was Bach and Abel and then Bach and Roath until the 1890s. Around 1900 Bruno St. James founded his eponymous store here. He sold his business to his employee Bertha E. Muehlig in 1924 and for almost half of the 20th century the building was called "Muehlig's."

Bertha was from a pioneer German family who had come to Ann Arbor in the 1840s. Her family owned a hardware store on Main Street and a furniture enterprise that later became the Muehlig Funeral Chapel (see #67), the longest surviving business in Ann Arbor. Bertha lived in one of the family homes a block away on Main Street. Never married, she was famous for her Christmas gifts to children, her support of the Donovan School, and later of the Northside School. After her death in the late 1970s, the business stayed in operation for about 10 years.

In 1981, the law firm of Hooper, Hathaway, Price, Beuche, and Wallace purchased the building and restored it for their law offices. John Hathaway, a local preservationist, was the force behind this venture. They unblocked windows, and a design in iron was created in front of the windows on Main Street to give the sense of its earlier form. Old interior features were kept as well. They received a Preservation Award from the Historic District Commission in 1984.

MSHD

94 201 S. Main
First National Building   1929

In February 1929, before the stock market crash and the beginning of the Great Depression, this building opened with a flourish and a special edition of the *Ann Arbor Daily Times News*. Sixteen floodlights made it a focal point of downtown at night. This Romanesque wonder sheathed in terra-cotta has carved lion heads, a sumptuous lobby with black terrazzo floors, black and gold marble, Italian travertine walls, bronze doorways, and a richly decorated coffered ceiling. It was designed by the local firm of Fry and Kasurin.

The First National Bank (see #92) was the first bank chartered in Michigan under the National Bank Act of 1863. After occupying other spaces, they built their own building only to succumb to economic realities during the Depression. In 1935, the former banking space was subdivided horizontally, creating retail space on the first floor with offices above. The massive bronze door and bronze grilles were removed. It was substantially remodeled in 1940, resulting in the loss of the grand entry which was cut in half. In 1981, First Martin Corporation acquired the building and began an award-winning restoration of the exterior. They also restored the interior floors, walls, elevators, and even the bronze mailbox to their original condition in the lobby. The decorative ceilings were cleaned and repainted as well.

NR, SR, MSHD

301 S. Main
Binder's Orchestrion Hall

95

1871/1908

A photograph of this corner from 1868 shows Henry Binder's home just before he tore it down to build a three-story brick Italianate building which was completed in 1871. Binder built many buildings on Main Street and all featured the carved stone lintels and elaborate cornices then in style. Binder's Orchestrion Hall was a saloon on the third floor that had an orchestrion, a large mechanical instrument like a barrel organ that could imitate many musical instruments. Such halls were very popular at the time and another existed on E. Washington Street at Rettich's. Binder, his wife, and their eleven children lived on the second floor. He died in 1894 and his wife soon built a house on E. William Street.

In 1877, S. and J. Baumgartner's Bakery and Grocery opened shop on the main floor. They expanded and built a brick building in the back (along Liberty) in 1880. Despite great success and reputation, they closed in 1892 and the storefront was rented to the Ann Arbor Organ Company whose factory was on First Street (see #63).

In 1908, the building was remodeled into its current form. It shed its frilly Victorian look for a simpler Roman-style facade. The German-American Bank was the first occupant but by 1916 it became Hutzel's Ladies Apparel, which occupied the corner for the next 70 years. In 1990, the Selo-Shevel Gallery purchased the building. A variance to the sign ordinance allowed them to keep the old Hutzel's sign and simply change the name. They closed in 2014.

MSHD

96 306–310 S. Main
Stephen Pratt Block   1896

In 1893, Stephen Pratt, a "Manufacturer of Steam-Boilers, Smoke-Pipe, etc." in Detroit, purchased this property, and in 1896 built this lovely terra-cotta and brick building to house the Crescent Works Corset Factory and other businesses. Built in a somewhat Renaissance Revival style with framed blocks of double windows surrounded by classical motifs in terra-cotta, the factory was featured in the 1896 *Headlight*, a magazine of the Michigan Central Railroad. "The product of this factory consists of high grade Custom Corsets and Waists, and the excellence of their goods has given them an enviable reputation…They deal direct with the consumer and every article is made to individual measure…their new factory…is the finest business block in Ann Arbor…" The building was designed by Detroit architects Malcolmson and Higginbotham, famous for their school buildings in Detroit and Ann Arbor. They also designed the U-M School of Education Building (see #227).

By the "roaring 20s" corsets were definitely out of style, and in 1924 this building became Kline's Department Store, which lasted 70 years until 1995. In 1961, white panels were placed over the original facade to give the store a more modern look. When the property was purchased by Ed Shaffran in 1995, he removed them and restored the original terra-cotta elements. He completed the award-winning project in 2011 with the restoration of the cornice, done by the Detroit Cornice and Slate Company—the same company that fashioned it in 1895.

MSHD

319–325 S. Main
Marchese Brothers Building

97

1925

Ann Arbor architect Herman Pipp designed this brick and terra-cotta building for the Marchese Brothers in 1925. It has Gothic details in its pointed pinnacles and sculpted Gothic arches between the spandrels. The marquee is particularly elegant, with Gothic touches in the hanging pendils and pointed pinnacles. Pipp also designed Nickels Arcade (see #104); many houses (see #59) in downtown, Burns Park, and Barton Hills; and sororities and fraternities.

Demetrio and Anthony Marchese had their tailor shop on the first floor and residences above. The Depression forced them to sell, and the building was purchased by Henry A. Whitaker in the 1930s. It was known as the Whitaker Building into the 1990s. Many remember Grinnell Bros., a combined musical instrument and sheet music store, that was here from the 1930s. They began in one of the three storefronts and eventually occupied the entire ground level until they moved to Briarwood in 1975. In the 1990s, the Curtis Brothers (owners since the 1980s) discovered that the original marquee was about to collapse and replaced it with a replica that uses a copper that doesn't oxidize and still gleams as new. They received an award from the Historic Distric Commission.

MSHD

98 | 120 Packard
Wines-Dean House   1848

William Wallace Wines and his brother Daniel E. Wines, natives of Connecticut, married two sisters and brought them to Michigan in the 1830s, when Michigan was the American frontier. They operated a lumber mill in Ypsilanti but later moved to Ann Arbor. William built this simple Vernacular cottage similar to homes back east in 1848. Daniel built his two years later next door at 126 Packard. He entered the sash, door, and blind (shutter) business and became a contractor and builder. William founded a clothing company known as Wines and Worden.

This house may have been built by Daniel for his brother. It is a simple clapboard structure with a center entry and gables facing sideways. A large addition to the house has altered this plan, but this may be a very early part of the home. The scalloped trim along the roofline is unusual and may be later than the 1840s. Another unusual feature is the brick nogging in the walls, more common in 1830s houses. It has a square parlor window bay with a multi-paned upper sash, and the porch on the east is Greek in form with Gothic details. There are some Queen Anne details on the west elevation. The front portico has the columns grouped as sheaves, a common feature of the Gothic Revival style beginning to be popular in the 1840s.

Nelson Strong, another pioneer, purchased the house in the 1870s after William constructed a grand brick house at William and Main (demolished in the 1960s). Strong then sold it to Sedgewick Dean, his son-in-law and a local merchant. Dean's daughter Elizabeth left her mark on Ann Arbor with the Dean Fund, a two million dollar grant to the city to plant trees. Elizabeth sold the house to Rev. Stellhorn, the minister of Zion Lutheran Church, and he and his wife lived here for 40 years. They made many modifications and changed the window to the right of the door to a picture window. In the 1960s, Donald Van Curler (see #11), a local architect, purchased the house with his wife Lottie. They restored the house, preserving the high ceilings, chandeliers, and marble washstands. Lottie has received several awards from the Historic District Commission.

Former IHP

330 Packard
W.S. Perry School

99

1902/1923

W.A. Otis of Chicago designed this beautiful Colonial Revival red brick building. It was completed in January of 1903, the first of many school buildings constructed in the fast-growing city. The original 1902 building, the portion closest to the corner of Packard and Madison, was built on the site of Hanover Park, the city's first municipal park. The school was named after Walter S. Perry, superintendent of the Ann Arbor Public Schools from 1870 to 1897. The original portion of the building features multiple flared hipped roofs and an octagonal tower with round-topped windows and a flared conical roof supported by large brackets in the eaves.

In 1923, the size of the building was greatly increased by a matching addition that runs at a diagonal along Packard Street. Great care was taken to blend the old and new construction with matching brick, windows, and rooflines. The two sections are virtually indistinguishable. In 1963, the building was sold to the University of Michigan because families with children were leaving the neighborhood for other parts of town. Later, the University extensively renovated and restored the building, replaced the windows, and added a large Post-Modern addition to the south elevation.

Former IHP

100 213–217 S. State

Brown House/Foster's House of Art   1872/1913

In the mid-19th century, this block of State Street was lined with homes of wealthy business-men and professors. The set-back part of this building is the last remainder of this residential neighborhood. The visible parts of the second floor show classic features of the Italianate style: double brackets under the eaves, frieze windows in the attic portion with stylized Grecian flowers, windows with peaked caps, and a symmetrical floor plan. The home was built in 1872 by the Hon. Benjamin Brown, an Englishman by birth, emigrant from Rochester, NY, and former state representative. His daughter Mary later married Fred Taylor, a well-known economics professor, and continued to live in Ann Arbor. You can see the original staircase as you enter the building.

By the early 20th century these homes were being converted into doctors' offices and eventually demolished for commercial structures. In 1913, instead of demolition, James P. Foster commissioned University of Michigan Professor of Architecture Emil Lorch to design a commercial addition to the Italianate Brown house. The addition is in the Arts and Crafts style, reminiscent of some buildings in Chicago and even Scotland. Colorful art glass patterns form the upper register of the front plate-glass windows. They are lovely in the late afternoon when the sun shines through them (despite the awning).

Foster's House of Art was *the* place to buy cutting-edge products in the first half of the 20th century—lamps, furniture, picture frames, china, art, pottery, jewelry, textiles—you name it. They also ran a tea room, lived in the back, and provided housing for girls in the old part of the house. When Mr. Foster died in 1949, his wife Clarice, the artistic one of the duo, put his money into a foundation which is now the Ann Arbor Area Community Foundation.

The building later housed a branch of Goodyear's department store, who added a slate roof for a "Normandy" effect, and maintained the tea room for many years. Eventually other shops came and went and it's been home to many restaurants and retail establishments over the years. Today, it maintains the eclectic nature of Ann Arbor businesses.

SSHD

233 S. State
State Theater

1940

This former movie theater with its jazzy Art Deco exterior of accordion-folded yellow brick and red stripes was begun in 1940 and opened in 1942, in the midst of World War II. An impressive sketch by the architect C. Howard Crane (designer of Orchestra Hall and the Fox Theater in Detroit) appeared on the front page of the November 1940 edition of the *Ann Arbor News*. The exposed brick at street level was originally covered in glass-like red vitrolite panels, but otherwise the exterior is remarkably intact. Also intact are the marquee and sign, the elaborate bathrooms of dubonnet, and the green tile on the second floor. Some recessed lighting remains on both floors, as do some of the floor tiles in the main entry.

The theater was built for the Butterfield Company, a Michigan theater chain. They operated the State until 1979, when ownership was transferred to the George Kerasotes Corp. In reaction to the multiplexes that began to appear in the 1970s, this theater was divided into four units. It still couldn't compete, and the theater closed in 1987. The building was sold a week later to Tom Borders of the Borders Group. They gutted the first floor and leased it to Urban Outfitters. Two theaters in the former balcony are still showing movies, but changes are in the works. The theater is owned by a group of private investors but movie showings are handled by the Michigan Theater Foundation.

In 1990, the Borders Group restored the marquee and sign to its original brilliant green, yellow, and red colors and reactivated the neon, receiving an award for their efforts by the Historic District Commission. The two-sided vertical sign is an icon and has appeared in numerous publications touting Ann Arbor.

SSHD

102 312–322 S. State
College Block and University Block   1886/1888

At one time, six pressed-tin facades linked these two groups of buildings constructed in the late 1880s. Fires and changing tastes have altered two of the six, but today some still retain not only their pressed-tin facades but their cornices as well. The four southernmost buildings (316–322) known as the University Block are bigger than the two to the north (the College Block) and can be seen on maps from the time period. The 1888 Sanborn Fire Insurance map notes that the University Block "burned in May 1888 and being rebuilt in June 1888. Taken from plans."

The University of Michigan, which is directly across the street, opened its doors in 1841. Growth was slow in the beginning and most of State Street and North University had houses belonging to professors and businessmen. The first commercial building on State Street appeared in 1874, after the Civil War, when student admissions soared. It provided a dining hall and a gymnasium. More commercial buildings followed in the 1880s, containing barber shops, bookstores, and grocery stores. Drugstores, restaurants, office supply, and clothing stores opened in the 20th century. Today these buildings still house businesses serving the campus community.

SSHD

317 S. State
S.W. Trick Building (Kresge's)   1937

103

This high-profile site at the corner of State and North University has been home to a single family house, a late 19th-century commercial building, and this Art Moderne yellow brick building with steel ribbon windows constructed in 1937. A steel sign in Art Moderne lettering at the State Street entry reads "S.W. Trick Building." Samuel W. Trick and his son Harold S. Trick (the owner of Moe's Sport Shop around the corner on North University) used plans supplied by Kresge's Five and Dime. Kresge's remained until 1987. In August 1989 Michigan Book and Supply moved in and remained until 2011. A Walgreens drugstore opened in 2014, recalling the first commercial use of this site as a drug store.

The closing of Kresge's prompted an editorial in the *Ann Arbor News* lamenting the disappearance of the five-and dime, "which is slipping into history" (another Kresge's on Main Street closed in 1974). The *Ann Arbor Observer* noted it had been a home for "unaffiliated intellectuals" and street people who all ate at their famous lunch counters. (Kresge's was founded in Detroit in 1899 by S.S. Kresge whose motto was "Nothing over Ten Cents.")

The building is one of a few commercial buildings in Ann Arbor in the Art Moderne style. In addition to the yellow brick and steel detailing, Art Moderne features include the curvature of the building and of the glass, and an aluminum fluted column at the corner entry. The upper floors have striated columns between the window units, breaking up the basic horizontality of the structure. When the store was remodeled for Michigan Book and Supply, local architect Richard Hermann restored the original curved windows at the corner entry, lengthening them to their full display window height. The red signboard (now brown-red tiles) that curves from State Street to North University once had large gold lettering spelling "S.S. Kresge."

SSHD

104 326–330 S. State
Nickels Arcade

1915/1918

This charming example of a glass-roofed shopping arcade in a Beaux Arts Classical style was designed by local architect Herman Pipp (see #59 and #97). It was built in terra-cotta in two stages, due to the onset of World War I. There are 18 shops in the Arcade and two have been there almost since it opened—Van Boven Men's Store and the Caravan Shop. Other long-term tenants include Bivouac, Maison Edwards, and the Arcade Barbers. Professional offices occupy the second and third floors.

The Arcade is named for the Nickels family, who owned a butcher shop on the site and demolished it to build the Arcade. The more elaborate portion at the entry was originally the Farmers and Mechanics Bank, which owned its portion. A bank occupied this space until 1960 when the Nickels family took it over. Today, descendants of the Nickels family still own the Arcade.

The building is essentially unchanged and was placed on the National Register of Historic Places in 1987. It remains one of Ann Arbor's most unique and attractive buildings.

SSHD

318 S. Thayer

Francis Hamilton Rooming House

105

1906

Sited on a narrow urban lot, sandwiched between three larger buildings, this building was built by Francis Hamilton in 1906 to serve as a boarding house. A bit of an architectural oddity, the home's style is hard to categorize; it has elements of the Colonial Revival in the small front porch, and Prairie style in the horizontal masonry bands and the low hipped roof. The front bay window seems to be a holdover from the long unfashionable Italianate style. The home is the lone survivor on a block once lined with residential dwellings, and is representative of a narrow urban style that was rare in Ann Arbor though more common in larger cities like Chicago and Detroit. The sand-colored brick is also a rarity used in very few buildings of the time.

Francis Hamilton graduated from the University of Michigan in 1869 and first worked as a school teacher in the city. He made his money through land speculation and development, developing land along Fifth Avenue, North University, William Street, and Hamilton Street, which was named after him. Hamilton served as first ward alderman for six years and as mayor of the city of Ann Arbor from 1905 to 1907. Hamilton bequeathed the city of Ann Arbor $1,000 to build a fine bronze drinking fountain that is still in use near the corner of State and North University. Hamilton's grand Victorian residence at 427 S. Fifth Avenue was recently demolished for the controversial City Place development.

For a majority of its history this home has been used as a student rental. It has been recently restored as a single-family residence and is owner occupied. The owner received a Rehabilitation Award from the Historic District Commission.

Former IHP

106 331 Thompson
St. Mary's Student Chapel   1924–1925

Designed by U-M Professor of Architecture Albert J.J. Rousseau (see #350) in 1923, this unusual Art Deco-style Roman Catholic church was dedicated in 1925 to serve the students of the University of Michigan. Despite the fact that Rousseau had been trained in Paris at the École des Beaux-Arts, he had a modernist streak, which is visible on the exterior. Inside he used heavy timber "scissors" trusses, as in the tithe barns of medieval England, to support the roof. The rest of the interior is not original. The Art Deco touches on the exterior include the yellow brick building material and the sculptural stone crosses over the windows, which had projecting brick jambs. Dual angels were used for ornament at the ends of the mullions and jambs of the windows.

The Student Chapel was established by students and faculty in 1914 under the leadership of Father Bourke, a bishop from Detroit. They believed a separate congregation for Catholic students at the University of Michigan was necessary. It was once affiliated with St. Thomas the Apostle Church (see #155), but became a separate parish in 1940.

A Newman Club for Catholic students was later formed for educational and social activities. They built the Fr. Gabriel Richard Center on Thompson Street in 1953. The buildings were joined together in 1995.

WSHD

200 E. Washington
Ypsi-Ann Building

107

1927

The early 20th century brought a wave of tall building construction to America's major cities and Ann Arbor did its best to keep up—specifically with the Glazier Building of 1906 (see #91) and the First National Bank Building of 1929 (see #94), both prominent on Main Street. Built in 1927, the Ypsi-Ann Building was the second tallest office building in Ann Arbor, coming over twenty years after the Glazier Building. The seven-story building was built for J. Karl Malcolm (see #294), Roscoe Bonisteel, Barney Hawkings, Charles Sink, and William Benje, directors of the Ypsi-Ann Land Company. The Ypsi-Ann Land Company developed many subdivisions in Ann Arbor and Ypsilanti.

They chose Bulgarian-born architect Ralph S. Gerganoff of Ypsilanti to design the building. Gerganoff designed many landmark buildings in Ann Arbor and Ypsilanti, including the Kingsley Post Apartments (see #185) and the Washtenaw County Courthouse (see #87). The construction of the building was handled by the Townsend-Daily Company, with materials provided by the Ann Arbor Construction Company.

The building's details are restrained, with some Arts and Crafts and Art Deco influences. The exterior is clad in brick with limestone blocks between the window courses. The street level is done in simple, unadorned limestone, somewhat in the Art Deco style, but the cornice is where the building really shines. The extensive use of stone and brickwork laid in decorative patterns known as "tapestry brick" are reminiscent of Albert Kahn's Arts and Crafts-style work on the Hatcher Graduate Library (see #232) and the Natural Science Building (see #229). The remainder of the cornice is limestone, and is executed in the more modern Art Deco style. In the 1930s the building was renamed the Wolverine Building, and is now called the Washington Square Building.

MSHD

108 201 E. Washington
Hoelzle Meat Market   1893

Since 1893, the octagonal tower with its tent-shaped metal roof has served as a sign for businesses. Originally, a cow-shaped weather vane proclaimed the Hoelzle Meat Market's wares. The building is brick in the Queen Anne commercial style with a large arched window taking up the second floor width on the Washington Street side. An old photo shows the building before the bricks were painted. Over the years it was Geisendorfer's Meat Market and then the Washington Meat Market (a portrait of Washington graced the side of the building). A small brick addition was added behind in the 1930s.

Later occupants were less kind to the turret and it was boarded up and the weather vane removed. After 1984 it housed Metzger's German Restaurant, which restored the weather vane and the building in general. Since 2002 it has housed the Arena Restaurant and Bar.

MSHD

216 E. Washington
Frederick Sorg Block

109

1871

This "block" for paint and glass dealer Frederick Sorg was such an instant success that a second building at 218 was added in 1872. The *Ann Arbor Courier* in July of 1871 noted "a new brick block is going up rapidly." It is a pared-down version of the Italianate style, with windows set into arched recesses on the second floor. Sorg was so proud of this building he featured it in many of his advertisements, and the 1874 *Atlas of Washtenaw County* features an engraving showing the delicate shadings on the thin brick pilasters on the second floor.

Sorg was a "house, sign and ornamental painter dealing in paints, oils, varnishes, glass, etc." Paper hanging, printing, and glazing were other specialties. The family lived upstairs, and his son Albert continued the business until 1886. Then milliner Edgar Munyon ran his shop here, also living upstairs. Throughout the 20th century it housed many businesses, including a barber shop, tape recorder store, donut shop, shoe store, and coal store.

In 1985, Robert Tisch acquired the building for his insurance and investment services firm. Architect Daniel H. Jacobs removed the porcelain enamel panels that had covered it since the 1950s, and the cast-iron facade was restored using the drawing from the county atlas. They also replicated the wood cornice with brackets. They received an award from the Historic District Commission in 1986.

MSHD

110 219–221 E. Washington
Weinmann Block   1867/1892

Michael Weinmann and John Gall (see #160) opened a meat market just after the Civil War at 221 E. Washington, an example of a high-Italianate brick commercial building. With a pedimented roof over the central portion that contains an oculus window, heavy and ornate stone arches over the second floor windows, and brick corbelling under the bracketed cornice, this building still makes a statement. The owners lived above the store and sold their meat from a plate-glassed storefront that has seen many remodelings since it opened.

They were prosperous enough that Weinmann was able to construct the building next door at 219 in the more flamboyant style of the 1890s. It has pressed-tin arches over the second floor windows, very rare in Michigan. The new building was careful to continue the cornice line and second floor designs of the older building. The corner building was known as the Weinmann-Geisendorfer Meat Market until 1937. Known for having the best frankfurters in town, it was popular with high school kids walking home from their school at Washington and State. The buildings were added to the National Register in 1983.

In 1937, another venerable Ann Arbor institution moved into both buildings. Fischer Hardware, in Ann Arbor since the 1860s, operated here until 1982. It was then purchased by developer Peter T. Allen who began to restore the buildings to their 1890s appearance. The cornice was restored, windows were unblocked, shutters replaced, and the storefronts were refurbished to emphasize the differences in the two buildings.

NR, MSHD

315 E. Washington
Michigan Bell Telephone Building

111

1925

This wonderful example of a Spanish Revival-style building in red brick with terra-cotta ornament was designed by William Kapp of the renowned Detroit firm Smith, Hinchman and Grylls. The firm designed many of Michigan Bell's buildings. Kapp was trained at the School of Beaux Arts in Paris, as witnessed by his use of terra-cotta rather than stone for the window arches and roof trim. The molds for the terra-cotta tiles were designed by Mr. Kapp himself. Kapp's other buildings include the University Club and Players Club in Detroit, Meadowbrook Hall in Rochester, and the Rackham School of Graduate Studies (see #242) at the University of Michigan.

The first telephones arrived in Ann Arbor in 1880, and an exchange was established in 1881. Only a small group of businesses used them at first. By 1915, the Ann Arbor Exchange had over 4,000 phones in service, and continuing demand led to the construction of this building in 1925, which had new automatic switching equipment for the now over 8,000 customers. In 1976, there were over 118,000 phones in service.

This building still serves to house telephone equipment. A large faceless and windowless addition on the rear, facing Huron Street, was added in the 1970s. This building has maintained its architectural integrity, and is still owned by Michigan Bell Telephone Company.

Former IHP

112 322 E. Washington
Jacob Hoffstetter House   1883

In July of 1882 the *Ann Arbor Argus* announced that the new Hoffstetter residence was to cost $5,000 and be built on Washington Street. Other papers followed the construction, and the *Ann Arbor Democrat* announced in October of 1883 that the house was enclosed, and that the mason was J.D. Dow. By May of 1884 the two papers announced that Mrs. Hangsterfer and family "will occupy the new brick residence of Mr. Hoffstetter on Washington Street." Such were the vicissitudes of new house construction. In 1888, they rented part of it to the Alpha Tau Omega fraternity, which was here until 1894. Jacob Hoffstetter had a grocery and saloon on Main Street as early as 1872. He was the son of German immigrants who arrived in 1854, and was part of a small group of Germans who were Presbyterian rather than Lutheran or Catholic.

This wonderful Queen Anne brick house is set on an ashlar stone foundation and has windows capped by stone segmental arches with carved keystones. An oculus window and kingpost, pierced with a trefoil design, decorate the front gable. This same pierced trefoil design is found on the side gables as well. Bracketed cornices crown the bay windows and porches, both features of the style.

The house is an unusual survivor of the residential buildings that once graced this street. It was converted into apartments in 1937. There was extensive interior remodeling but much of the original wood trim remained intact. In 1980, the house was purchased and restored by Peter and Rita Heydon, who also restored the former parsonage next door and the Graves garage in the rear (see #113). In 2008, the Heydons placed preservation easements in perpetuity on the properties with the Michigan Historic Preservation Network. They were declared "Preservationists of the Year" by the Historic District Commission in 2008.

NR, Former IHP, MHPN Preservation Easement

332 E. Washington
Methodist Episcopal Parsonage

113

1858

This is an extremely well-preserved example of the late Greek Revival style in Ann Arbor. Built of clapboard and designed in the front-facing temple with pediment style, it has a triangular window in the attic space, shutters, and a typical Greek Revival entry with sidelights and transom. It also has a full entablature with dentils. The transformation of the Greek Revival style to the more picturesque Italianate and Gothic styles can be seen in the unusual scalloped trim around the gables and returns.

It was built as the home of the Methodist Episcopal (this was later shortened to Methodist) minister Seth Reed, who was a leader of the Methodists in Michigan. He began his ministry in 1844, and had a large circuit throughout Michigan. He was appointed here in 1857, and despite only a two-year stay, he managed to enlarge his church at Ann and Fifth. The home was used by other ministers until 1881.

Shoe merchant William Allaby purchased it in 1882, and lived here until 1910. Albert Graves then acquired it and built his garage in the back. He died in 1927, but Mrs. Graves remained and divided the house into two apartments in 1957.

In 1980, Peter Heydon bought the property (see #112) and undertook a massive restoration project. In 2008 he and his wife Rita received the Preservationists of the Year Award for putting these properties under a protective historic easement in perpetuity with the Michigan Historic Preservation Network.

NR, Former IHP, MHPN Preservation Easement

114 606 E. Washington
Zenas and Eliza Burd House   c. 1862

Moved in 1916 to make way for construction of Lane Hall (see #216), this house originally stood near the corner of State and Washington. The home was constructed by Zenas and Eliza Burd in about 1862. Built in the Italianate style, three-bays wide with a hipped roof, the home features arched four-over-four windows with dog-eared trim. The windows on the original front facade are paired, a common feature in early Italianate buildings, as are the dentils of the cornice, though the paired brackets appear to have been altered. The home still features its fine original front entry with painted glass sidelights and transom.

Zenas Burd was an early settler of Ann Arbor and the Michigan Territory, arriving from Oneida County, New York in about 1826. He eventually settled in Northfield Township where in 1856 he married his third wife Eliza Newman, a native of England. Zenas Burd farmed and served as justice of the peace in Northfield Township until 1862, when the couple moved to Ann Arbor. An elder and trustee in the Methodist Episcopal Church, Burd aided in the building of the church building that once stood across Washington Street from his residence. Zenas Burd died in 1870, and Eliza continued to live in the house until her death in 1898. For years the property has been used as a student rental.

Former IHP

112 W. Washington
William Herz Paints
115
1880

This commercial Italianate two-story brick structure was constructed in 1880 by William Herz, a house, sign, and fresco painter. Herz began his paint business in Ann Arbor in 1869, the same year he arrived from Germany to join his parents. Herz married Sophia Muehlig in 1874 and they had one son, Oswald, who ran the business from 1913 until his death in 1954. He willed the business to four faithful employees who continued to run it until 1963. When the firm closed, it had been at the same address throughout its 93-year existence. During that time their devoted customers included the elite of Ann Arbor who often went on vacation leaving their keys with the company so they could wallpaper, paint, and fresco their houses without inconvenience to either party. In 1950, the firm provided the red cypress for the Frank Lloyd Wright house on Orchard Hills Drive (see #344), one of Ann Arbor's most important architectural landmarks.

The cast-iron entry, brick corbelling, fancy wood-bracketed cornice, brick pilasters, and original one-over-one windows capped by a hood molding of raised brick with floral-patterned stone "ears" and a keystone, were all kept intact by the next owner, Herman Goetz. Until the 1970s it was one of the few unremodeled 19th-century commercial buildings in Ann Arbor. For a brief time it was the Town Bar and in 1972 the Cracked Crab opened there—one of the first restaurants in Ann Arbor to serve fresh fish. It expanded into the space at 114 W. Washington in 1978 and the fronts were remodeled to look Colonial. Luckily, when this remodeling was undone in 1995 by Jon Carlson, the ornamental cast-iron columns on the front facade were still intact. It has been Café Zola since 1996.

MSHD

116 119–123 W. Washington
Germania Hotel   1885

This typical late-Italianate brick structure with traditional round-arched windows (now picked out with limestone at the corners and centers of the arches) was once only three stories tall. It was built by Michael Staebler, a farmer from Scio Township who hired architect George Schwab to construct a building to house his coal and farm implement business and a hotel. Staebler's Germania House had the largest "sample rooms" in the state, where traveling salesmen could exhibit samples of their goods. There was also a saloon and dining room. A huge hunk of coal stood in front of the building to advertise the coal business, while the third floor (with taller windows) contained an auditorium for musical performances.

The hotel was remodeled in 1895, and a fourth floor was added. It still has the original fancy bracketed cornice. The name was also changed to the American House, owing to the anti-German sentiment developing before World War I. The Staeblers later ran a bicycle shop and an automobile dealership from here too. A small one-story building was added to the rear in 1918 to house their dealership. This now has an Ashley Street address and once housed the Bird of Paradise Jazz Club.

In 1954, the hotel was sold to Earl Milner who had a chain of hotels, and it was renamed The Earle. It became a shabby flop house, and was closed in 1971 for fire code violations.

In 1973, Ernie Harburg and Rick Burgess (owners of the Del Rio Bar across the street) purchased the hotel, intending to restore it. David Rock and Dennis Webster were also early investors. At the beginning it was a struggle to get loans from banks for the renovations. Soon, a group of investors known as the limited partnership group of Marvin Carlson and Tom Garthwaite sold shares to help defray the costs of renovation. The owner of record today is Cooperative Investments LLC.

The Earle restaurant opened in the basement in 1975 and is still thriving. This restoration and restaurant inspired the renovation of many buildings west of Main and began the influx of high-end restaurants that remains a feature of the area. It has also served as a jazz club that has featured famous headliners.

NR, MSHD

146

122 W. Washington
John Wagner Jr. Blacksmith Shop   1869

117

Blacksmithing and related activities were already concentrated along Ashley (known as Second Street until 1889) when Wagner built his carriage and wagon shop in 1869. He was expanding the trade of his German-trained father who lived kitty-corner from here. John Wagner Sr. arrived in Ann Arbor in 1837. His son did well, building a fine commercial Italianate brick structure of three stories with the traditional segmental arches over the windows on the second floor and round arches on the third. Each had a limestone keystone in the center for aesthetic effect.

Wagner's advertisement in 1872 claimed: "CARRIAGE AND BLACKSMITH SHOP keeps on hand and manufactures all kinds of CARRIAGES, WAGONS AND SLEIGHS. Custom work and horse shoeing done promptly and in a satisfactory manner...Corner Washington and Second Streets."

By 1874, probably because of the Depression of 1873, the shop became the property of John Schneider Jr., another early German pioneer and blacksmith. In July of 1884 Schneider opened the Union Hotel and moved his blacksmithing business around the corner. In 1888, it advertised a good meal for 25 cents and bottled beer for 10 cents. By 1899, the bottling works, also run by Schneider, was the only tenant.

Dietz's Saloon occupied this spot in 1895, followed by a variety of saloons and restaurants including the Barrel House, Dietz's Soft Drinks (during Prohibition), Flautz's Restaurant, Metzger's German-American Restaurant, and the Del Rio Pizzeria which opened in the 1950s.

In 1969, Ernie Harburg, his wife Torrey, and Rick Burgess made a dream come true. They bought the Del Rio in what was then a rough and dangerous neighborhood and turned it into a bar, restaurant, and music venue with free jazz on Sundays. They restored the front facade of the building and the interior as well and encouraged the renovation of many buildings in the vicinity (see #116). The bar closed in 2004 after 25 years. It has been the Grizzly Peak Brewing Company since 2005.

118 608 E. William
First Congregational Church   1876

The First Congregational Church was organized in 1847, and according to church history, it split from the Presbyterians over slavery. The secession was led by a small group of liberals who differed with the Presbyterians on questions of faith and dogma. They built a church in 1849, but voted in 1870 to build a new one. In 1871, the University of Michigan hired James B. Angell, a Congregationalist, to be its new president, which must certainly have given impetus to build a sanctuary worthy of this office as well. The church opened in 1876, the same year as the Centennial of the United States was being celebrated.

They hired famous Detroit architect Gordon W. Lloyd, who also designed St. Andrew's Episcopal Church (see #149). He chose the Gothic Revival style, using multicolored fieldstone and Indiana limestone. The slate roof with lozenge motifs in various colors is also a hallmark of the style, and was meticulously replaced in 2005. Inside, the use of wooden hammer and collar beams adds to the effect, as do the pointed arched windows, also a feature of the style.

In the 1940s and '50s, stained glass grisaille windows and the front entry steps were added. In 1953 a parish house was completed and named the Douglas Memorial Chapel, after Dr. Lloyd C. Douglas, a former minister and author of two popular books, *The Robe* and *The Magnificent Obsession*, which became hit movies. The architect was Ralph Hammett of the University of Michigan School of Architecture.

In 1986, the church undertook a three-year renovation of the collar beams and installed the Wilhelm tracker pipe organ, as well as handicap-accessible ramps and an elevator.

The church hosts numerous concerts open to the public and retains its liberal stance on most social issues. It graces a major corner opposite the original University of Michigan campus and makes a lovely transition between "town and gown." It is one of several "downtown" churches that have remained and serve a vital function for the community. They received a Preservation Award from the Historic District Commission in 1989 and again in 2006 for the restoration of the slate roof.

Former IHP

611 E. William

Delta Kappa Epsilon (ΔKE) Shant

1878

This Gothic red brick building with unusual gabled dormers, stained glass, a date stone, a cartouche with a scroll spelling out "ΔKE," and fancy chimneys was designed by William LeBaron Jenney, a Chicago architect who is considered the inventor of the modern skyscraper. Jenney was on the faculty of the University of Michigan (1876–1879), though continued to live in Chicago where he designed his path-breaking buildings. Jenney described the building as a copy of a 13th-century French church. The interior was described as "chapel like" with beautiful collar beams. Jenney's other Ann Arbor buildings have been demolished and this is believed to be his only remaining building in Michigan.

The ΔKEs used their "shant" for regular meetings until the University of Michigan chapter was deactivated in the 1960s. While empty, it was vandalized and many items were stolen. In 1971, Wilfred V. Casgrain and other Omicron chapter members raised funds and renovated the structure to function again as an on-campus club for ΔKEs. It has been used for alumni gatherings, receptions for parents of graduating seniors, and secret fraternity rush rituals, as well as initiation rites. It is also the oldest freestanding fraternity house in the country still used for its original purpose.

Jenney's original design has not been altered and thus the stone foundation, brickwork, and woodwork make it a rare 19th-century Victorian eclectic building. The brick wall was added in 1901, and shelters a tiny marble tombstone for "Abe," the ΔKE's mascot of long ago.

DSHD

149

OLD FOURTH WARD/ KERRYTOWN/ NORTH MAIN

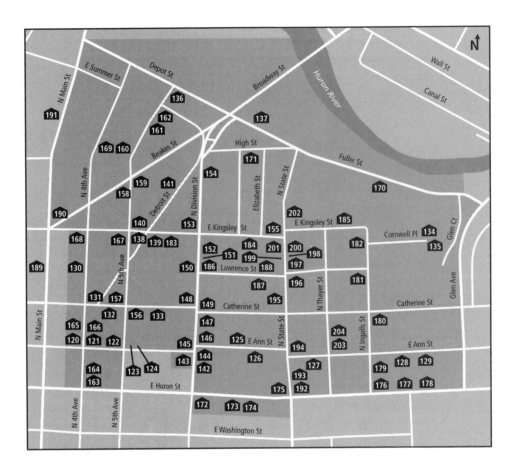

The Old Fourth Ward neighborhood contains Ann Arbor's most impressive collection of 19th- and early 20th-century residential buildings. Exceptional examples of Greek Revival, Gothic Revival, Italianate, Queen Anne, Shingle style, and Colonial Revival buildings can all be found in the neighborhood, as well as a number of fine early 20th-century apartment buildings and historic churches. From the 1820s through the late 19th century, many of the city's prominent citizens called this neighborhood home, including professor and mayor Silas Douglass, who built a fine Gothic Revival home on E. Huron in 1848 (see #173), the first architect-designed home in the city, and Judge Robert S. Wilson, whose home is considered by many to be one of the finest Greek Revival houses in the country (see #144). Ann Street between Division and State is the only residential block in town containing only 19th-century buildings (see #125 and #126). Following University of Michigan President Henry Tappan's 1852 edict closing dormitories on campus, students began moving into the neighborhood. A number of buildings were built as rooming houses (see #176 and #195) and many more were converted to this use. Large apartment buildings were constructed in the early 20th century to deal with the post-World War I population boom (see #185 and #196). Students make up a majority of the neighborhood's population today, though there are a number of owner-occupied residences.

Historically, the Kerrytown and North Main areas have had a more industrial flavor due to their proximity to the Huron River and the Michigan Central Railroad (see #137 and #159), which arrived in 1839. Lumber yards (see #136), breweries (see #162), steam planing mills (see #141), and slaughterhouses employed large numbers of Irish, German, and African-American laborers. The area was a center of the African-American community throughout Ann Arbor's history, with churches (see #158, #162, and #171), black-owned businesses (see #120), and the Colored Welfare League (see #165) located in the neighborhood. While much of the North Main area remains unrestored rental properties, Kerrytown has undergone a major transformation, with popular shops and restaurants, including the world-famous Zingerman's Deli (see #139). The area also hosts significant nightlife with the Kerrytown Concert House (see #168) and the bars and restaurants of Braun Court (see #130).

120 109–119 E. Ann
Hoban Block   1871

"Fire on Rotten Row," screamed the headline of the *Michigan Argus* on December 30, 1870, as wooden commercial structures went up in flames. By March of 1871, the *Peninsular Courier* was announcing that ground had been broken for a new building, and by the summer it was completed. Mrs. Hoban, owner of the new block of brick buildings, was described by the 1881 *History of Washtenaw County* as having "built a substantial business on Ann St. in 1871 at a cost of several thousand dollars."

The buildings remain today, shorn of their elaborate bracketed wood cornices, the epitome of Italianate commercial architecture. Brick window hoods, arched half circles on the third floor, and segmental arches on the second are typical of the style. Brick corbelling unites the facades of five of the six storefronts; the building at 109 E. Ann was probably built a few years later.

Throughout their 140 years, they have housed restaurants, groceries, saloons, and butchers. These were often the businesses of new immigrants, including a Chinese laundry, a Greek restaurant, and a Jewish dry goods store. The building also housed a number of African-American-oriented businesses as the neighborhood became the center of black commercial life in the early 20th century. One example was the barber shop at #117, run by Henry Wade Robbins, who came to Ann Arbor from Canada in 1884 and became a successful businessman.

This part of town was notorious for its bars and pool halls as early as the 1890s, and was plagued with drugs, prostitution, and crime. In the 1960s, a blues bar named Clint's Club attracted patrons from all of Ann Arbor with "Washboard Willie" as the headliner. *Down Beat Magazine* noted in 1967 that Louis Armstrong had played a free concert on Ann Street with flutist Art Fletcher.

An extensive restoration was completed by the Bilakos family in the 1980s. Several of the original cast-iron storefronts were restored. The Bilakos family continues to maintain and preserve their buildings, where Peter Bilakos now maintains his law office.

FAHD

201–207 E. Ann
Bank of Washtenaw/Chapin House

1836

Land sales boomed in the 1830s and this required capital. Banks with little real capital but the ability to print money (known as "wildcat banks") sprang up in the Michigan Territory. One such bank was the Bank of Washtenaw, founded by local businessmen in 1835. They constructed this building to house their banking rooms and their head cashier. When the entire banking system of the U.S. collapsed in the Panic of 1837 (the same year Michigan became a state), the Bank of Washtenaw died as well. The building stood empty for almost a decade until it was sold in 1847 to local businessman and early settler Volney Chapin, a native of upstate New York, who converted it to his residence. He and his wife Chloe made it their home for over 25 years and it became a showpiece property, surrounded by exotic catalpa trees and a garden that stretched along rose-bordered paths all the way to Catherine Street.

This brick Greek Revival-style house, covered in stucco scored to resemble masonry, is the earliest example of this style in Ann Arbor and was copied in the building that is now the University of Michigan President's House (see #235). Although it has been enlarged on the west, the Greek Revival details can still be seen in the Ann Street entry with its simple Doric columns supporting a dentillated entablature.

By the 1880s, the area had become very commercial and the house became the Arlington Hotel, then the Catalpa Hotel, and later the Peters Hotel. Joe Parker's saloon occupied the corner space ("Joe" is spelled out in tile at the former corner entry) from 1913 until 1920 when Prohibition drove him out of business. The Ann Arbor Chamber of Commerce bought the building and later sold it to Christ Bilakos in 1942. Many different businesses have occupied the street-level retail spaces while apartments were rented on the second floor. In 2000, the Bilakos family still owned the building and undertook a massive restoration job, returning the building to its former glory and receiving an award from the Historic District Commission.

FAHD

122 223 E. Ann
Ann Arbor Armory

1911

In 1910, the State of Michigan passed a law allowing local communities to house military units. The City of Ann Arbor donated the land to the state, while a fund drive raised $25,000 for an armory building. Built by the Koch Brothers (see #51) and designed by Jackson architect Claire Allen, the Armory opened in 1911. It housed a drill room, reading room, billiard room, captain's office, orderly rooms, locker rooms, an indoor shooting range, and a kitchen in the basement. For many years it was the scene of musical events, especially for the African-American community, with rock and roll, R & B, and gospel groups putting on shows. It housed the National Guard until 1990. It sat empty until 1997, when it was rehabilitated and converted to condos by Ed Shaffran, who received a Rehabilitation Award from the Historic District Commission in 1999.

This brown brick building is in the castle-like Collegiate Gothic style, with smooth stone bordering the windows, staggered stone quoins around brick sections, and turreted towers flanking the entry (the turrets were removed long ago). This militaristic style was favored for many armories.

NR, SR, OFWHD

311 E. Ann
James F. Royce House

123

1866

This house was constructed in 1866, just after the Civil War, by local pioneer James F. Royce. Royce had come to Ann Arbor from Connecticut in 1830 and was a skilled cabinet maker who had a chair-making business. He later operated a carriage factory, and his daughter married prominent citizen Philip Bach. In the early 20th century, it was the home of Electa and Harriet Knight, descendants of the pioneer Rufus Knight of Scio Township. It became a rental in 1960.

A textbook example of an Italianate building, the house is cube-shaped with a low hipped roof, paired brackets under the eaves, a symmetrical arrangement of windows and doors, and ornamental sawn woodwork, often called "gingerbread," on the front and side porches. Also typical of the style are the chamfered posts on the front porch and the lack of railings. The siding on the front porch is shiplap, while the rest is simple clapboard. French doors leading to the porch with large flanking shutters are also typical of the style, but rare in Ann Arbor. The house has not been remodeled much and even has most of its original window glass.

OFWHD

124 317 E. Ann

Mills-Corselius-Breed House   1831

Cornelia Corselius, a local historian, wrote that her family was occupying this house in 1838, while deeds note a Dr. Randall living there in 1834. The house was probably built by Sylvester or Willard Mills in 1831, making it one of the oldest houses in Ann Arbor. George Corselius, Cornelia's father, became editor of Ann Arbor's first newspaper, *The Western Emigrant* (owned by John Allen and Samuel Dexter), after arriving from upstate New York in 1829. He is also credited with starting the first lending library. The house was occupied and expanded by the Bower family in the 1840s. The Breed family, who lived here from the 1880s until 1937, included local teachers and Congregational ministers.

The original house is simple in what local historian Lela Duff called the "New England style." In architectural terms, the original was an I-House, meaning it had a central hall, was two rooms wide, one room deep, and two stories tall. It was studied by University of Michigan Professor of Architecture Emil Lorch, who referred to it as the Catherine Breed House. He noted that the pilastered doorway was from 1938, but the door was the original walnut one, and that the joists in the basement were still covered with bark. The plastered walls were 10 inches thick and the triangular field in the side gables once had Federal-style fan lights. Lorch refers to the style as "post-colonial." The six-over-six windows are likely original, as are some doors and interior trim. The Lorch Collection at the Bentley Library includes measured drawings and old photos of the structure. It became a rental after 1937 and was covered in aluminum siding in the 1950s.

OFWHD

511 E. Ann

Willcoxson-Easton House

125

c. 1827

This simple clapboard house (formerly with shutters) has some classical features, which put it in the Greek Revival mode: an entry with sidelights and transom, six-over-six windows, and cornice returns at the gable ends. It also suggests an older New England style in that the gable ends do not face the street. The house is on a brick foundation, and the chimneys are at the center and end gable.

The house is thought to have been built by Gideon Willcoxson in about 1827 at Division and Ann. Willcoxson purchased the property from town founder John Allen in 1825. It then included the entire block bounded by Division, Catherine, Ann, and State Streets. In

the 1820s, this site was just east of the township/town boundary (hence the name Division Street). Fellow attorney George Jewett managed the property for his children after Willcoxson's sudden death in 1830. The house is believed to have been moved to Ann Street in 1858 when the block was platted and Ann Street was extended from Division to State (before that Ann Street had been a cow path).

The 1853 map shows the only house at the northeast corner of Division and what was later Ann being occupied by George Sedgwick, mayor of Ann Arbor in 1851. Sedgwick purchased the Division Street property in 1852. It is possible that this house was moved to Ann when Ebenezer Wells purchased the property and built his grand home (see #146).

Charles Easton, a grocer, purchased the home in 1863. Martha and Widdicombe Schmidt purchased it in 1975, and preserved the original hand-blown glass of the windows. The Schmidts were part of the driving force behind the creation of the Old Fourth Ward Historic District.

ASHB

126 602 E. Ann
Gerhard and Rosena Josenhans House   1885

The 1906 book *Past and Present of Washtenaw County, Michigan* states that "Mr. and Mrs. Josenhans have a beautiful home at No. 602 East Ann Street, and it is noted for its hospitality, being the center of a cultured society circle." Gerhard Josenhans was born in Leonberg, Germany and came to Washtenaw County as an infant in 1855. He began working in his teens for Mack and Schmid, Ann Arbor's largest department store, starting as an errand boy and working his way up into management. He married Ann Arbor-native Rosena Bross in 1881, and four years later built this home on E. Ann Street.

Like many German-built Victorian homes in Ann Arbor, the Josenhans House combines a variety of architectural details on what is essentially a gable-front Folk house. The home's window trim is borrowed from the Stick style, while the porch sports Italianate brackets and posts, as well as Gothic Revival gingerbread. Another architectural detail of note is the use of a "blind window" on the front facade, which gives the house a more symmetrical appearance, though there are only two windows on the second floor.

The home remained in the Josenhans family until 1975 and remains a single-family house today.

ASHB

712 E. Ann

127

Moses and Jane Gunn House

1851

Jane Gunn wrote in her memoir of 1889 that in 1851, she and her husband Moses "had purchased a roomy house nearly completed," and the long pillars in front "suggested a style of Grecian architecture now almost obsolete." Gunn arrived in Ann Arbor in 1846 and helped establish the University of Michigan Medical School in 1850. He became Professor of Anatomy and Surgery and his portrait by Revenaugh hangs proudly in the University Hospital. Gunn was a native of East Bloomfield, New York and married Jane Terry, the daughter of a local doctor, in 1848.

Moved to its present site in 1898, the house originally faced State at the corner of Ann and State. Purportedly it was a twin of Governor Felch's house next door and built by the same builder, Andrew DeForest (see #148). It is built in what University of Michigan Architecture Professor Emil Lorch called the "domestic" Greek Revival, with square rather than round columns, pilasters at the corners, "eared" trim around the windows and doorway with a fine entablature, and a pedimented roof above the portico. The interior is remarkably unaltered and has original doors, windows, and trim.

Gunn moved to Detroit in 1854, but remained on the University of Michigan faculty until the Civil War. The house was then owned by Richard Hooper, a local brewer, and later by William H. Payne, Professor of the Science and Art of Teaching. Payne's papers at the Bentley Library have provided the oldest known photograph as well as reams of material about his career and his purchase of the house. Following the 1898 move, the house became a rental until 1945 when it was purchased by orthodontist David James and his wife Naomi. They lived here for almost 45 years and raised their two daughters in the house. In 1987 it was purchased by Lars Bjorn and Susan Wineberg, who have lived here since. Susan was one of the founders of the Old Fourth Ward Historic District and both are historic preservation activists.

OFWHD

128 920 E. Ann
Keating Family Home

c. 1860/1873

This is a good example of a Vernacular "upright and wing" structure, which has both a gable portion facing the street and facing the side. The side wing has a porch with chamfered columns, lacy gingerbread, and no railing, typical features from the 1860s. A smaller house appears on the 1866 Birdseye Map, and the property jumped in value in 1873, indicating the front-gabled addition. The house has its original working shutters and original wood siding. For over 100 years it was the home of only two families, the Keatings and the Donegans.

Builder and mason Timothy Keating appears in the 1860 *City Directory*. John Keating, with James Cole, published the 1872 *City Directory* that lists John living here with his brothers Thomas J., a cigar maker, and Timothy. John was well known for his medical journal, *The Physician and Surgeon*, which he published from 1873–1915. The journal had a national circulation and was edited by Keating and University faculty members. The Timothy Keating family continued living here and Timothy's widow shared the house with Dorcas Donegan and blacksmith James Donegan. Dorcas and her sister Marie lived here until 1973. In 1993, the home was purchased by Mary Ivers and Tony Ramirez, who restored the home and received a Preservation Award in 2007.

OFWHD

1010 E. Ann
Phi Beta Pi/Phi Alpha Kappa Fraternity House 1929

129

The Phi Beta Pi fraternity house is somewhat unusual among Ann Arbor Tudor Revival buildings of the time period due to its mostly homogeneous building materials. The house is built primarily of randomly laid, cut ashlar, topped with a slate roof, and has very little of the false half-timbering and stucco typical of the style. Two large bays with castellated parapets protrude from the front of the structure. The left bay features a recessed entry with a Gothic arch. Half-timbering does make an appearance on the building in an unusual upper side wing, which creates a porch space on the first story, and in a third-story shed dormer in the back of the house.

Phi Beta Pi was a medical fraternity founded in 1891, with the University of Michigan branch organized in 1898. They built this house near the University hospital in 1929. In 1945, this building became the home of the Phi Alpha Kappa fraternity. Phi Alpha Kappa was a Christian fraternity formed by alumni of Calvin College in 1929, and started at Michigan as a fraternity for graduate students. First limiting its membership only to those who graduated from Calvin College, the fraternity soon began accepting members from other colleges if they were of Dutch or Christian Reformed Church backgrounds. Because of a large Dutch influence in the fraternity's early days, the fraternity house was called the "Dutch House" by its members. The fraternity received a Preservation Award in 1993.

OFWHD

130 313–327 Braun Court

Braun Court   1915–1918

In the early 20th century, the character of this portion of town was primarily industrial, with machine shops, planing mills, and lumber yards occupying much of the Kerrytown neighborhood we see today (see #141). Between 1915 and 1918, carpenter and contractor Samuel M. Braun began constructing these front-gabled Craftsman-style workers' houses on a former industrial lot on N. Fourth Avenue. Braun's workshop originally stood in this row of homes, but it was demolished in the 1970s. Like the working-class houses on Mulholland and Murray Streets (see #277), the Braun Court buildings were all originally identical, built of wood frames covered in stucco, with front-gabled roofs and full-width front porches. What makes Braun Court unique is the common, central "mews" between the facing rows of the buildings.

In the 1980s, Braun Court was converted to commercial use, and today hosts a number of interesting bars, shops, and restaurants, and is the center of Kerrytown's nightlife. Some of the buildings still exhibit many of their original features.

Former IHP

201 Catherine
Davis Block/Agricultural Hall
1856

131

This simple brick commercial building's construction was announced in the September 19, 1856 issue of the *Michigan Gazetteer* (a statewide publication): "the excavation is being made for...the erection of a fine brick block to be used as an agricultural implements warehouse. It will be a fine improvement." The builders, Davis and Greenman, dissolved their partnership three years later and in March of 1860 the *Michigan Argus*, a local newspaper, noted that Moses Rogers had purchased the Davis Block and was moving from Washington Street to have "an extensive agricultural implement manufactory in his new quarters." It is the oldest commercial building in central Ann Arbor.

Rogers was an emigrant from New York State who had arrived in 1831 and operated several agricultural implement factories here before buying this building. This hall became the headquarters of the Soldier's Aid Society for Civil War Relief, and Rogers allowed many social events to be held there to raise money during the Civil War. A planned celebration of the Union victory in 1865 went ahead despite the assassination of Lincoln. Rogers' home and later factory location are elsewhere in this book (see #138 and #143).

The building was sold to John Finnegan in 1867 and became known as Agricultural Hall. Finnegan specialized in agricultural machinery, mowers, reapers, and binders, machines unheard of 50 years earlier. In 1892, the Hall was sold to the Hay and Todd Manufacturing Co. of Ypsilanti, which specialized in making underwear. By 1916, Horace Prettyman had converted it to the White Swan Laundry and the building was known by this name for most of the 20th century.

The building was extensively rehabilitated in 1988 by Michael Vlasic, and a Post-Modern addition, designed by local architect Frederick H. Herrmann, was added to the north.

Former IHP

132 216 Catherine
Anton Eisele House   1872

Anton Eisele, a German immigrant, opened a stone-cutting business with his brother John W. in 1868. They specialized in American and Italian marbles, and the unusual carvings in the stone lintels above the windows of Anton's home are testimony to his art. They were prosperous enough to be included in the 1874 *Atlas of Washtenaw County*. Most of their work was for tombstones, and samples of them appeared when a nearby building was being renovated in the 1990s. The house is a simple brick rectangle, with symmetrically arranged windows and large carved stone lintels. A rear wing that served as the kitchen was removed in a remodeling in 2003–2004 and replaced by a garage.

Eisele died in 1887, and his stepson John Baumgardner took over the business. He constructed a fancy brick office across the street on the island at Catherine and Detroit and advertised being the successor to Eisele, specializing in cemetery monuments, building stones, and slabs for sidewalks. "Estimates cheerfully furnished," he proclaimed in one ad. The main building was demolished in the 1930s for a gas station that now serves as Argiero's Restaurant, but the stables survive today at the corner of Fifth and Catherine (see #157).

OFWHD

324 Catherine

133

William G. and Mary Foster House

1870

This two and one-half story brick building is a simple version of the Italianate style, with its double-carved brackets under the eaves of a hipped roof, eyebrow windows on the third floor, and cube shape. The classical doorway with transom and sidelights is more in the Greek Revival style. The porch is not original and the windows have been changed. The house was converted to apartments in the late 1940s.

The house was built for attorney William G. Foster and his wife Mary. He died suddenly in 1873, and Mary obtained a law degree from the University of Michigan in 1876. She opened her practice in this home and became Ann Arbor's first woman lawyer. She is one of the few women featured in the 1881 *History of Washtenaw County,* which included an engraving of her. Mary Foster was active in the temperance movement and local historical societies and had a paper published in 1880 by the Pioneer Society of Michigan. Since 1988, the Women Lawyers Association, Washtenaw Region, has presented an annual award in her name.

OFWHD

134 1009 Cornwell Place
Wirt Cornwell House   1886

In the 1880s, Cornwell Place was developed by the Cornwell family on a ridge overlooking the beautiful Huron River with views of the unspoiled countryside beyond. Professors, businessmen, educators, and medical personnel flocked to build their mansions in this idyllic setting. Only two houses remain of the ten that graced this street in the late 19th century. They are now owned by the University of Michigan and 1009 serves as a residence for students in the Center for International Business Education.

The Cornwell family owned paper mills (see also #154) in Ann Arbor and Ypsilanti and had large real estate holdings. Wirt was director of the First National Bank. Wirt's father Harvey lived nearby on Ingalls Street in a house later demolished to build St. Joseph Mercy Hospital. Wirt, Mary, and their descendants owned the property for nearly 40 years. It was divided into apartments after being vacant for almost a decade. Their daughters created the "Wirt and Mary Cornwell Prize in Pure Science" to reward University of Michigan undergraduates who showed great intellectual curiosity.

The house is a clapboard and brick affair in an almost Shingle/Queen Anne style, with a "jerkin head" or clipped gable in the front and a second-story porch over a veranda. It displays a typical Queen Anne sensibility with its asymmetry within symmetry, unusual rooflines, varying window shapes and sizes, and the use of different materials. The fieldstone porch was altered in the 20th century but the house retains much of its original splendor. The property at 1013 Cornwell has a similar clipped gable and was probably the carriage house for the Cornwell mansion.

OFWHD

1014 Cornwell Place
Dr. George Dock House

135

1894

Perched on a steep bluff overlooking the Huron River Valley and Glen Avenue, this elaborate Queen Anne house was built in 1894 for Dr. George Dock, Professor of Clinical Medicine and Pathology at the University of Michigan. The irregular massing, the polygonal tower with tent roof, wraparound porch, cross gables, windows in varying shapes and sizes, and the combination of materials including clapboard, board and batten, and cut shingles are all features of the Queen Anne style. They give the house a busy look, typical of the late 1890s. The house is a twin of one formerly on S. Main Street and now located on Huron Parkway.

Dr. Dock taught and practiced at the nearby University of Michigan Medical School, which was then located on Catherine Street. He later sold the house to Dr. Albert Barrett, director of the State Psychopathic Hospital, also located on Catherine. It housed the Gamma Alpha fraternity from 1925 to 1950, and then became known as Clark's Tourist Home. It was purchased by the University of Michigan in 1986 to house foreign students.

OFWHD

136 304 Depot
Wood and Perrin Building   c. 1872

Sellick Wood came to Michigan with his parents as a young man in 1834. The family established a farm in Lodi Township near the home of Captain John Lowry, a devout abolitionist and conductor on the Underground Railroad. Wood aided Lowry on the Underground Railroad, often carrying runaway slaves in his wagon by night to the Detroit River and freedom in Canada. In the late 1860s, Sellick Wood and his wife Ellen (Bliss) moved to Ann Arbor where Sellick became a produce dealer. He was in business with Hiram Perrin and the pair constructed this brick building in about 1872.

The building is a simple Italianate/Vernacular structure, unique because it is only one story tall, built on a tall stone foundation. Its only architectural details are the arched brickwork above the windows and the brick dentils that wrap around the building just below the frieze. A series of very old sheds and connected buildings stand behind the main brick building, including a Greek Revival building that likely predates the Wood and Perrin building. By 1878, the company was named S. Wood and Co., and included Sellick's son Frank. The father and son manufactured barrels and sold a huge variety of products, including pork, lumber, fire bricks, wool, drainpipes, and plaster.

Frank Wood continued in the business until 1916, when the building became the home of the Washtenaw Lumber Company. Since 1986, the building has been the home of Casey's Tavern, who renovated the building while preserving its historic character.

Former IHP

401 Depot
Michigan Central Railroad Depot/Gandy Dancer   1886

137

Detroit architects Spier and Rohns designed this Richard-sonian Romanesque train station that opened in 1886. Diagnostic of the style are the heavy stone walls, the deep-set openings, and the large arched entry into the building. The heavy construction represent-ed the solidity, strength, and prestige of the railroad. Stained glass windows, two fireplaces, and beautifully carved woodwork graced the interior of the waiting rooms and baggage areas. It was considered the finest station on the Michigan Central Line (and later the New York Central Line) when it opened.

The station was a port of entry into Ann Arbor for visiting students, tourists, and presidents of the United States. Cabs met them there and traveled up State Street to the main campus. Soldiers left from here during both world wars. After World War II, passenger service declined and the station closed in 1967.

In 1968, Chuck Muer bought the property and restored it, opening a seafood restaurant with a railroad theme called the Gandy Dancer. It was an instant hit and continues to serve great seafood and a famous Sunday brunch. Muer soon realized he needed to expand and enclosed the former platforms with glass and attached the baggage room to the main dining room. Patrons still applaud when the trains pass through.

NR, DSHD

138 417 Detroit
David Henning Cooper Shop   1864

Barrel and stave manufacturer David Henning built this commercial Italianate building in 1864 during the height of the Civil War. Marked by its decorated arched brick windows (with evidence of a former cornice with brackets), it is typical of the style. Henning was born in Ireland and came to Ann Arbor in 1836. He was enriched by lucrative contracts with the Union Army and became one of Ann Arbor's wealthiest citizens. His tombstone at Forest Hill Cemetery, surrounded by smaller ones of family members, greets entrants to the cemetery and makes a stunning impression.

The building was sold to agricultural implement maker Moses Rogers (see #143 and #131) in 1871. The business continued after his death in 1888 under the able leadership of his daughter Katie Rogers, better known as a skilled portrait painter. She sold the business in 1895.

Throughout the 20th century the building deteriorated as the neighborhood became less important. It served as a warehouse, creamery, machine shop, pattern works, and art gallery. Poverty is a friend of preservation and this building still has its old hand-blown glass windows.

Along with 419 Detroit, it was renovated in the 1960s by Travis and Demaris Cash, preservation-minded folks who also operated the Treasure Mart at 529 Detroit (see #141) and The Tree next door. They salvaged the wrought-iron fence from the Rominger property on S. Fifth Avenue (site of the parking structure) and rented to the Ann Arbor Ecology Center for over 25 years.

OFWHD

Old Fourth Ward/Kerrytown/North Main

422 Detroit
Desderide Grocery/Zingerman's Delicatessen 1902

Italian immigrant Rocco Desderide constructed this brick-veneered building in 1902 to house his grocery and confectionery business after he moved an older building to the rear of the property. His store quickly became a local "hangout" for neighborhood kids, according to Milo Ryan's *View of a Universe* (1985). Bands of corbelled brick radiate from above the second-floor windows, which were originally arched. Bands of brick decorate the lower half of the building as well, giving the exterior a very lively texture. A date of 1902 appears under the cornice line, setting the date in stone.

Desderide was a local character who lived nearby on Kingsley Street. He lived to be 105, despite smoking a cigar every day. The store passed into the hands of the Diroff family in 1921 and they operated a true "mom and pop" grocery there until 1980. Art Carpenter, who developed Kerrytown, then opened a short-lived deli.

In 1982, Ari Weinzweig and Paul Saginaw began Zingerman's Delicatessen, now an iconic food shop and a must-see for tourists. From this small space they have spun out eight other businesses and have an international reputation for fine food and service. Zingerman's built a small addition to the original building in 1986 and expanded into the other buildings on the site, including the building Desderide had moved and a former home next door. Another recent addition has doubled the size of the deli. It still serves as the neighborhood hangout as in the days of Desderide.

OFWHD

140 501–507 Detroit
Stofflet Block   1900

This handsome brick structure at the corner of Detroit and Kingsley, with its finial-topped tower and double porches, was built by news and book dealer Francis Stofflet for his children (he lived nearby on Lawrence). It is in a Colonial Revival style, and was originally four attached townhouses. The octagonal bays at each end sit atop high fieldstone walls as do the porches.

The name "Stofflet" appears in stone on the Detroit Street facade. Stofflet was a well-known local businessman who arrived here in 1869 and received a law degree two years later. In 1881, he began a newspaper distribution business that expanded to include magazines as well. Stofflet News Service continued to be run by his sons until 1970.

Two of the apartments were occupied by his children until the mid-1920s, and his widow Mary moved into one unit and divided the other three into eight one-story flats. In 1934, the mortgage was foreclosed and the building fell into disrepair. Taylor Collins purchased it in 1938 and lived there with his wife until 1973. By then all the occupants were black, as the neighborhood had become the main African-American residential part of town.

When Taylor Collins sold the building in 1973, it was renovated and renamed the Olde Town Apartments. In the mid-1980s, it was converted into eight condominiums called the Brownstone Condos, which utilized space in the basements and attics so that each unit had two stories. Lush landscaping and mature trees are set off against the beautiful red-brown brick, now over 100 years old.

OFWHD

529 Detroit
John G. Miller Planing Mill/Treasure Mart

141

1869

This Italianate brick building with its heavy, triple-arched windows and door openings was built by John G. Miller for a planing mill, specializing in "sash [windows], doors, blinds [shutters], molding and scroll work [gingerbread]." It replaced a wooden mill from 1853 that burned in July 1869. The earlier mill had made carriages and sleighs using a new steam process for bending wood. The brick mill was built within months of the fire.

Detroit Street hummed with industrial activity with its many mills, machine shops, and carriage factories—there were three at one time. Miller's mill was able to meet the booming demand after the Civil War. In 1878, he sold the mill to Herman Krapf, who renamed it the Detroit Planing Mill, and operated it until his death in 1906. Krapf also lived next door at 521 Detroit, a home he built in the 1880s, described in a 1906 local history as a "beautiful home."

This part of town went into steep decline after World War I. The industrial focus remained, as old mills and factories became warehouses for toys, fruit, and machinery. In 1960, the building was leased to Mrs. Demaris Cash for her now-famous Treasure Mart Consignment Store. She purchased the former mill in 1983, and her descendants continue this Ann Arbor institution.

OFWHD

142 | 120 N. Division
George and Emma Wahr House   1894

This exuberant Queen Anne house is one of several built and occupied by book dealer and stationer George Wahr and his wife. After purchasing the Wilson house at 126 N. Division (see #144) at a tax auction in 1892, Wahr built this house on the side lot. Projecting gables, varying window shapes and sizes, a semicircular porch with spindle work at both top and bottom, and a general asymmetrical organization of the spaces are typical features of the Queen Anne style. A twin of this house, also built by Wahr, stands at 445 S. Fourth Avenue (see #69).

Wahr was the son of pioneers from Germany who arrived in Washtenaw County in 1835. He apprenticed in the book business and eventually owned two bookstores—one on Main Street and one on State Street. He specialized in student supplies and also had a publishing business. His success was mirrored in this residence, which was in the most fashionable part of town.

The house remained in the Wahr family until 2002, when it was purchased by local historian Ray Detter who was one of the founders of the Old Fourth Ward Association, the Old Fourth Ward Historic District, and the Downtown Street Exhibits Program.

DSHD

121 N. Division
Moses Rogers House

143

1861

This Italianate structure, built as the Civil War was just beginning, has the classic features of the style in the double brackets under the extending eaves, the symmetrical arrangement of doors and windows, and the cube shape with hipped roof. It is one of the few that has its original porch, a dormer, and clapboard.

It was built for Moses and Letitia (Sweetland) Rogers who lived here with their daughters Katie and Ellen. Moses' brother Randolph Rogers was raised in Ann Arbor and went on to become an internationally famous sculptor. His "Nydia" can be found in the University of Michigan Museum of Art, and some of his other works can be found in art museums around the country. Randolph Rogers also designed the bronze doors of the Capitol in Washington, D.C.

Moses was more business-minded and specialized in manufacturing agricultural implements, though he too exhibited artistic talents. He is associated with several other historic buildings in town (see #131 and #138) and was active in local politics and the Unitarian Church. Katie became an accomplished painter and graduated from the Chicago Academy of Art. She dutifully took over her father's business upon his death.

The Weinberg family restored and maintained the home as single family throughout the 20th century while modernizing the interior.

The house is part of a dynamic foursome of houses at the corner of Ann and Division, which represent the Gothic Revival, Italianate, and Greek Revival styles.

DSHD

126 N. Division
Wilson-Wahr House

1835/1844/1863

This most iconic of Ann Arbor's historic houses started out as a small house facing Ann Street built around 1835 and purchased by Judge Robert S. Wilson in 1840. Wilson was a judge of probate and an early settler from upstate New York. The original kitchen was in the basement of this section which still contains the original Dutch oven.

Wilson expanded the house toward Division Street and built the Ionic-columned, pedimented Greek Revival house we see there today. The house has appeared in many books on architectural history as the epitome of a Greek Revival structure, with a pediment supported by two-story fluted columns, a doorway with sidelights and transom, and its stucco-over-brick structure scored to resemble stone masonry. It was praised for its perfect proportions by noted historian Fiske Kimball and appeared on the cover of Rexford Newcomb's *Architecture of the Old Northwest Territory*. A rear wing was added in the 1860s. The house was studied by Emil Lorch of the U-M School of Architecture and drawn as part of the Historic American Buildings Survey (HABS) in 1934.

Wilson sold the house to John A. Welles in 1850 and moved to Chicago. In 1861, it was sold to Susan Welles, his sister-in-law, who also donated the land for what is now Ann Street. In 1892, the property was purchased at a tax auction by local bookseller George Wahr. It remained in his family for over 100 years. In 2002, it was purchased by preservation architects Ilene and Norm Tyler who have restored the building to its original glory and have received awards from the Historic District Commission.

DSHD

178

205 N. Division
Palmer-Ryan House

145

1868/1876

One of the finest Gothic Revival houses still remaining in Ann Arbor, this beauty was designed by prominent Detroit architect Gordon Lloyd (see #149, #255, and #343). Its pointed gables with elaborate wooden fretwork and kingposts, its steeply pitched roofs and dormers, and triple-banded columnar porch posts are all features of the style.

A native of upstate New York, Dr. Alonzo Palmer came to Ann Arbor in 1852, after 10 years in Tecumseh, to help found the University of Michigan Medical School. He was affiliated with the University for more than thirty-five years. With his first wife, he purchased an 1868 brick house that faced Ann Street. His wife died a few years later and he married Love Root Palmer, whose fortunes allowed him to attach the Ann Street house to a new, grand house facing Division Street in 1876. He was Dean of the Medical School twice, from 1875–79 and from 1880–87. The house was purchased in 1901 by Tobias and Sarah Staebler Laubengayer, who commissioned a mural along the interior stair to record the Staebler immigration from Germany to Ann Arbor. Their daughter Wanda and son-in-law Mack Ryan lived in the home until 1970.

Ownership has changed many times since the 1970s. It became a rooming house and was later converted to apartments. Despite the intense residential use, the interior retains many of its original features, including ornate marble hearths, elaborate crystal chandeliers, and walnut stairs. It has its original shutters and entry door, and a beautiful wrought-iron fence.

DSHD

146 208 N. Division
Wells-Babcock House   1866/c. 1927

This beautiful Italianate-style brick house, with pressed metal Ionic pilasters at the corners, was built for physician Dr. Ebenezer Wells around 1866. The building replaced an earlier structure (visible on old maps) that had been built by Gideon Willcoxson in the 1820s and purchased in 1852 by George Sedgwick, Ann Arbor's first mayor. Wells served as Ann Arbor's ninth mayor from 1863–64, shortly after organizing and later becoming president of the First National Bank (see #92). His brother-in-law J.D. Baldwin (see #305) named Wells Street after him.

Wells was a major figure in business and social circles in Ann Arbor and Bay City, as well as physician to the elite. The October 19, 1877 issue of the *Ann Arbor Courier* noted that American educator and historian Charles Kendall Adams was to deliver the first of a course of six lectures on the colonial history of America at the residence of Dr. Wells on N. Division.

Wells died in 1882, and his widow Margaret sold the home to James L. Babcock in 1891. A native of Massachusetts, Babcock had come to Ann Arbor in 1861. He was the manager of the wool business of his uncle Luther James of Chelsea, and was his constant companion in his declining years. Babcock paid close to $10,000 for the property, "which was surrounded by beautiful and extensive grounds, richly adorned with flowers and ornamental trees and situated in one of the most delightful portions of the town" (*Past and Present of Washtenaw County,* 1906).

Luther James died in August of 1888, and his will required Babcock to marry within five years to double his inherited fortune. Babcock obliged in 1892. He and his wife Ella remodeled the house in 1894 using imported leather wallpapers, beveled and etched glass, and elaborately carved woodwork throughout the home. The entry hall is a tour de force of 1890s interior design. On the north side of the rear addition is a stained glass window with the Babcock coat of arms. Mrs. Babcock is mentioned in a 1905 School of Music publication as being the president of the Ladies' Musical Club. Other publications mention that the Babcocks entertained frequently and were active in the social life of the city.

After James' death in 1912, Ella continued to live here, later with her second husband. She moved to California where she died in 1927. The house was sold to George Weeks and a third story was added in such a seamless manner that it is difficult to notice. The mansion and carriage house were then converted to apartments. It was sold to the Lueck family in 1944.

A major renovation of the interior occurred in 2004 after a spectacular fire almost destroyed the building. The public was invited to view the results and old photographs from descendants were discovered, showing the house standing only two stories high, with an elaborately carved Italianate-style entry porch. Still a rental, this impressive 19th-century structure sits on a huge double lot surrounded by mature trees and a 19th-century iron fence.

DSHD

218 N. Division
John W. Maynard House

147

1844

When John W. Maynard constructed his center-entry, side-gabled brick house in 1844, it was in the middle of a large undeveloped block. Catherine Street and Ann Street were not yet extended between Division and State and this section east of Division was not yet within

the city limits. Maynard was a successful grocer with a store on Main Street. He arrived in Ann Arbor in 1824 as a child, only months after the town had been established by John Allen and Elisha Walker Rumsey. His father Ezra, who lived in Pittsfield Township in a cabin that is now the dining room of the Cobblestone Farm (see #328), wrote the first eyewitness account of the emerging village. Maynard Street perpetuates the family name.

The house was described by the *Michigan Argus* in 1849 as exhibiting "…a style of architecture which is an ornament to our village and evinces the taste, judgment and liberality of their owners." Today this house is part of a row of buildings along Division that hint at how the elite lived in the 19th century.

Maynard family members lived here for half a century. In 1908, Russell T. Dobson, publisher of the *Ann Arbor Times*, purchased the house and in 1910 remodeled it to Colonial Revival style, moving the door to the side, changing the windows to beveled glass, and erecting the large porch across the front. From the 1950s through the 1970s it was used as Canterbury House, an outreach program of St. Andrew's Episcopal Church next door. It was later used as a drop-in center for people with mental illness. In 2001, it was purchased by developers Allen and Kwan, who moved the door back to the center but gutted the original interior. Today it is a single-family residence.

OFWHD

148 303 N. Division
Andrew DeForest House   1845

This center-entry Colonial Revival-style house was built in 1845 as a Greek Revival, front-gabled, side-entry house facing Catherine Street. Builder Andrew DeForest worked as a contractor in town for 15 years, "erecting many of the substantial buildings that now stand in the city," according to the 1881 *History of Washtenaw County*. Early maps show a colonnaded portico across the front, similar to that at 712 E. Ann (see #127). The house retains some of its Greek Revival features in the corner engaged columns, the multi-paned windows, and the crosettes in the corner blocks of the interior woodwork.

DeForest sold the house in 1888 to druggist Henry Brown, who hired University of Michigan Architecture Professor Louis H. Boynton to remodel it. Brown's wife Jane stayed on until 1933. In 1936 it became the Colonial Inn, a tea house. Tea rooms fell out of fashion and it became the home of Sue Horner's antiques business until the 1970s. It served as a rental for many years, but is now a single-family residence.

DSHD

306 N. Division

149

St. Andrew's Episcopal Church   1867/1880/1903/1951

This is a perfect example of an English Gothic Revival church and was designed by pre-eminent Detroit architect Gordon Lloyd in 1867. It resembles many of the fieldstone churches built by Lloyd throughout Michigan, including Ann Arbor's First Congregational Church (see #118). The massive fieldstone building features a basilica-style floor plan, steeply pitched roofs with chevron slate designs, pointed windows so characteristic of the Gothic, trefoils and quatrefoils as decorative elements, and a Celtic cross at the end of the iron-ornamented ridgeline. The interior is noted for its butternut pews, Pewabic tile floor, and stained glass windows.

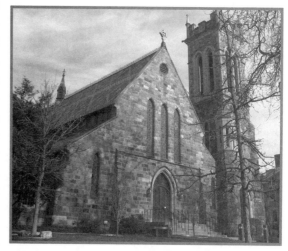

The tower was built in 1903, in memory of Dr. Alonzo Palmer by his wife Love Root Palmer, neighbors down the street (see #145). In 1880, Page Hall, designed by James Morwick, was built along Catherine Street and used as a chapel. The most recent addition is the Parish Hall designed by Ralph Hammett and Frederick O'Dell in 1951.

St. Andrew's was organized in 1828, four years after the first settlers arrived in Ann Arbor. Its members were usually the business and political elites. Pews were rented on an annual basis. The Corselius family (see #124) donated the land on Division and the first church building was built in 1839. This is the only church in Ann Arbor still on its original site. It has managed to weather the storms of trendiness, maintaining a major presence in the downtown community. It has done much outreach, with services for the homeless, the disabled, and students (see #175). It underwent a massive restoration in 2009 and received many awards, including Project of the Year from the Historic District Commission in 2010.

DSHD

150 401 N. Division
Jones School/Community High School   1922

The post-World War I years brought a huge influx of people to Ann Arbor. The city's public schools responded by undertaking a massive building program that built four new school buildings during the 1920s. Finished in 1922, the Jones School was the first of these to be completed, and was named after Elisha Jones, University of Michigan professor and super-intendent of the Ann Arbor Public Schools from 1867 to 1870.

A school had been on this site since 1846. The previous Jones School was constructed in 1869. This Colonial Revival-style building, designed by architect L.H. Field of Jackson, was built in the H-shaped floor plan typ-ical of schools of the period. The building is sided in red brick, with subtle limestone accents, including window sills, cornice, and arched entry pediment and pilasters. The original dentils in the cornice have been covered in a maroon, enameled steel band.

By the 1960s, the neighborhood was the home of Ann Arbor's growing African-American population, and 80% of the students of the Jones School were black. In order to remedy the racial segregation of Ann Arbor's public schools, Jones School was closed in September of 1965, and the students were bussed to other schools in the district.

The school was reopened in 1972 as Community High School, an alternative, magnet school that encouraged students to develop individual ways of learning and to use the entire com-munity as a classroom. The product of an era of liberal social and educational reform in the city, Community High is still going strong today, one of the oldest magnet schools in the country.

OFWHD

406 N. Division
George Rinsey House

151

1913

This house was constructed on the side lot of the David Rinsey house at the corner of Lawrence and Division (see #186) by his son George. Built in the then-popular Craftsman bungalow style, it is quite a contrast to the grand Queen Anne structure of his parents next door, which continued to be occupied by George's mother and sisters. It was designed by local architect George Scott and features an open low-roofed porch above which a cat-slide roof extends. The dormers on the upper floor are also typical of Craftsman-style homes. It was deeply recessed on the lot to preserve the enormous original burr oaks on the property. The emphasis on nature and on horizontality rather than verticality was a feature typical of the style. A lovely pergola remains intact on the south side of the property.

George Rinsey was in the insurance business. His wife continued to live in the home after his death in 1940, and remained until the 1970s. It was then purchased and turned into a rental property. Despite this use, the interior is remarkably intact. The current owner has the original plans for the house, dated 1913.

OFWHD

152 412 N. Division
Kingsley-Rinsey House

1835/1890

Behind what appears to be an 1890s Queen Anne is a very early home of one of Ann Arbor's founders and most prominent early citizens, James Kingsley. Kingsley came to Ann Arbor in 1826, was the first member of the Washtenaw County bar, and was appointed judge of probate in 1828. He was a member of the Territorial Legislature, and once Michigan became a state, he served in the State Legislature and the State Senate. He was later elected mayor of Ann Arbor and to the University of Michigan Board of Regents. In 1835, he built this home on the corner of Division Street and Bowery (today's Lawrence Street).

After Kingsley moved to a farm just south of town, the home was bought by the Jamaican-born Emanuel Henriques and his wife Harriet (Hunt), and was later the home of their son Edward who was in the medical school at the University.

In 1890, the house was moved north on the lot to its present location by David Rinsey to make room for his stunning Queen Anne home (see #186). The Kingsley house originally had a hipped roof and back wing, with the long front facade of the house facing Division. Rinsey appears to have completely reworked the house, converting it into a front-gabled structure, though the door surround with sidelights, as well as window placements, may be original. The highlights of this Victorian house are the ornate front gable, with its sunbursts and alternating bands of siding, and the stone front porch with Doric columns, which probably dates to the early 1900s.

OFWHD

505 N. Division
Clark Girls School

153

1865

The most famous and the most permanent of the many private schools in 19th-century Ann Arbor was the Misses Clark's Seminary for Young Ladies. This simple brick building, now converted to apartments, was the sixth and final location of that school, and was built in 1865.

Mary Clark, the founder, established the school in 1839 with sisters Chloe and Roby. All three were graduates of the famous Emma Willard Female Seminary in Troy, New York.

They brought a new philosophy, exposing girls to science and math as well as other subjects, and "many prominent women owe their high culture to the facilities enjoyed in the [Clark] Seminary." The curriculum was heavy on the observation of nature. Mary Clark, an avid botanist, took her students on trips through what later became the U-M Nichols Arboretum and gave her plant specimens to the U-M Herbarium where they are still used. The philosophy emphasized morals, and boarders at the school were not allowed to receive male callers, except on Wednesdays or Saturdays, so as not to "promote an undue love of society."

Mary Clark died in 1875, and the school closed. By 1900, the building had been converted to apartments. Called the Oakwood in 1910, it was further subdivided in the 1920s into eight units and renamed the McLean Apartments. The McLean family added the brick front porches.

OFWHD

154 538 N. Division
Henry Cornwell House   1894

This Queen Anne/Colonial Revival house was built entirely of bricks, but its owner had earned his fortune as a lumber man. Only the lavish wood inside the seventeen-room interior hints at his occupation. Henry Cornwell established a paper mill on the Huron River with his brother Harvey, and by the 1860s they were already wealthy men. The house here replaced an earlier Italianate structure which to them, no doubt, was hopelessly dated. This house was highlighted in the train brochure of 1896 known as the *Ann Arbor Headlight*.

Henry's son Frank remained in the house with his family until after World War I. The house was sold in December of 1927 to the Beth Israel Congregation, and served as its first synagogue for nearly 20 years. In 1946 the congregation moved to the Burns Park area and sold the house to a local realtor. In 1947 it was purchased by the Pentecostal Church of God and then sold in 1951 to St. Thomas Church.

Bulletins from St. Thomas show pictures of the house in use as a Teen Center in the 1950s, with bobby soxers and jukeboxes. William DeBrooke bought the house and restored it in the 1970s and then sold it to Deucalion Resources Group, a computer software company. In 1998 it was sold to the law firm of Ferguson and Widmayer, who remain today.

OFWHD

517–540 Elizabeth, 515 N. State

St. Thomas the Apostle Church Complex

1899/1902/
1911/1929

The history of St. Thomas the Apostle Church is intimately tied to Irish immigration to Washtenaw County. Initially the Irish were concentrated in Northfield Township but by the 1830s they began to appear in larger numbers in Ann Arbor. Louis W. Doll's *History of St. Thomas Parish* reports a momentous meeting in 1835 that resulted in the first effort to build a Roman Catholic church in Ann Arbor. It took ten years until the first church was built on Kingsley Street in 1845. In 1868, the parish purchased the former public school at 324–326 E. Kingsley (see #183) for their first parochial school. By 1886, the school moved to a new building on Kingsley and the old one was sold.

When Father Kelly arrived in 1891, the parish was badly in need of a new church due to increased immigration from Ireland, as well as a large influx of Italian and German Catholics. Prominent businessmen such as Moses Seabolt and David Rinsey (see #186) helped the energetic Kelly raise the money. In 1897, the Detroit firm of Spier and Rohns designed a handsome Romanesque building, reminiscent of Italian hill churches, with a large stained-glass rose window above the entry. The cornerstone was laid in 1898, and the church was dedicated in 1899. This firm also designed the nearby Michigan Central Railroad Station (see #137). The local firm of Koch Brothers constructed the church of granite fieldstone and Bailey bluestone and proudly showcased it in their advertisements.

Only a few years later in 1902, the yellow brick rectory was constructed behind the church at 515 N. State. This Georgian Colonial Revival building is a long rectangle with a projecting center capped by a highly decorated full pediment with brackets and dentils. Two small pedimented dormers add to the impression of a country estate. Note the pointed arches of the windows and the keystones above them.

The last building constructed under Father Kelly's tenure was the 1911 convent for the Sisters of the Immaculate Heart of Mary at 517 Elizabeth. It resembles the rectory in general form and materials but more pronounced are the pedimented dormers, embellished on the sides with fish-scale shingles, and finished off with unusual green clay tiles on the roof. The Roman star design on the balustrade above the porch is particularly handsome. Built by parishioner and local contractor Henry G. Pipp, the total cost of the convent was $8,600.

A new school in orange brick was built in 1929, designed by the Detroit firm of Donaldson and Meier in the Art Deco style. An award-winning restoration accompanied the Centennial Celebration in 1998. A Michigan Historic Marker graces the front entry.

OFWHD

156 220 N. Fifth
Jacob Vandawarker House   1844

Jacob Vandawarker came to Ann Arbor in 1834 from Herkimer County, New York (center of the Old Dutch part of New York State). He wasted no time in getting married and setting up a shoemaking business on Main Street. In a decade he was able to purchase two large lots and construct this fine brick New England Federal-style house. An elaborate front door surround with transom and sidelights is sometimes a Greek Revival element but the simple rectangular shape and gable returns facing to the side rather than the front of the house hark to the earlier Federal style. Other features mingling these styles include the modillion detailing under the eaves, the six-over-six windows, and the simple stone lintels over the windows. The front porch, with its fine gingerbread designs and thin chamfered columns is later, and dates to the 1860s.

The *Ann Arbor Courier* wrote of Vandawarker's death in 1881: "soon none will be left to tell the tale of the early settlement of Michigan." Local artist Charles Ciccarelli immortalized his old store in a pen and ink drawing for Ann Arbor's Sesquicentennial in 1974.

Sons Edwin and Frank Vandawarker took over their father's business and continued to live in the house until World War I. By the Depression it had been converted to a rental property. In 1978, it was restored inside and out by local realtors Casey and Myra Jones. It has been used for commercial purposes since then and current owner Susan Gardner received a Preservation Award in 2009.

OFWHD

301 N. Fifth
Baumgardner's Barn

157

1887

This Italianate brick barn with an 1887 date stone under the eaves and rounded windows topped with alternating colored stones in the lintels is the last surviving building of a complex that once dominated this small triangle of land bounded by Catherine, Detroit, and Fifth. The buildings were part of John Baumgardner's stone and marble business that specialized in sidewalks, tombstones, sills, and lintels. His business was the successor to that of his stepfather Anton Eisele. Their craftsmanship can be seen across the street at Eisele's house (see #132). Though the hayloft door remains intact, the large garage door below was replaced after a car smashed into the corner in 1978. The original windows were replaced in the 1980s.

The complex later became the Wurster Dairy and the barn was used to stable the delivery horses and wagons. In the 1930s, the other buildings were razed for a gas station, and in the 1950s both gas station and barn served as a used car lot with paint and bump shop. They too were almost demolished by urban renewal, which had targeted this part of town for "improvement." Today the barn is a rare survivor in the heart of Kerrytown.

OFWHD

158 | 521 N. Fifth
Second Baptist Church   1952

This orange brick former church is one of the few Art Moderne buildings in Ann Arbor. It was designed by the local firm of Kasurin and Kasurin (see #94 and #322) for the Second Baptist Congregation, one of the oldest African-American churches in Ann Arbor. It replaced an older church on the site that had been constructed in 1883. Second Baptist remained here until moving to their current quarters at 850 Red Oak in 1980. The church served as a relief agency for poor people, and in 1965, when it celebrated its 100th anniversary, dignitaries from around the state attended. By the 1980s, the congregation moved and the buildings (a parsonage of the same vintage is attached on the south side) became a pre-K school, which it remains today.

The building has typical Art Moderne features, including an almost-triangular shape with a corner emphasized by a tower, although the main entry is off Beakes. Both sides have built-in crosses and sets of long narrow openings of glass block, allowing lots of light into the interior sanctuary. Plans for the church appeared in the *Ann Arbor News* of September 6, 1952, indicating it would "replace the overcrowded red brick church recently torn down." Kurtz Building Co. were the general contractors. Local artist Milt Kemnitz featured it in a drawing in his *Ann Arbor Then and Now* (1972). The congregation was pictured worshipping in the open air across the street while the building was under construction.

530 N. Fifth
Michigan Central Railroad Depot

159

1868/1886

The Michigan Central Railroad first came to Ann Arbor in 1839, and the first station was built on the current site of the Gandy Dancer Restaurant on Depot Street (see #137). Fire destroyed it in 1845, and a second wood structure was built. In 1868, an addition was added for railroad customers to eat in. It is believed that this building was that addition. Old photos show the building as an Italianate cube, with hipped roof and paired brackets in the eaves, attached to the end of the older depot.

In 1886, a much grander station was built and this portion of the old depot was moved to the corner of Beakes and Fifth. For most of its history the building appears to have been used as a rooming house. Today, the paired Italianate brackets are gone, the roofline has been lowered, and the house appears to have been "bungalowized" in the early 20th century, with the addition of a front porch and a large front window. Remarkably, the house still retains many of its original six-over-six windows, a testament to recent owners who have done a wonderful job of maintaining the building and caring for its historic significance.

Former IHP

160 605 N. Fifth
Chester and Sabrina Tuttle House   1835

Second only to the Josiah Beckley house on Pontiac Trail (see #26), the Chester and Sabrina Tuttle house is thought to be one of the oldest brick residences remaining in the city. Built in a classic New England style, with double-end chimneys, classical sidelights, and gable returns, the Tuttle house is a superb example of what the more substantial early dwellings in the city looked like.

Chester and Sabrina (Kidney) Tuttle came to Ann Arbor from Cuyahoga County, Ohio in 1835 and built this house soon after their arrival. The Tuttles sold the house to Nelson and Catherine Imus in 1839, and moved to Chelsea. Nelson Imus was a blacksmith in Ann Arbor until "gold fever" struck in 1849, and like many early Ann Arborites he left the city for California in search of riches.

In the 1860s, John and Julia (Neathammer) Gall purchased the home. A native of Wurttemberg, Germany, John Gall was a successful butcher who along with partner Michael Weinmann built a fine business block on E. Washington (see #110) to house their butcher shop. John Gall died in 1896, but his widow Julia continued to live in the house until her death in 1903.

Though somewhat dwarfed by a recent series of large additions, much of the home's historic character remains intact. It has been the home of Michael Bielby, a local builder, since 1988.

Former IHP

716 N. Fifth
John Adam Volz House

161

1873

This exceptionally handsome and symmetrical red brick Italianate house, with its bracketed eaves, segmental arched windows, and brick detailing, was built for John Adam Volz in 1873. The intricate carving of the wood entry porch is still in fine condition. Side additions were added in 1880 and 1890. The house retains its original shutters, a rarity in Ann Arbor.

Volz was the proprietor of the Ann Arbor Central Brewery located next door at the corner of Fifth and Summit since 1858. Water for the brewing operation came from a spring behind the house. Volz sold the brewery the same year he built the house and two years later he sold the house. No doubt this was due to the financial Panic of 1873 that put many people out of business. The new brewery owners, Jacob Beck and John Jacob Muehlig (married to Volz's daughter), also purchased the house. The Muehligs were the parents of the well-known local businesswoman Bertha Muehlig (see #93).

In 1885, another young German emigrant, Frederick Walter, a miller by trade, purchased the house and raised his family here. His descendants occupied it for over 80 years. The house was famous for its lilacs, begun with cuttings from the U-M Nichols Arboretum. The house was purchased in 1970 by Reynold and Judith Lowe, pioneers of the recycling movement and owners of Materials Unlimited in Ypsilanti. The Lowes completely restored the interior and preserved the exterior.

DSHD

162 724 N. Fifth
Central Brewery

1858/1898

Breweries were one of the first buildings constructed in a new town, just after sawmills and grist mills. They were an important element of the economy of Ann Arbor from the earliest days of settlement in the 1820s. The first mention of this brewery is in the 1860 *City Directory* under Lawrence Trube. The 1868 *City Directory* lists John Adam Volz as the proprietor, who was successful enough to build the Italianate brick house next door (see #161) just prior to the Panic of 1873. The larger of the building's two wings is a fairly simple example of the commercial Italianate style with arched windows and projecting brick window hoods. The gable roof is unusual for this type of building, as is the foundation of dressed fieldstone.

The brewery business expanded quickly after the Civil War, but the economic panic and the growing influence of temperance societies were squeezing many local brewers. This brewery ceased operations in 1870 and by 1883 it was Bert Stoll's Ann Arbor Pop Works, specializing in bottled ginger ale, root beer, and excelsior water. In 1886, it was Ross and Welch's Bottling Works, and in 1899, it was converted to residential use, a year after the construction of the brick veneer wing along Summit Street.

This part of town was a gateway for many ethnic groups and the center of African-American Ann Arbor in the 20th century. The building first housed many German families, and later became known as "Little Italy." From 1921–56 it was owned by Italian clothier Daniel Camelet. After World War II it housed Japanese-Americans released from internment camps.

It was first restored in 1975 by local architect David Byrd with owner Mallory Thomas. In the late 1970s, John Hallowell and Robert and Nancy Harrington renovated the building into six contemporary apartments and renamed it "Brewery Apartments," for which they received a Preservation Award from the Historic District Commission in 1993. It was sold to Morgan and Nelson in 2007.

Former IHP

106 N. Fourth
Land Title Building

163

1927

The Art Deco facade of this building was designed by local architect and University of Michigan Professor of Architecture Albert J.J. Rousseau. He was a graduate of the École des Beaux Arts in Paris, a distinguished professor of both architecture and design, and well known for his public commissions. Also in his portfolio are St. Mary's Student Chapel (see #106), his own home (see #350), and the Trotter House (see #352). He also designed the fabulous Masonic Temple on Fourth Ave. that was demolished in 1973 and the Anberay Apartments on East University that were demolished in 2007.

In 1909, attorney Arthur Brown, a former mayor, and his wife Cora purchased this lot for Washtenaw Abstract Company, a company he founded in 1893. At first it was a small building known as Brown's Little Old Office, then expanded several times, and in 1927 the Browns added the Art Deco facade (older photos show the earlier front). Typical of Art Deco is the use of smooth limestone, an emphasis on verticality and geometry, and a crenel-ated cornice of stone panels. The leaded glass windows are several stories high, also a Deco trademark.

After 1900, Gertrude Norris ran the place and employed only women until the 1930s. Her tenure ended in 1956 when the Abstract and Title Guarantee Company took over. In 1960, it was Lawyers Title. The title business moved out in 2000.

FAHD

164 110 N. Fourth
YMCA Building   1904

The history of YMCA in Ann Arbor begins in 1858, when a group was started on the University of Michigan campus and eventually housed at Lane Hall (see #216). In 1892, the Ann Arbor YMCA was founded, and in 1904 the group built this building.

Designed by Pond and Pond, with elements of the Italian Renaissance Revival and Beaux Arts styles, this building was home to the YMCA from 1904 to 1959. The building originally housed a swimming pool in the basement and a gymnasium on the top floor. Pond and Pond was founded by brothers Irving K. and Allen B. Pond of Ann Arbor. They designed numerous buildings in Chicago, as well as a number of Ann Arbor landmarks, including the Student Publications Building (see #212), Michigan Union (see #223), Michigan League (see #231), and 1410 Hill (see #303). Pond and Pond were known for their elaborate brickwork, which can be seen in the YMCA building with its contrasting layers of hard-fired glazed brick, red brick, and limestone. The glazed brick is utilized on the street level, and is continued upward in the striped, brick pilasters and corner quoins. In characteristic Renaissance Revival fashion, the windows of each story are different, with paired windows at street level, paired main floor windows with an interesting square muntin arrangement and multi-paned arched tops. The third floor features two-over-two windows with limestone pediments, while the upper floor features simple keystones. The cornice is limestone with brick dentils, and the entrance features an interesting stepped pediment, a detail repeated in the front parapet wall.

In 1959, the YMCA moved to a new building on Fifth Avenue and William (since demolished). Today the old YMCA building serves as the Washtenaw County Annex.

FAHD

209–211 N. Fourth

Kayser Block

165

1874/1899

The date stone in the cornice line says 1899, but a newspaper article from that year reveals that it was a remodeling of an older structure built as a saloon in 1874 by William B. Tock. Charles Kayser made improvements and added a third floor in 1899. The article noted that the roof framing showed the old solid style. The sunburst brick patterns fanning out from the windows on the upper floors stand out as an exuberant display of the bricklayers' art.

By 1905, the building was known as Forester's Hotel and the area was becoming a hub for Ann Arbor's African-American community. According to city directories, the managers were listed as "colored" beginning in the early 20th century. In 1921, it housed the Colored Welfare League, an organization dedicated to helping African-American migrants and World War I veterans find work and housing. The League was the brainchild of Rev. Ralph Gilbert, pastor of the Second Baptist Church. He also helped create the Dunbar Center for recreational activities at the southeast corner of Fourth and Kingsley.

John Ragland, a 1938 University of Michigan Law School graduate active with the NAACP, described the Kayser Block's transition from a hotel to a community center in a 1978 interview that can be found among his papers at the Bentley Historical Library. This and the Dunbar Center became the locus of African-American activities in Ann Arbor following the segregation in housing patterns that took place after World War I. Many African-American businesses flourished here, including barber shops, bars, billiard halls, a tea room, and a beauty salon. The area reached its heyday as a cultural center in the 1950s and '60s.

It was purchased in 1966 by J.D. Hall, a barber, who renovated the building. It later served as the home of the Community Leaning Post, an organization to help ex-offenders find homes, which was run by Hall's sister Lucille Porter for over 20 years. In 1996, Ms. Porter organized the African-American Downtown Festival, a community block party to raise money and celebrate the black history of the area. Hall sold the building in 2002 and Ms. Porter died in 2007, but the annual African-American Downtown Festival continues.

Former IHP, FAHD

166 210–212 N. Fourth
Greene Block/City Offices   1893

This late 19th-century cut fieldstone and brick building was designed by local architect George Scott in 1893 for offices of the city of Ann Arbor. It was the "first time all the city offices were in one building on the second floor over two stores on North Fourth Avenue," wrote George Scott in an undated memoir at the Bentley Historical Library. City offices remained here until a new city hall was built at the southwest corner of Fifth and Huron in 1907, and the buildings were converted to commercial use. Early shops included Modder's Bakery (1918), the Livernois Market (1931), and the Lindemann Meat Market (1910). The building was the first home of the People's Food Co-op, which opened in 1975 along with the Wildflour Bakery. The People's Food Co-op moved two doors north in 1994.

The cut fieldstone building has two bays and a center, each having large arches of cut stone with keystones in the center. Even the doorway is of large blocks of colorful cut fieldstone topped by a lunette with a cut stone arch with key-stone. The storefronts have changed dramatically over the years.

FAHD

410 N. Fourth and 405–415 N. Fifth

Kerrytown

167

1860s/1899/1936/1980s

"Kerrytown" is a grouping of old and new buildings that came together as a concept for an urban marketplace in 1974 by Art Carpenter, a local attorney and developer. Under the auspices of the Arbor-A company, Carpenter and O'Neal Construction first renovated the

old Washtenaw Farm Bureau building, built in 1942, that abutted the Farmers' Market. Then they tackled the Luick Lumber Mill at the corner of Fifth and Kingsley in 1974. The goal was to show that investment in the downtown area could be socially and financially successful. Carpenter sold the company in 1980 to O'Neal Construction, who still owns it today. It has succeeded beyond their wildest dreams and now includes the former Godfrey Storage Building at 410 N. Fourth Ave. A lovely garden lined with benches along brick paths, with an old carriage stoop from one of the Luick homesteads, unites three of the buildings today. Notice also the 1950s "Jack and the Beanstalk" wall tiles in the elevator lobby, which were rescued from Arborland when it was rebuilt.

In 1860, a small woodturning shop of Alpheus Roys was at the southwest corner of Fifth and Kingsley, and the brick mill building just to the south was built that year by Wines, Hallock, and Douglass. By 1868, the firm was Wines and Douglass' Ann Arbor Steam Planing Mill. In 1873, Gottlob and Emanuel Luick, sons of German immigrants, bought the mill and began to manufacture wood products including sashes (windows), doors, crown moldings, "gingerbread" sawn designs, blinds (shutters), and lumber for house building.

The Luick Mill operated from 1873–1931, and expanded several times both to the north and to the west. The open spaces now forming the Ann Arbor Farmers' Market were the Luick lumber yards. They were donated to the City of Ann Arbor by Gottlob Luick, who had been an alderman as well as mayor of Ann Arbor from 1899–1901.

The commercial brick building at 410 N. Fourth Avenue was built in 1899 as the Godfrey Moving and Storage Company. It was built by Charles Godfrey to store furniture, pianos, and even hay balers, so it was built to last. It still retains the wide plank floors, brick walls, and beams of solid trees that provide much of the ambience for the Kerrytown shops.

168 415 N. Fourth
Burns-Martin House   1866

The Burns-Martin house is home to one of Ann Arbor's most beloved institutions, the Kerrytown Concert House, which began holding classical and jazz music performances here in 1984. Though the interior spaces in the house have been opened up to provide more space for the performances, the renovation sensitively maintained the home's original staircase, as well as the house's exterior details.

Though a small house stood on this lot as early as the 1840s, the current structure appears to have been built by Ellen Burns, who purchased the lot in 1866. The house is a large, yet simply designed gable front and wing structure, with a muscular frieze band and small window pediments. The frilly front and side porticoes date from the late 19th century.

Next to nothing is known about Ellen Burns, except that she was related in some way to Ellen (McMahon) Martin and her children John F., Ellen, and Michael J. Martin, who were long associated with the property. Ellen Martin lived in the house next door at 409 N. Fourth, and both properties appear to have operated as rooming houses during the 1860s and 1870s. Ellen Martin died in 1883, and Ellen Burns appears to have died in 1884, leaving the house to Ellen Martin's children. Michael J. Martin practiced law and continued to live in the house until 1897. His son John F. Martin, a dentist who had an office on N. Fourth Avenue, lived in the house following his parents.

Winnie Martin was the last survivor of this family to live here. She sold it in the 1940s and in the 1950s it became the home of James and Parthenia Parker. They sold it to Carl Brauer in 1983 and he sold it to the Kerrytown Concert House in 1999.

632 N. Fourth
Bethel AME Church

169

1891–1896

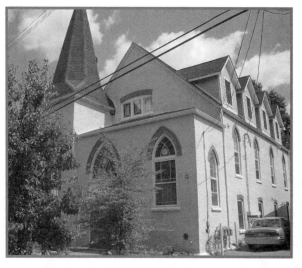

Before the Civil War, African-Americans in Ann Arbor worshipped in a small Greek Revival church known simply as the Union Church (see #171). Eventually two congregations evolved from this initial group, Bethel AME (African Methodist Episcopal) and Second Baptist. Both built sanctuaries in the general vicinity of Beakes and Fourth/Fifth Ave. This church building was begun in 1891. The cornerstone was laid by Bishop Henry McNeal Turner, the first black chaplain in the U.S. Army, appointed by President Lincoln. It is built of brick in a modified Gothic style, with Gothic pointed windows and a witch's hat-topped belfry next to the main entrance.

Much drama surrounded the completion of the church as its funds were depleted by the Depression of 1893. One member of the community mortgaged his own home to save the church and many white businessmen helped as well, with many windows in the foyer dedicated by them. The building was opened in 1896.

A fixture in what had become a segregated neighborhood, former members recalled that "our lives revolved around the church. We socialized there, did our homework there." The congregation eventually prospered and built a new church on Plum Street (now John A. Woods) in 1971. The old structure became the New Grace Apostolic Church, and in 1995 some minor interior changes were made. It was sold to a developer in 1998 who converted it into condominiums. Michael Bielby and Lisa Profera won an Adaptive Reuse Award from the Historic District Commission in 2004.

Former IHP

170 916 Fuller
Washtenaw Light and Power Building   1902

This small brick structure resembling a bell tower for a Romanesque church was built in 1902 as a relay station for the Washtenaw Light and Power Company. It became a substation for Detroit Edison, which owned many properties along the Huron River. People have always been intrigued by this building. Local architect David Osler (see #373) was so intrigued that he bought it in 1961 and maintained his architectural practice here until 2008. He maximized the space inside and made it fun and lively. He also built an addition in the rear, which is attached by a small passageway that creates an atrium. Now the offices of several clinical psychologists, it still maintains its air of mystery to the casual passerby.

Former IHP

504 High
Union Church

171

1854–1857

This small brick structure appears on the 1854 map of Ann Arbor labeled as "Union Church." It was not finished until 1857, as the *Michigan Argus* of December 25, 1857 report-

ed: "The Union church has been completed by the Colored People of the City and is to be dedicated Sunday by Rev. J.M. Gregory. S.H. Estabrook will officiate." Although its simple classical lines have been obscured by a later porch, the building serves as a fine example of the Vernacular Greek Revival used for non-residential buildings.

By 1871, two congregations split off from this original group and became Second Baptist Church and Bethel AME Church. Both churches still exist and trace their roots to this building. The Baptists continued to use this building until 1881, when they relocated to the southwest corner of Fifth Ave. and Beakes (see #158). Bethel AME built its own church in the 1890s (see #169). Both of these African-American churches have built newer buildings elsewhere.

In 1884, this building was sold to Michael Kearns who converted it to a residence. When his widow sold the property in 1907 it was still referred to in the deed as "the church lot." An addition to the east was probably added in 1910.

OFWHD

172 412 E. Huron
Parkhurst-Root House   c. 1848

This New England-style clapboard house, with side entry and a single chimney, was likely constructed in 1848, shortly after Asahel Parkhurst purchased the land. It was purchased by Tracy Root in 1855 and was his family's home for over half a century. The Root family added the double brackets under the eaves (a distinctly Italianate feature).

Tracy Root was the son of pioneer Erastus Root who arrived in Ann Arbor in 1832. Erastus Root ran a grocery store and his son was educated in town, becoming a well-known lawyer. Moving from his childhood home on Spring Street to Huron Street was, at the time, a symbol of wealth and success. Nearby were houses of other wealthy men and the First Presbyterian Church. Tracy Root served as County Clerk in 1862 and as Circuit Court Commissioner in 1872. His home is one of a handful that survives from this era of gentility on Huron Street.

During the 20th century it became a rental and was occupied for years by University of Michigan Astronomy Professor Richard Sears. Since 1985 it has been used for commercial purposes.

OFWHD

502 E. Huron

173

Silas and Helen Douglass House   1848/1856/1864

This pristine example of the Gothic Revival style is one of the best documented homes in Ann Arbor. Built in 1848 by U-M Professor of Chemistry Silas Douglass, it was designed by local architect Arthur Marshall and was expanded with various wings in 1855, 1856, and

1864. It has steeply pitched rooflines with decorative bargeboards, stucco walls scored to resemble masonry (a holdover from the Greek Revival), and Gothic motifs including quatrefoils and trefoils. A picturesque porch along the east wing was removed in the 1920s and restored in 1995 using old photographs from the vast archive at the Bentley Library. There was great fanfare and public enthusiasm for the restoration project.

Douglass was not only a professor of chemistry, but also the overseer of the construction of the Detroit Observatory (see #206), twice mayor of Ann Arbor, founder of the Ann Arbor Gas Company in 1858, Dean of the Medical School, and builder of the pioneer chemical laboratory and library on campus. When founding the gas company, he was quoted as saying, "Ann Arbor had groped in the darkness long enough." While mayor in 1871–1872, he reorganized the city's tiny police force and introduced a licensing system to regulate liquor (he was a strong temperance man).

He and his wife raised their seven children here. Marie Douglass, the last survivor, died in 1941 and the house was willed to University of Michigan for a Washtenaw County Historical Society Museum. They were unable to raise the funds to accept this responsibility and in 1942 the local Baptist Guild acquired the property. It is still owned by the Baptist Church and houses the Campus Center, a student outreach program for music, study, discussion, and prayer, and sometimes meals and movies. As an aside, *The Ann Arbor Observer* had its birth in this house when the church's janitors, Mary and Don Hunt, decided to write a local news magazine.

The house has had several additions attaching it to the Baptist church and school in the rear, and is now referred to as part of the First Baptist Campus.

OFWHD

174 | 512 E. Huron
First Baptist Church   1880

Organized in 1828, this was the third building for the Baptists, who had previous structures on Wall Street and Catherine.

The Gothic-style fieldstone church was constructed in 1880 with the help of parishioners who personally chose and arranged the fieldstone into beautiful color combinations. The architect was Elijah Myers of Detroit, also the architect of the State Capitol in Lansing. University of Michigan Mathematics Professor Olney mortgaged his home to help pay for the construction.

The carved wooden hammer beams on the interior with hanging pendils reflect a Gothic sensibility, although the floor plan with its spread-out, semicircular seating arrangement does not. Prominent balconies sweep down to meet the altar on each side. Upon entering, one feels as if the church has welcomed you with open arms. The sanctuary seats 400 and has a pipe organ, grand piano, choir loft, pulpit, and lectern. A large rose window is featured above the Gothic arched entry. Corner buttresses have gabled stone caps. The building is in a magnificent setting surrounded by centuries-old oaks.

Although some remodeling has occurred, the church is remarkably intact, with its old stained glass windows and slate roofing. It now forms the center of a four-structure campus that includes a school, student center, and meeting rooms. It is one of several older congregations that have committed to remaining downtown and serving the large student population.

OFWHD

617 E. Huron
Harris (Hobart) Hall

175

1886

This red brick and limestone example of Richardsonian Romanesque architecture, complete with arched entry on an ashlar foundation, arched windows topped with colored glass and checkered patterns of brick, and elaborate brick chimneys, is a sober example of the style. It was designed by Detroit architect Gordon W. Lloyd (see #118, #145, #149, and #343) who was always ready to meet the needs of his clients. Here the client was St. Andrew's Episcopal Church, which wanted a student center and parish hall closer to campus. Not only was there much religious ferment on campus at the time, but the reviled Unitarians were building a church just across the street (see #192). The stated purpose was a student center "to establish Christian teaching in the midst of a great secular university."

The hall was finished in 1886 and named for Rev. John Henry Hobart, the first bishop to officiate in the State of Michigan. It was soon changed to Harris Hall to honor Bishop Samuel Harris who died in 1888. The building also housed church offices, a Sunday school,

and meeting spaces for the student Hobart Guild. Students were encouraged to use the three parlors, dining room, kitchen, and billiard room. A bowling alley and gymnasium occupied the basement. A library was established and lectures by national and local figures were given in the large assembly hall on the second floor.

Times change, and by 1943 it was used by the USO to serve soldiers in training. After 1946, the University leased the building for its marching band and wind instrument departments. In 1974 St. Andrew's sold the building. The exterior is remarkably intact. The interior was restored by the firm of Buckheim and Rowland who purchased it in 1980. They received a Preservation Award in 1984.

NR, SR, OFWHD

176 903 E. Huron
Harvey Bannister House 1858

This simple brick Greek Revival with a front-facing gable, pedimented roof with classical returns, six-over-six windows, and modest side entry is typical of the late Greek Revival houses built in Ann Arbor. This one is special because it was one of the first buildings created for student housing after University of Michigan President Henry Tappan decreed students could no longer live in campus buildings.

It was built by Harvey Bannister to be a rooming house. Bannister, a mason and plasterer, helped build the First Presbyterian Church nearby. He was also a strong abolitionist, which was mentioned in his 1895 obituary.

The University of Michigan began admitting students in 1841 and housed them in dormitories at South and North Halls until 1856, four years after Tappan became president. He thought students would benefit from living with "private families where they would be subject to home influences." He also thought it would make students better citizens and reduce crime and disease. This policy set off a building frenzy in areas near the campus, but few of these structures survive.

In the 1920s, the house was occupied by Catherine Meier who, with her daughter Joy Meier, lived here for over 50 years. It is a rental for students once again.

OFWHD

1001 E. Huron
University Reformed Church
1960–1964

177

Sometimes disparagingly called the "Holy Toaster" for its boxy, monolithic, toaster-like shape, the University Reformed Church is slowly being recognized as a landmark of modern architecture. The building was designed by the acclaimed Latvian-born architect Gunnar Birkerts, who studied under the modern master Mies van der Rohe. By the early 1950s, Birkerts had settled in Michigan where he worked in the offices of Eero Saarinen and Minoru Yamasaki. He came to Ann Arbor to teach at the University of Michigan in 1961.

For the University Reformed Church, Birkerts used poured concrete as the primary building material, making this church, along with the Power Center (see #209), among the few Brutalist-style buildings in the city (*brut* is a French word for rough or raw). Birkerts had worked with Kevin Roche and John Dinkeloo, architects of the Power Center. Birkerts' innovative church featured no cross, no stained glass, and no altar. The massive poured concrete walls were softened by the use of wood in the floors, doors, and pews. Birkerts utilized indirect lighting in the form of concrete light boxes in the upper portions of the building, which funneled light down to the sanctuary. Unfortunately, recent renovations have covered up the light boxes and removed many of the original features, including the birch pews, wood floors, and light fixtures.

Other notable Birkerts designs include the south wing of the Detroit Institute of Arts, the underground addition to the University of Michigan Law Library (see #224), and the Federal Reserve Bank in Minneapolis. After over fifty years in the business, Birkerts is still designing buildings from his studio in Bloomfield Hills, Michigan.

OFWHD

178 1007 E. Huron
Charles Whitman House   1891

This house is one of Ann Arbor's few late 19th-century houses designed in the Shingle style, which is expressed through its broad expanse of roof, use of saw-tooth shingles, multi-paned windows of curved glass, and emphasis on the long and the low. Built in the transitional period between the Queen Anne and the Colonial Revival, the home shows the influence of both styles. It was built by railroad tycoon and State Commissioner of Railroads Charles Whitman in 1891.

The house retains much of its original character both outside and in, with a porch of cut fieldstone, unusual shingle patterns, and bowed windows on the first floor. The attached porte-cochére on the west is a unique feature and unusually decorative. Featured in the 1896 *Ann Arbor Headlight,* the house is reputed to have cost $10,000. In 1898, the home was sold to the Chi Psi fraternity. Later it became the Psi Omega fraternity before being purchased by the University of Michigan for the Human Adjustment Speech Clinic in 1936.

Still owned by the University, it has served many units, including the Counseling Center and the Center for the Child and Family.

OFWHD

114 N. Ingalls
John and Electa Carman House

179

1880

This transitional Italianate brick structure, built by retired farmer John Carman in 1880, shows traces of Gothic influence in the steeply pitched roof and elaborately pierced saw-cut wood gingerbread below the front gable. A careful observer can see the outline of the arched windows that were squared off sometime in the 20th century, when the current porch was also built.

Carman and his wife Electa raised several children here, the most well known of whom was Georgianna, principal of the Fourth Ward School in 1883, and later principal of Perry School (see #99). The Carman family continued to occupy the house until 1909, when daughter Mary sold it to Charles and Anna Rankin. It later became a nursing home, and by the late 1920s, a rental to mostly students. Despite additions and alterations, the house has been wonderfully landscaped and retains the flavor of the late 19th-century period in which it was built.

OFWHD

180 220 N. Ingalls
Phi Rho Sigma Fraternity (Zeta Chapter)   1929

Myron Pugh was hired by the fraternity in 1928 to design this English Tudor-style building. The 84-foot-long building is mostly sandstone laid in random ashlar courses. The gables are faced with half-timbering in wood and tapestry brick and the roof is of rough slate. Other features of the Tudor style include leaded glass, oriel windows, quatrefoil designs, and an arched doorway with quoins. With joists of steel and walls of stone, brick, and hollow tile, this structure was built to last—so much so in fact, that in 1950 when St. Joseph Mercy Hospital coveted their land for hospital expansion, the building was picked up from its original site at the northeast corner of Ingalls and Catherine and moved to the southeast corner. The move was so smooth that the china in the cupboards remained unbroken.

The Phi Rho Sigma medical fraternity, organized in 1897, has always been located near hospitals and medical facilities. They were located in various parts of the Old Fourth Ward until they bought the Stevens property at 300 N. Ingalls and remodeled that house in 1911, demolishing it in 1928 when the current structure was built. Old photos in the *Michiganensian* show the previous building. In the same house since 1928, the fraternity became co-ed in 1975, making it officially a medical society.

OFWHD

321 N. Ingalls
Reuben Kempf House

181

1887

This house is the epitome of what people think of as "Victorian." Built of brick on a high foundation of cut stone, it is the Queen Anne style embodied, with asymmetrical arrangements of windows, doors, and gables, and elaborate gingerbread on several porches, with turned posts and lattice spindle work. Stained glass and half-timbering in the gable contribute to the style, as do windows of varying sizes and shapes, and the use of different materials. Also of note is an octagonal tower with a combination weather vane/finial with a crown and banner motif. Original porches are extremely rare anywhere, so these are unique survivors. For many years the house was painted one color and the details were lost to the casual viewer. A major renovation by dentist James McNamara took place in 1992 which accented various details with other colors, thus restoring the glory of this fabulous building.

It was originally built in June 1887 as the home of Chelsea banker Reuben Kempf, not to be confused with the Reuben Kempf associated with Kempf House (see #53). The home remained in the family until 1918. It was later purchased by Edith Hagerman for her husband, Dr. George Hagerman, who was affiliated with St. Joseph Mercy Hospital across the street and ran his medical practice from here. In 1992, Dr. McNamara established his dental practice here, and along with his wife Charlene, made the building their residence. They received an award for their work from the Historic District Commission in 1993.

OFWHD

182 415 N. Ingalls
Efner-Grant House   1850

The exact age and origin of this house cannot be completely documented, as it was moved to its current location sometime between 1906 and 1910. Evidence points to the house being moved from the corner of Ingalls and Kingsley Streets, where it is thought to have been built by George W. Efner in 1850. The house may be the earliest example of an Italianate cube remaining in Ann Arbor, though the house was built with classical corner pilasters, a nod to the earlier Greek Revival style that was still very much in fashion at the time. The fanciful "steamboat" porch was a later addition to the house, probably dating from the 1880s or '90s. George Efner was a carriage painter and he and his wife Rosa lived in the house for sixteen years, renting out rooms.

One of their tenants in 1860 was a University of Michigan student named Claudius B. Grant. Grant was a man on the make when he left his prominent positions as postmaster, Ann Arbor school teacher, and school principal to fight in the Civil War, where he would eventually attain the rank of colonel. In 1866, following his service, Grant and his wife Caroline, the daughter of former Michigan Governor Alpheus Felch, bought this house from the Efners and made it their home for the next seven years. During those years, Grant began his rise to become one of the most distinguished men in the State of Michigan. He was admitted to the bar in 1866, then became postmaster again in 1867, and was a member of the state legislature from 1871 to 1874.

In 1873, Grant left Ann Arbor and became prosecuting attorney in Houghton, and then circuit court judge. In 1889, he was elected justice to the Michigan Supreme Court, a position he held for twenty years. Though he left Ann Arbor, Grant never lost his connection to the city and the University of Michigan. In later years, he served as chairman for the construction of Alumni Memorial Hall (see #222) on the University of Michigan campus. He was buried in Forest Hill Cemetery in 1921. It was purchased and rehabilitated by Michael Bielby, who received a Preservation Award in 1987.

OFWHD

324 E. Kingsley
North District Public School

183

1846

This simple brick Greek Revival building was originally a school, built in 1846 after citizens voted to tax themselves to build public schools for the "Upper Village" (Lower Town was across the river). A second public school for the South District was located in the "Old Academy" at Fourth Avenue and William Street, now the site of a parking structure. Previously, most educating had been done at private academies which flourished in the early days of settlement. This austere building with simple gable returns resulted from the philosophy of schooling that emphasized the seriousness of education, or more likely the lack of money. The paired arched windows probably date to the 1870s when it was used as a school by St. Thomas Parish. The porch was added in the early 20th century when it was converted to a duplex.

Ann Arbor became a city in 1851, and the public school system began in earnest to keep up with the growth of the city. Later, Jones School was built in 1869, on Division Street (see #150), and St. Thomas Church (see #155) purchased the North District Public School in 1868. By the 1880s, they had built a new school on Elizabeth Street and sold the building to John Pfisterer (see #280) who converted it to a residence. After World War I, it was converted to a duplex. Among the notable tenants were the Pastorino family who lived here over 35 years. Rosa Pastorino was the daughter of Rocco Desderide, owner of an eponymous store next door (see #139). Desderide lived to be 105 and made model ships in the little potting shed that still stands in the backyard.

OFWHD

184 506 E. Kingsley
Sarah Schumacher House

1890s

John Schumacher was a prosperous hardware dealer who had a store on Main Street that sold stoves, tinware, plumbing, home furnishings, and furnaces. In operation from 1870 to 1940, Schumacher's Hardware had enough inventory to fill three storefronts. Schumacher and his wife Sarah (Harkins) had a home on this lot for a number of years before John's death in 1890. Son Burt continued to run the family hardware business.

Sometime after 1890, the widowed Sarah Schumacher built this grand Queen Anne home. The home is built with a central hipped roof bisected by a double cross gable. The hipped roof is topped with an unusual three-sided dormer. The different types of siding are characteristic of the style, with clapboard on the first story, "fish scale" shingles on the second story, and square shingles on the third. The lower wraparound porch features turned posts with brackets and a unique crossed balustrade, while the upper porch is centered above the front entrance, with three arched openings sided in shingles.

Sarah Schumacher lived in the house until her death in 1910. For much of the 20th century, the home was covered in asbestos siding. Current owners Jeff and Chris Crockett removed the asbestos and have done a remarkable restoration of the home. They were rewarded by the State of Michigan and the City of Ann Arbor for their efforts. Chris Crockett has been president of the OFWA since 1985.

OFWHD

809 E. Kingsley
Kingsley Post Apartments

185

1929

This Art Deco/Spanish Revival brick and stone apartment building, created in a burst of apartment construction in the 1920s, is now one of a handful remaining in Ann Arbor. It was built in 1929, just before the Great Depression, and was designed by Ypsilanti architect R.S. Gerganoff. Gerganoff created many public buildings, especially schools, and later gained fame as the architect of the Washtenaw County Courthouse (see #87). His use of orange brick, terra-cotta panels, diamond-shaped accents in green and blue glazed tile, tapestry brick, and black wrought-iron railings epitomizes the Spanish influence characteristic of this style. Some Moorish influences can be seen in the multi-colored stone entry, which recalls the Alhambra, and in the long windows topped by Islamic arches. Many similar apartment buildings were built in Detroit in that era, especially in Palmer Park.

Mainly serving the medical campus nearby, its 37 units overlook the Huron River Valley with magnificent views of the river from its perch on a bluff. It has been owned for decades by the Pappas family, who received a Preservation Award from the Historic District Commission in 2011.

OFWHD

186 401 Lawrence
David Rinsey House   1890

This epitome of the Queen Anne style was built by grocer David Rinsey in 1890 when Division Street was still a very fashionable address. It is an asymmetrical wooden clapboard house with many gables, a variety of materials and surfaces, varying window sizes, and cutaway corners, which are features of this style. The interior is stunning in its use of oak paneling on walls and ceilings, tile fireplaces in every room, cherry and maple parquet floors on the main floor, and lincrusta wall coverings (a product made to look like embossed leather). It was a symbol both of the owner's good taste and prosperity. Mr. Rinsey was so proud that he placed a large "R" in the gable facing Division Street.

Rinsey, a German Catholic, was a true American success story—arriving penniless at age 16 and owning his own grocery by 1867. His partner Moses Seabolt, also a German Catholic, lived on Lawrence Street too, no doubt so they could easily walk to St. Thomas Church (see #155) a few blocks away. Rinsey became president of the Ann Arbor Savings Bank and the Ann Arbor Fruit and Vinegar Company.

When Rinsey purchased the property, he moved and remodeled the house already there to the north of the lot (see #152). The property was so large that Rinsey's son George was able to build a house on the side lot in 1915 (see #151). His mother and sisters continued to live in the family house until 1938, during which time the address was changed to Lawrence (from 402 N. Division), and the elaborate Queen Anne porch was altered to the simple one there today. Following the Rinseys, the home was converted to apartments. In 1990, owner Ray Detter received a Preservation Award from the Historic District Commission for superior maintenance.

OFWHD

602 Lawrence
Mitchell-Gregory-Prettyman House

187

1848/1914

Nestled among some of Ann Arbor's finest landmark burr oak trees, this 2½-story Greek Revival house has a gabled front roof with cornice returns and dentils at the top of the frieze band. The low pitched roof and the stucco exterior, scored to resemble stone, were part of the local Greek Revival tradition. This house is unusual in that it is constructed of adobe brick. There probably was once a front entry where one of the windows is today. Also typical of the style is the attic window—a triangular opening with diamond-shaped panes of glass. In about 1914, the house was "bungalowized" and the owners rounded off the corners of the window trim and added porches on both the east and west sides with columns done in the style of the time—tapering with the bottoms wider than the tops.

The house was built in 1848 by Thomas and Margaret Mitchell shortly after Henry Bower platted the area and named the street Bowery after himself (the name changed to Lawrence in 1887). They gave the house to their daughter Mary Gregory and her husband Hubbell Gregory in 1853. The house remained in the Gregory family until 1914 when Horace and Jennie Prettyman bought and ran it as a boarding house. Abby Shaefer bought it in 1946, and operated a rooming house known as Abby House. In 1961, it was sold to the Inter-Cooperative Council and renamed Vail Co-op for Stephen Vail (Stephanos Valvanis), a former ICC president who died young in a tragic accident. For many years it was an all-female house.

OFWHD

221

188 603 Lawrence
Margaret Kearney House

1882

In 1879, Miss Margaret Kearney purchased this lot, which had an older home on the site. She soon built this elaborate brick Italianate house with Eastlake features, including the fancy bargeboard carvings of stars, steeply pitched roof, and large attic. The long round-topped windows (now unfortunately with modern replacements) and entry door are diagnostic features of the Italianate style, as are the paired eave brackets. The wood portico with chamfered columns is from after 1939 when the full front porch was removed. A side porch is now the entry for a second unit and has Italianate features as well.

The Kearney family had a long association with this part of town and was typical of the Irish Catholics who settled in the area to be near St. Thomas Church (see #155). Margaret's brother Ambrose Kearney was a grocer and owned the property at 411 N. State (see #199). These two properties abut in the rear. The first tenant listed in the 1883 *City Directory* was Rev. Russell Pope, pastor of the Methodist Church. A notice in the May 1882 *Ann Arbor Courier* notes that the ladies of the Methodist Church were negotiating with Miss Kearney for a residence for Rev. Pope. Margaret is listed here in 1886 with Ambrose. In 1892, Margaret's nephew Thomas D. Kearney joined her, and soon became the city attorney. The house was empty for part of the Depression, but then Ambrose N. Kearney, an insurance salesman with Tuomy and Tuomy (his cousins), lived here until the 1960s. The house was converted to a duplex in the early 1950s.

OFWHD

415 N. Main
Thomas Earl House

189

1857

This fine example of a gable-front Greek Revival house maintains a major presence along this part of North Main Street. It is unusual in that it still has its original shutters. Also unusual is the window in the attic and the flat stone lintels above the original windows with many six-over-six panes still intact. The porch was added in 1908. The door surrounds have sidelights and a transom, and the front has beautifully proportioned gable returns and wide frieze board.

The house was built for Thomas Earl, an immigrant from Ireland, who became wealthy as a farmer in Northfield Township before moving to Ann Arbor and running a grocery. He and his wife Mary lived above their store until they built this house, which had a side lot for an orchard. Earl also served as alderman. Mary outlived him by many years and died in 1899. She willed the house to St. Thomas the Apostle Church (see #155) and it sold later at auction to Fred Schaible for $1,300 in 1900. The Schaible family lived in the house for most of the 20th century, and preserved the pewter numbers "57" from the previous house numbering system.

In 1990, the house was purchased and restored by Peter Fink, who converted it to office use and received an award from the Historic District Commission in 1991.

NR, SR, Former IHP

190 500 N. Main
Kellogg-Warden House   1835/1839

This house was moved from 1015 Wall Street in 1990 by the Washtenaw County Historical Society to be its museum and headquarters. It is a finely preserved example of an 1830s
house, not remodeled in any way since the last addition was added to the front in 1839.
During a meticulous renovation, an original doorway was found in the central portion. It
is now outlined on a wall in the front parlor. The house is in a style one could call Federal.
Its few Greek features are the door and its surround with sidelights and transom and gable
returns on the sides. However, it is more a townhouse than a typical Greek Revival and
displays other New England characteristics including "nogging," or bricks within the walls
and accordion lath, which is unsawn and was used when saw mills were scarce. Channel
and corner block trim grace the interior, which has a beautiful staircase right out of Asher
Benjamin's pattern book.

The oldest portion of the house was built by Ethan Warden (married to a Kellogg) in 1835.
He sold the property to his brothers-in-law Dwight and Daniel Kellogg, whose large family

moved here from Auburn, New York.
They were a family of millers and built
a flour mill on the Huron River in the
1830s. Dwight Kellogg was a partner
of Anson Brown before he died. The
patriarch, the Hon. Charles Kellogg,
arrived in 1839 after the front portion
was built. He ran a dry goods store on
nearby Broadway.

The house was later occupied by the
Ruthruff and Greiner family who purchased it in the 1890s. That family
remained until the University of Michigan purchased the home in 1988. The
historical society rushed to save the house from demolition, and was given it by the University (with funds to help move it). The site was provided by the Ann Arbor Parks Department. Today it is a thriving museum, with changing exhibits, hundreds of visitors, and a gift
shop. It was the Historic District Commission's "Preservation Project of the Year" in 1991.

NR, Former IHP

611, 613, 615 N. Main

191

John J. Robinson Houses/Sinelli Grocery 1885/1914

In 1885, John J. Robinson purchased the obsolete 1835 Washtenaw County Jail and converted the front portion of the jail, which was originally used as the sheriff's residence, into his own home. Robinson tore down the back portion of the building and used the bricks to build these two houses. The two Queen Anne/Vernacular homes are built of solid masonry, with front-gabled roofs and full-width front porches. Though both porches have been altered, they still retain their original decorative brackets. Though dilapidated, the front gables of the two houses feature decorative trusses in the Queen Anne style, and the arches above the windows feature carved wood trim.

Both homes appear to have been used as rentals from the beginning. In 1914, Louis and Angela Sinelli added the masonry storefront to 611 N. Main, in which they operated a grocery store. By 1938, Thomas Kusserelis operated a grocery store out of the storefront, known as Tom's Market, and in 1963 it was McCoy's Market. Though somewhat rundown after years of being used as rentals, the buildings still retain many of their original features and charm. The side of the market still exhibits a weathered and faded Vernors Ginger Ale sign that was painted on the building decades ago.

Former IHP

192 100 N. State
First Unitarian Church   1882

When this fieldstone church, designed by the Detroit firm of Donaldson and Meier, was dedicated in September of 1882, the *Ann Arbor Register* noted that "the structure is thoroughly churchly in look, picturesque in outline, and certain to be one of the most admired architecturally of our public buildings." The builders, Walker Brothers of Ann Arbor, were also responsible for the Michigan Central Depot (see #137). Both are done in the Romanesque style associated with Henry Hobson Richardson and known as Richardsonian Romanesque. Towers, turrets, and an asymmetrical form characterize the style. Note the horizontal row of small black stones that are carefully placed to form a girdle around the church.

The Unitarian church was always controversial—very liberal, supportive of free speech and civil liberties, and sometimes not even considered Christian. In reaction to the Unitarian presence, numerous other church denominations felt the need to build or operate spaces for their own stu-

dent congregants in the neighborhood. By 1946 the Unitarians' numbers had dwindled and they moved to a former residence on Washtenaw (see #355). The church was purchased by Grace Bible Church, which remained here until they built a new church in 1975. The church had badly deteriorated (the sanctuary had been used as a basketball court!) and was empty for 10 years. It was saved from demolition by a coalition of preservationists and the architectural firm of Hobbs and Black, which repurposed it for their headquarters. The former sanctuary is now a three-story atrium. The award-winning renovation uncovered a forgotten Tiffany window from 1900 that now graces the east wall of the reception room. They received an award from the Historic District Commission in 1987 and continue to operate today.

NR, OFWHD

110 N. State

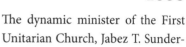

First Unitarian Church Parsonage 1883

The dynamic minister of the First Unitarian Church, Jabez T. Sunderland, requested and got a parsonage built for himself and his family a year after the church opened. The Detroit firm of Donaldson and Meier was again employed and designed a Queen Anne house with red brick veneer on the first floor and cut shingles on the second, with stone quoins around the first floor windows, giving it a Gothic effect. Two large and elaborate chimneys were unfortunately removed during a renovation.

In a rare instance of direct evidence, the diary of the mason Warren Walker at the Bentley Library records Sunderland's input: "...Sunderland asking for brick veneer and boulder stone trimmings around doors and windows and also to build corners of stone for first story only. I told him we could." A later entry noted that Sunderland was concerned about the color of the mortar.

When the church was sold in 1946 to Grace Bible, the parsonage was part of the package. For a while in the 1970s, the church used the home as a bookstore. As deterioration set in, they were forced to vacate the building. It was renovated with the church next door by Hobbs and Black in 1986 (see #192).

NR, OFWHD

194 | 200 N. State
Wil-Dean Apartments   1928

A twin of Duncan Manor Apartments (see #196), this is one of a handful of remaining apartment buildings constructed in the 1920s. It was built by Harold Zahn and Dugald Duncanson, real estate salesmen from the firm of Allan Paton Co. They hired the architect Gardiner Vose, a graduate of the University of Michigan School of Architecture. The building is a Tudor Revival, with steeply sloped rooflines, half-timbered gables, round-arched entries, balconies, and a general asymmetry common to the style. Multi-paned steel casement windows were another feature of the type. When constructed in the Roaring Twenties, no expense was spared: the roof was slate, and the pierced brickwork, color tiles, and sandstone details were added in the spirit of modernity and good taste.

The stock market crashed in 1929, and Zahn just managed to hang on until 1946 when he sold the building to Elizabeth Lueck. Mrs. Lueck kept the apartments affordable and many were rented to nurses who worked at the nearby St. Joseph Mercy Hospital or to University of Michigan staff and faculty. The Lueck family, under the name Draprop, continues to own this property as well as its twin further down the street.

OFWHD

307 N. State
Hanorah and Ellen Morse House

195

1882

In the booming 1880s, students needed places to live within walking distance of campus. A dynamic woman named Ellen Morse filled that need by building many of the rooming houses along this stretch of N. State. A newspaper in 1879 noted that, "This house being

constructed makes the seventh large and commodious house erected by Miss Morse…she orders her own lumber and personally supervises the erection of her houses…" As with her other houses, the builder was probably William Lawrence. Miss Morse charged $1.75 a week, with students furnishing their own wood for heat. Local historian Louis Doll, who grew up nearby, reported that she often did her own cleaning, and was often seen walking down State Street with a mop and pail.

In 1881, Ms. Morse and her mother Hanorah purchased a large property on State and built 301 and 307 in 1882. Miss Morse later became nearly penniless through a bad investment but managed to hang on to some of her properties. Living to the age of 87, she donated her last home (see #201) to the Sisters of Mercy who founded St. Joseph Mercy Hospital there.

Miss Morse sold 307 to Alexander and Lena Wallace in 1915. Their daughter, Minnie Wallace, continued the boarding house tradition, and in 1970 the Inter-Cooperative Council (ICC) purchased the house and named it "Minnie's Coop" to honor her care for generations of students. It is a local landmark because their rules require the house to be painted purple.

The house is a good example of the simple Queen Anne style, with multiple gables, clapboard, shingles, bay windows, porches with gingerbread, a tower, and a more symmetrical arrangement of features than in later examples.

OFWHD

196 # 322 N. State
Duncan Manor Apartments   1928

Like its twin, the Wil-Dean Apartments (see #194), this Tudor-style apartment building was constructed in 1928 and opened in 1929, just before the stock market crash. The only difference between the two buildings is the color of the brick. Built in the Tudor Revival style, it features a steeply sloping roofline, casement windows, arched entry and balconies, and patterned brick and half-timbering. It was constructed by Dugald Duncanson, a real estate salesman, and designed by Gardiner Vose, a recent University of Michigan School of Architecture graduate. They moved the house that was here to 506 N. State (see #202).

Duncanson was unable to keep the property after the 1929 stock market crash. Later it was purchased by Mrs. Rosa Lueck, who also purchased the twin Wil-Dean Apartments, and it remains in the hands of her descendants today. Mrs. Lueck was known for preserving her historic properties and for providing affordable housing.

OFWHD

406 N. State
Enoch and Keziah Terhune House

197

1858

This house illustrates the transition from the Greek Revival to the Italianate style that was occurring in the late 1850s. In massing and plan the house is an "Italianate cube," but in detail many Greek Revival elements remain, including the engaged corner columns or pilasters, the central entry with wide architrave, and the six-over-six windows. The interior has a beautiful curved staircase of butternut.

It was built by Enoch Terhune, an 1831 emigrant from Seneca County, New York, who grew up in the Pittsfield area. He became a builder and contractor in 1842 and his obituary claims he was the first to bring planing mill machinery to Ann Arbor. This upset the local carpenters who thought they would lose business. In the mid-1840s, he became a successful dealer in sashes, doors, and blinds and also dealt in agricultural implements. "For over a quarter of a century he was one of the active business men of Ann Arbor," reported the *Ann Arbor Argus* in 1899. Terhune's grandfather was an ensign in the Revolutionary War and is buried in the tiny Terhune Cemetery in Terhune Park, owned by the City of Ann Arbor and maintained by the Pittsfield Chapter of the Daughters of the American Revolution (DAR).

As early as the 1890s, they were renting rooms to law students. After the turn of the century, the property passed into the hands of grocer Jay Herrick of Herrick and Bohnet. Mrs. Herrick was active in the suffragette movement. A program from the Ann Arbor Equal Suffrage Club from 1911 lists a meeting at this house.

The house was converted into apartments in the 1950s.

OFWHD

198 410 N. State
Society of Friends Meeting House   1851/1866

An 1851 deed confirms that Richard and Robert B. Glasier, trustees of the Society of Friends (Quakers), purchased this property on behalf of the Society. The Glasiers, who lived on Glazier Way, were active abolitionists involved in the Underground Railroad. This house has an exciting history. It was used as a church by the "colored people" of Ann Arbor and was the site of a riot in the winter of 1860, when avid abolitionist Parker Pillsbury spoke there. A mob broke up the speech, wrecked the furniture, and drove everyone out. Pillsbury remarked: "It is hardly possible now to believe that in 1861 free speech was in such a precarious condition in Ann Arbor…" An engraving from 1861 shows the riot and the Greek Revival building, which was five bays across and only one story tall, with gable returns on the side.

In 1866, the Quakers sold the building to tobacconists Charles and Frederick Horn, who likely repaired and enlarged it in the Italianate style, with carved brackets supporting the wide overhanging eaves, a hipped roof, and two pairs of long, narrow, double-hung two-over-two windows. The original Greek Revival doorway is intact. The porch supports a balcony with a single balustrade which is probably early 20th century.

The Horns sold it ten years later and after that the house changed hands frequently. By 1931, it had been divided into 10 apartments.

OFWHD

411 N. State
D.L. Wood House

199

1858/1868

Despite its unassuming appearance, this house has an interesting history. It was purchased by Ellen Morse (see #195 and #201) in 1873. After 1877, it was for many years the home of the Kearney family who were grocers. It was sold in 1922 to the Doll family who rented rooms. Their most famous tenant was Pulitzer Prize-winning playwright Arthur Miller, who wrote of the Dolls in his biography *Timebends*. Miller remembered them as a family of giants ducking in every doorway. He also noted that Jim Doll's enthusiastic response to his first attempt at playwriting left him running through Ann Arbor in the dead of night in a physical reaction to this approval: "The magical force of making marks on a piece of paper and reaching into another human being, making him see what I had seen and feel my feelings—I had made a new shadow on the earth." Miller maintained a close tie with Ann Arbor and the University of Michigan and was photographed in front of this house years later. The Miller Theater on North Campus honors his strong ties to the University of Michigan.

Louis Doll published many books about Ann Arbor history, including a history of St. Thomas Church, a history of Ann Arbor newspapers, and a history of Frank Glazier of Chelsea.

Under the inappropriate aluminum siding is an Italianate structure whose roof and porch were altered in the early 20th century. The bay windows on two sides and the paired windows with four-over-four panes are Italianate features and are original.

OFWHD

200 418 N. State
Newton A. Prudden House   1854

The Prudden house is one of a small number of surviving stucco-over-brick Greek Revival houses in Ann Arbor, which was referred to in a local newspaper as "...a little stucco village" in 1849. It is a simple house with a Greek Revival side entry. An unusual feature in the construction is the use of both adobe brick and tabby (see #187), making the stucco necessary to keep the structure dry. It originally had a gable front, which was altered to a hipped roof after the Civil War.

Prudden was a local fruit dealer, beekeeper, and manufacturer of water filters. His talents as a bee-keeper were lauded in the *Ann Arbor Courier* of September 1877 and the local beekeeping association was founded in this house in 1880. After his death in 1888, his nephew Newton F. Prudden took over his business affairs and lived in the house with his aunt until 1893 when he traded it for a farm in Chelsea. They had already been

renting parts of the house. Visiting nurse Emily Hollister commented about the family in her diary and noted that Mrs. Prudden gave away her card and comb to her nephew and her spinning wheel to the Methodist church. Hollister also commented on the decrepit and neglected state of the house and that it gave her a creepy feeling.

Like most houses on this block it became a boarding house. It was owned by Charles Kempf in 1896. Miss Ellen Morse (see #195) spent her last years here. After a series of tenants, Helen Tracy and her daughter Frances, a nurse, moved into the house in 1926. In 1938, local author Louis W. Doll (see #199) purchased it and renovated it as best he could, creating three apartments. His new entry door was featured on the cover of *House Beautiful Magazine* in September 1937. Doll owned it until 1992.

OFWHD

419 N. State
Hanorah and Ellen Morse House

1878

Hanorah and Ellen Morse ran boarding houses on State Street for almost a quarter of a century. They moved around a lot, living on Catherine, Thayer, and Lawrence Streets, and in this house on North State. In appearance it looks like an 1890s Colonial Revival with a tower in the back in an odd place, but perhaps the house was radically altered in the late 19th century. It has the cross gables, simple returns, and symmetrical arrangement of windows that are characteristic of this style.

The house has a very interesting history. Miss Morse sold the house to the Sisters of Mercy in 1911. They converted it to a 17-bed hospital that eventually became St. Joseph Mercy Hospital. A picture of this house often appears in their promotional materials. In 1919, when they outgrew this building, it became the Old Ladies Home, which later moved to W. Liberty and became the Anna Botsford Bach Home (see #274). Today the building is covered in aluminum siding, and is a dilapidated rental property.

OFWHD

202 506 N. State
Mary Ann Thayer House
c. 1854

This house was built on the southeast corner of State and Lawrence Streets, but was moved in 1928 for the construction of the Duncan Manor Apartments (see #196). The home dates to about 1854, and appears to have been built by Charles T. Gorham for Mary Ann Thayer. Wealthy banker and abolitionist Charles T. Gorham of Marshall technically held the property, as trustee of minor Mary Ann Mart, later Mrs. Charles Thayer. Charles Thayer had used his wife's inheritance inappropriately, and was forced to relinquish this property to the former trustee who was to use or sell the property exclusively for Mary Ann's benefit. It is believed that Gorham built the house as an investment property in 1854.

In 1857, the house was sold to Luther and Lucy Dodge for $1,200. Dodge was an express agent and an assistant assessor for the federal government. In 1871, it became the home of Ernest J. and Roxanna (Potter) Knowlton. Knowlton was a genius and manufacturer of "Knowlton's Universal Bath," a flexible, portable bathtub that could be suspended between two pieces of household furniture like a hammock. Knowlton's bath was inexpensive and very successful in the mid- to late 19th century, when bathtubs and plumbing were almost non-existent in private homes.

Like its former neighbor at State and Lawrence, the Terhune House (see #197), the house exhibits characteristics of both the Italianate and Greek Revival styles. The house is very much Italianate, with its cube-like shape, shallow hipped roof, bracketed cornice, and porch. At the same time, the porch is much more muscular than later Italianates, with its square columns and heavy frieze, and draws from the Greek Revival style. Other details, including the wide corner pilasters, the classical entry, and six-over-six windows, are also typical of Greek Revival buildings of the time period.

OFWHD

206 N. Thayer
Thomas Ready House

203

1858

When Thomas Ready constructed this Greek Revival cottage in the late 1850s, its only neighbor was the former Ellsworth Boarding House up the street at the southwest corner of Catherine and Thayer.

In the 1840s, Irish Catholics were also moving to this neighborhood to be close to St. Thomas the Apostle Church (see #155) on Kingsley, as indicated by a string of Irish names on the deed documents. In 1885 the Patrick O'Hearn family purchased the house and lived there for 70 years. In 1888, O'Hearn built another house on the north half of the lot, which

he used as a rental and never lived in himself. O'Hearn, who died in 1899, had been a supervisor with the city government and the first assessor. A huge turnout at his funeral included all of the city council and its staff. He was lauded as a kindly man, a man without enemies, and of incorruptible integrity.

Simple in shape and tiny in size, the house's old age is seen in its sagging roofline with one single ridgepole in place. Charming features of the house are the flowery Italianate porch (note the lack of a railing), and the shutters. For years it was the home of Cecile and Joe Hogan, who were rewarded by the Historic District Commission for their preservation efforts.

OFWHD

210 N. Thayer
Patrick O'Hearn House   1888

Patrick O'Hearn, who lived next door (see #203), built this rental house in 1888 in the Queen Anne style so popular at the time. Consisting of clapboard and shingle with intersecting gables, windows of varying sizes and shapes with multiple panes and stained glass, some half-timbering in the gable, plus an elaborate porch with turned columns and carved trim, the house is a fine example of the style and has never been remodeled on the exterior.

O'Hearn's first tenant was Dr. Jacob Reighard, professor of zoology at the University of Michigan. Around 1905 Reighard became the director of the Zoological Lab and Museum and built himself a much finer house in Burns Park (see #291). After he left, it was rented to a series of tenants until the 1940s when it was purchased by two widows. From 1969 through 2000 the Hogan family, owners of 206 N. Thayer (see #203), owned the property and were rewarded for their preservation by the Historic District Commission in 1989.

OFWHD

CENTRAL CAMPUS/ MEDICAL CENTER

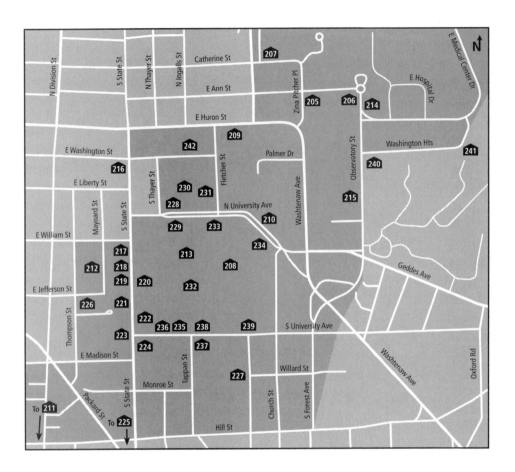

The history of Ann Arbor and the story of its architecture would be incomplete without a thorough study of the University of Michigan. Founded in Detroit in 1817, the University moved to Ann Arbor shortly after Michigan became a state in 1837. The Ann Arbor Land Company donated 40 acres along State Street between North University and South University, with East University as the eastern border. The first buildings were constructed in 1839–1840. They included a classroom building along State Street with dorm rooms for students, and four houses for professors—two facing North University and two facing South University. The President's House (see #235) is the only surviving building from this era.

Under the visionary leadership of President Henry Tappan, hired in 1852, the University expanded its curriculum to include practical subjects like science, medicine, and law, which led to the construction of the Detroit Observatory in 1854 (see #206), a medical building in 1851, and a law school in 1859. Tappan also closed the student dormitories on campus to allow the rooms to be used as classrooms. This led to a large flow of students into the surrounding neighborhoods and to the rise of boarding houses. Little of the University's 19th-century building stock remains. Tappan Hall (see #236), the President's House, and the Detroit Observatory are the oldest buildings on campus.

The architectural character of the University of Michigan's Central Campus was defined during the post-World War I era—mainly by architect Albert Kahn—with the construction of Angell Hall (see #220), the Hatcher Graduate Library (see #232), the Natural Sciences Building (see #229), the Clements Library (see #238), Hill Auditorium (see #228), and the West Engineering/West Hall building (see #239).

A Central Campus Historic District bounded by State, Monroe, Huron, and Washtenaw was created in 1978 and is on the National Register of Historic Places.

The original 40 acres were insufficient by the early decades of the 20th century, and the University began expanding in all directions. Many old residences, schools, and churches along State Street, South University, and North University Avenues were demolished or moved to make way for new buildings. Hill Auditorium (see #228), Betsy Barbour House (see #217), Helen Newberry House (see #218), and Martha Cook Dormitory (see #237), were some of the first major University buildings outside the original 40 acres. The Law Quadrangle and Law School Buildings (see #224) were constructed in the 1920s–30s in a huge expansion off Central Campus. Ann Arbor's own Irving and Allen Pond, and their Chicago architectural firm Pond and Pond, designed the Michigan Union (see #223), the Michigan League (see #231), and the Student Publications Building (see #212).

The post-World War II era brought another huge influx of students, and a larger campus expansion. A more modern sensibility guided the architecture of the era, with the LSA Building (see #221) and Alden Dow's Fleming Administration Building (see #226) standing in stark contrast to their more traditional neighbors. The building boom continues at the University of Michigan, which remains the primary driver of Ann Arbor's changing landscape.

1300 E. Ann
Couzens Hall

1925/1955

With a bequest of $600,000 in 1923 from U.S. Senator the Honorable James Couzens of Detroit, a plan for a residence for nurses began to jell. The Georgian-style building opened in 1925 with 250 single rooms for women. Designed by Detroit architect Albert Kahn, this red brick building trimmed in limestone was built in the shape of an "H" and conveniently located across the street from Kahn's newly opened University of Michigan Hospital. The lobby was paneled in walnut, and it had a reception room and library. The rear overlooked a beautiful garden and the women's athletic field. Each of the two side sections of red-brown brick has a stone, four-story central portion with quoins and classical detailing. The central portion and entry is particularly handsome, with a stone arch flanked by pineapple-filled bowls over the side walls. Attached columns with Ionic capitals form the central portion, which is topped by a stone balustrade with stone balls and a slate roof. A curved, balustraded wall at entry level welcomes the visitor.

In 1955, after University of Michigan Housing acquired the building from the U-M Hospital, an addition was made to the original building on the east elevation that doubled its capacity. In 2011, after a $49 million renovation, Couzens reopened as one of the U-M's "Heritage Halls." Improvements were made in fire suppression, air conditioning, bathrooms, and study spaces—including a 24-hour lounge. It is now a co-ed residence for 525 students and houses a multicultural lounge, a Community Learning Center, and the Health Sciences Scholars Program (HSSP). Inside there are graphic wall panels illustrating the history of the building with old photographs and keepsakes.

1398 E. Ann
Detroit Observatory

1854

This stucco-over-brick building—scored to resemble a stone Greek Temple—has both Greek Revival and Italianate details, including classical columns and eave brackets. Its construction was the high point of University of Michigan President Henry Tappan's presidency. Tappan's efforts resulted in funds from Detroit business interests (hence the name) to purchase a 6-inch Pistor & Martins meridian circle and a 12 5/8-inch Henry Fitz refracting telescope, which in their day were among the largest in the world. A point of pride was that the Fitz telescope was made in America to European standards. The Observatory was the centerpiece of Tappan's efforts to transform the University of Michigan into a great research university. He would marvel today at how well he succeeded. Tappan was fired a few years later due to personality and philosophical clashes with the Regents. He lived out his life in Europe, never returning to the U.S. His Observatory, however, continued to expand until the 1930s.

In 1976, the University of Michigan demolished all but the original building of the Observatory complex. Under the watchful eye of Patricia Whitesell, the Observatory was meticulously restored in 1998 and was the Historic District Commission's "Project of the Year" in 1999. Today it is a division of the Bentley Historical Library and open to visitors on weekends. Docents explain the instruments and demonstrate how the heavens were observed in the mid-19th century by pulling a continuous rope to turn the dome.

NR

207 1111 E. Catherine
Victor Vaughan Building   1939

This red brick building was constructed in 1939 on the site of the old Homeopathic Hospital that was destroyed by fire in 1927. It was built with funds from the federal government and designed by Wirt C. Rowland (of O'Dell and Rowland). Previously, Rowland, as the head designer at Smith, Hinchman and Grylls (1922–1930), designed the Guardian, Buhl, and Penobscot Buildings in Detroit. The building served originally as a dorm for male medical students but changed during the war years to one for females and was later co-ed. In the last 50 years it has been the home of various University of Michigan institutes and departments, most recently serving as a speech clinic that helps victims of stroke. It was named after Victor C. Vaughan, Dean of the Medical School from 1891–1921.

The building is very Art Deco, with a streamlined look created by thin, horizontal stripes of dark red terra-cotta on the red brick framing on what were once steel casement windows (replaced in the 1980s). The zig-zag pattern of the exterior is shaped by triangular bays alternating with flatter parts. A limestone entry with the incised name "Victor Vaughan House" has stone horizontal bands flanking the doorway leading up to a flattened

arch over the door. Original terrazzo floors can be found in some areas, as can some original wood doors. An elevator wing was added in the 1950s, but the building is a remarkably well-preserved and unusual example of Art Deco on the U-M campus.

440 Church
West Medical/Dana Natural Resources Building   1903

208

The stone and brick West Medical building was designed in a classical style by Detroit architects Spier and Rohns (see #219 and #236). The first two courses are of dressed fieldstone while the upper levels are of pressed brick, molded brick arches, and ornate cornices. Ornamental entrances on the east and west are of Bedford limestone. The building was the second on campus for the U-M Medical School (the first being an 1850 Greek Revival building just to the south of this one). The Medical School was the first professional school opened at U-M.

In the 1950s, a restructuring led to new medical buildings closer to the Main Hospital on Catherine at Observatory. This building then became the home of the School of Natural Resources & Environment (SNRE after 1992), teaching forestry, wood technology, and wildlife management with GIS, remote sensing, and micro-computer labs. They also have courses in landscape architecture and environmental design. The building was renamed for Samuel Trask Dana, professor of forestry from 1927–1953.

In 1998, the local firm of Quinn Evans was hired to remodel the building based on sustainable practices, resulting in the first LEED-certified building in Michigan when the "greening" was completed in 2004. They received an award from the Historic District Commission.

CCHD

121 Fletcher
Power Center

1971

The University of Michigan's Power Center is an example of the "Brutalist" (from the French word *brut* meaning rough or raw) style. It hosts many of the premier stage performances associated with the University of Michigan and the Ann Arbor Summer Festival. The building originated in a 1963 gift to the University of Michigan by Eugene and Sadye Power and their son Philip Power. Eugene Power was an early inventor and innovator in the microfilm industry, and founder of University Microfilms. He was also a U-M Regent.

The 1,381-seat theater was designed by internationally renowned architects Kevin Roche and John Dinkeloo, of the firm of Kevin Roche, John Dinkeloo and Associates. Both had worked in the office of Eero Saarinen (see #369). Roche and Dinkeloo designed over 200 projects around the world and won numerous prizes, including the AIA Gold Medal. As in much of their early work, Roche and Dinkeloo chose exposed concrete as the primary building material, a treatment that is softened somewhat by ivy. Massive concrete columns line the front, backed by highly reflective mirrored glass. During evening performances when the lobby is illuminated, viewers can see two fantastic spiral staircases, tapestries by Roy Lichtenstein and Pablo Picasso, and the huge concrete columns. No seat in the building is farther than 72 feet from the stage.

CCHD

1109 Geddes
Alexander G. Ruthven Museums Building   1928

210

Another of the many buildings designed by Detroit architect Albert Kahn, the Ruthven Museums Building (formerly known as the Exhibits Museums of Natural History) is prob-

ably the most well known to residents of Michigan. Here are the dinosaurs and planetarium that are visited by 85,000 school children every year. It houses the Museums of Anthropology, Paleontology, and Zoology, which are in the process of expansion to other locations. It also has exhibits on Michigan wildlife, Native American culture, and archaeology in Ann Arbor.

The building is in a Classical style and resembles the nearby C.C. Little Building (see #234). Both are on triangles of land facing each other across Geddes. It was renamed the Ruthven Museums Building in 1968 to honor former Museums Director and U-M President Alexander G. Ruthven.

The building is of Bedford limestone and maroon tapestry brick and the entry has beautiful animal carvings in stone. Below the cornice is the famous quotation of Louis Agassiz: "Go to Nature, take the facts…look and see for yourself." The bronze doors by U-M sculptor Carleton Angell have "Truth conquers by itself" inscribed over the leaves and are flanked by two black terrazzo pumas, also by Angell. The spandrels between the third and fourth floors have heads of pioneer American naturalists in relief. A beautiful rotunda with balcony greets the visitor upon entry.

CCHD

211 1201 S. Main
Michigan Stadium
1927/1956/2009

Michigan Stadium is one of Ann Arbor's best known and nationally recognized buildings. Called "the Big House" after the 1970s, the stadium holds an official capacity of 109,901 people and is one of the largest sports venues in the United States. It is built into the ground in an elliptical bowl shape to take advantage of the natural slope of the land. It surprises new visitors with its immense size.

The University of Michigan Wolverines are among the oldest college football teams in the nation, playing their first game on May 30, 1879. They are also the winningest college football team in the history of the game. U-M is part of the Big 10 Conference, which was organized in 1896 and is located primarily in the Midwest.

The stadium was the brainchild of U-M Football Coach Fielding Yost and was completed at a cost of $950,000. It replaced the nearby Ferry Field whose gates can still be seen today from State Street. The first game in Michigan Stadium was played against Ohio Wesleyan on October 1, 1927. Three weeks later, on October 22, 1927, Michigan Stadium was dedicated during a game against rival Ohio State.

The stadium was designed by Bernard Green, U-M Alum and President of Osborn Engineering of Cleveland, Ohio. The stadium's bowl shape made it subject to water problems due to underground springs on the site, and these problems have persisted until quite recently. It is rumored that a crane that sank during construction is still buried underneath the stadium. In 1930, the stadium became the first in the nation to employ an electronic scoreboard. Michigan Stadium originally held 72,000 people plus an additional 10,000 temporary bleachers. In 1956 press boxes and additional bleachers were added, which raised the capacity to over 101,001. The extra "1" seat was added in honor of athletic director Fritz Crisler.

The most dramatic change to the appearance of Michigan Stadium took place in 2008–2010, when large arched brick walls, vaguely reminiscent of the Colosseum in Rome, were added to the east and west elevations. This created a new press box, 83 luxury boxes, as well as additional and accessible seating. New lights have allowed night games for the first time in the Stadium's history. A massive new scoreboard was added in 2013.

420 Maynard
Student Publications Building   1931

212

The Student Publications Building was designed by the Chicago firm of Pond and Pond, which also designed the Michigan Union and the Michigan League. The red brick and lime-

stone building is in an Art Deco/Collegiate Gothic style and has many features also found at these other buildings, including the stylized stone flowers on the exterior and the polychrome tile flowers on the interior. Also like the others, it has large multipaned and multicolored glass windows. Unique is an interior checkerboard pattern of zenitherm (an asbestos product) in the huge composing and editorial room on the second floor. An iron staircase with Art Deco patterns, a terrazzo floor, and carved woodwork (more Collegiate Gothic than Deco) complete the interior.

The building houses the offices of *The Michigan Daily*, *The Michiganensian* (yearbook), *The Gargoyle* (a humor magazine), and *The Student Directory*. The building underwent a major renovation in 2008 and received a Rehabilitation Award from the City of Ann Arbor's Historic District Commission. Many interior features were kept, including the tile and travertine walls, and the colorful zenitherm which was carefully repaired. Wherever possible, original woodwork, tables, benches, cabinets, and doors were also restored and reused. It was renamed the Stanford Lipsey Student Publications Building in honor of the major donor.

213 Miscellaneous Locations
Public Art at the University of Michigan

From the Block M on the Diag to the Cube at the Fleming Building, from the small stone benches scattered throughout Central Campus to the large sculptures on North Campus, the University of Michigan has a vast array of public art that is both commemorative (as gifts from various classes) and aesthetic. Together with the mature trees and the many historical buildings it creates a pleasant whole. A website devoted to detailed explanations of this public art can be found at the U-M President's Advisory Committee on Public Art. See *http://www.public-art.umich.edu/the_collection/campus/central/60.*

102 Observatory
Simpson Memorial Institute

1926

214

The Simpson Memorial Institute, a lovely four-story granite structure in a Classical Revival style, is another of the many buildings on campus designed by the Detroit architect Albert Kahn. It was a gift to the University by Christine Simpson in honor of her husband Henry Simpson, who died of pernicious anemia. The building was endowed to house a facility to study and care for patients with this disease and to find a cure. After a cure was discovered, other blood diseases were studied, and it was here that Vitamin B12 was isolated for use in blood substitutes and the treatment of shock during World War II. Later research has focused on leukemia, and the building housed the Historical Center for the Health Sciences until 1992. Today it houses the Center for the History of Medicine.

The building has stone quoins at the corners, a pedimented entry, a band of dentillated stone separating the third and fourth floors, and a mansard roof punctuated by three dormers surrounded by a stone balustrade with four urns facing the street. Mrs. Simpson chose the Classical style which complemented the U-M Hospital nearby (now demolished), also designed by Kahn. She was present at the groundbreaking and the dedication in 1927.

215 324 Observatory
Stockwell Hall   1940

Stockwell, which became co-ed in 2009, was the last of the women's residence halls built on "the hill" overlooking Washtenaw Ave. Located at the intersection of Observatory and North University, this Tudor-style brick building was constructed in 1940 with federal funds (WPA) at the tail end of the Depression and was designed by C. William Palmer of Detroit. The dorm is named in honor of Madelon Louisa Stockwell, the first woman admitted to the University in 1871.

This red brick L-shaped building with tapestry brick details has limestone-framed windows in a quoin-like pattern and half-timber wood trim. Steeply pitched slate roofs in alternating heights punctuate both wings. A semicircular lobby formed by the right angle of the wings leads to an atrium two stories high, which is one of the unique features of this building. The wood-paneled lobby has alcoves containing lozenge-shaped colored glass and beautiful original light fixtures. The former dining areas are now community spaces, created in the recent upgrade in 2009 that restored many of the original light fixtures, the wood-paneled walls, and the two fireplaces. An outdoor portico of nine flattened limestone arches has a lovely blue and gold Pewabic tile mosaic with a central "S" in the wall, and benches that provide a great place to view Palmer Field and the city below. A Special Merit Award from the Ann Arbor Historic District Commission in 2010 recognized the restoration of the slate roof and infrastructure upgrades.

204 S. State
Lane Hall

216

1916

Lane Hall was built as a YMCA. The cornerstone for this Georgian-style building was laid in 1916 after a large donation from John D. Rockefeller. Several houses were moved from the site to Washington Street, just behind the current building. Otis and Clark of Chicago were the architects. This enterprise was widely supported by the University, as it wished to provide a non-denominational student center to complement those of the many churches nearby. Run by the Students' Christian Association (SCA), the building was formally purchased by the University in 1937, and renamed for Victor H. Lane, a member of the law faculty and longtime president of the YMCA.

In 1956, an office of religious affairs was created which merged with the SCA and moved to another building. Lane Hall became an international center for Chinese, Japanese, North African, and Middle Eastern area studies with a Japanese garden in the lobby. It now houses the Women's Studies Department and the Center for Research on Women & Gender.

The red brick Georgian building has typical features of the style: a symmetrical arrangement of openings with a central entry, and multi-paned windows that are capped by jack arches with a keystone in the middle. A stone-pedimented entry leads to a foyer and large lobby. Stone quoins are found at each corner of the building and on the front facade as well. It has a limestone water table between the basement and the first floor.

In 2000, the building was completely restored and an addition was added to the back in the same Georgian style. Quinn Evans architects were careful to preserve as much of the original fabric as possible, and in 2001, the University of Michigan received a Project of the Year Award from the Ann Arbor Historic District Commission.

217 | 420 S. State

Betsy Barbour House   1920

This Georgian-style building with a large setback off State Street was the third residence hall opened for women on the University of Michigan campus. Nearby Helen Newberry and Martha Cook, built in 1915, were the first two. It was the gift of Regent Levi L. Barbour and was named after his mother. Barbour had funded the education of two Chinese girls (Barbour Scholarships), and when one died he dedicated himself to providing safe, healthy living conditions. For years, his mother's favorite rocker sat in the first floor reception room along with many pieces of furniture from Regent Barbour's home in Detroit, including his library, paintings, and objects collected on his travels. Just over 100 women live here and its cozy spaces and convenient location make it a popular women's residence.

The building, designed by Detroit architect Albert Kahn, is a highly symmetrical design of light red brick with white trimmed multi-paned windows and a glass-enclosed porch along the State Street side. Despite the State Street address, the main entry is off Maynard. A classical Georgian entry with broken pediment and arched window greets the visitor. Completing the Georgian style is the brick belt course below the third and second floors, and the triple dormers on the steeply pitched slate roof with modil-

lioned cornice line. It has been modernized a few times to allow more women to live here, but it has retained most of its original fabric and design.

432 S. State
Helen Newberry Residence

218

1915

Built in 1915, the first of two residence halls built for women on campus, it is a Georgian-style four-story stucco-over-brick building with a center entry and symmetrically arranged windows of multi-paned glass. The Georgian features here include a high first floor of exposed red brick, three floors of gray-painted stucco with red brick arches over the windows, and a three-story exposed brick entry on the west. The steeply pitched slate roof has several dormers and exposed rafters.

The building was designed by Detroit architect Albert Kahn with the aid of Ernst Wilby, who had worked with him on Hill Auditorium. It sits far back from State Street, much like its neighbor Betsy Barbour, because at the time the old "West Hall" (originally a public school), was still standing. Also like Barbour, the main entry is off Maynard Street.

Funds for the dorm were donated by the children of Helen Newberry of Detroit to honor their mother. Mrs. Newberry had earlier donated funds for what is now the Kelsey Museum (see #219). The dorm was also part of the SCA until 1924 when the University purchased it. It has served continuously as a women's residence hall and houses 120 students, just across State Street from the original 40-acre campus.

219 434 S. State
Newberry Hall/Kelsey Museum   1888

This picturesque building in the Richardsonian Romanesque style was designed by the Detroit firm of Spier and Rohns after a long fundraising effort by the Students' Christian Association (SCA). It was named Newberry Hall (still spelled out in copper lettering typical of the late 1880s) after John S. Newberry, a railroad magnate, whose widow Helen contributed substantial funds. To the north stands Newberry Hall, a women's dorm named after her.

The building has typical features of this style—a tower with rows of windows of varying sizes, a heaviness projected by the use of fieldstone and Ohio bluestone, a deeply recessed round-arched entry, a heavy oak interior, and a beautiful Tiffany window that unfortunately faces north and is not easily visible. An archway in the main gable of checkerboard brick is particularly unique. The building was added to the National Register in 1972.

The Students' Christian Association was reorganized in 1904 as the YMCA/YWCA, and they used the building until 1919, when it became open to all religious groups. By 1920, they couldn't afford to keep the building, and rented space to the University which eventually purchased it in 1937. It was renamed the Kelsey Museum after Latin Professor Francis W. Kelsey, whose excavations in Egypt provided the first group of artifacts for the Museum. Later excavations in the Middle East by others provided even more artifacts and now over 100,000 items are housed here. In 2009, an addition to the Museum was built with the same fieldstone and named for the donor, William E. Upjohn. The building and the addition received a Rehabilitation Award from the Historic District Commission in 2010. The Museum welcomes schools and organizations for tours of the facility.

NR

435 S. State
Angell Hall

220

1924

Completed in 1924, Angell Hall was designed by the famous Detroit architect Albert Kahn to meet the increased classroom needs of the liberal arts division after World War I. It is designed in a muscular Classical style with eight Doric columns decorated with the traditional Greek meander pattern. There are sculptural reliefs for History, Arts, Philosophy, and Poetry by Ulysses Ricci of New York. Look for the owl, the book, and the lamp of learning between the main columns and the University seal, "Artes, Scientia, Veritas," over the main entry. The travertine marble lobby and the rich ceiling decorations were done by the DiLorenzo Studios of New York (who also did the Clements and the Hatcher Libraries). Also in the lobby is a relief of James B. Angell by Karl Bitter.

The building was originally a tribute to Kahn's friend Henry Bacon, the sculptor of the Lincoln Memorial, and meant to be much larger. Its design was constricted by the fact that it was built directly onto the front of University Hall (1871), formerly the main classroom building noted for its distinctive tower and large meeting spaces used for graduation and musical events. University Hall was demolished in 1950 and wings were added to the east, now known as Mason Hall and Haven Hall. The original cornerstone for University Hall is on display in the hallway linking Angell Hall with these buildings.

Angell Hall was named for the recently deceased (and longest serving) president of the University, James B. Angell, who had served for over 40 years. On the roof is a small observatory, and at the cornice line is a quote from the Northwest Ordinance of

1787, which was the backbone of the educational system in the territories settled after the Revolutionary War.

CCHD

221 500 S. State
U-M Administration Building
1948

This orange brick building, nicknamed the "salmon loaf," served as the U-M Administration Building until 1968 when the Fleming Building opened. Its long, low profile, ribbon windows, whimsical aluminum figures of baboons and other animals, and aluminum clock are features of the Art Moderne style. Seven stone reliefs on the west elevation representing Hiawatha, Aesop's Fables, the naturalist, adventurers, scientists, and musicians are also distinctly of the period. A "Student Motif" stone relief on the east facade is a pair of hands holding a diploma. All were from the studio of famed Michigan sculptor Marshall Fredericks. Others of his works can be found at the Michigan Stadium and the "Spirit of Detroit" in Detroit. Unfortunately, two bronze reliefs formerly on the east facade, known as the "Dream of the Young Man" and the "Dream of the Young Girl," were removed and placed in obscurity at the Bentley Library. Aluminum railings and doors and near ground-level lights flanking the entry complete the style and are original to the building.

The building, designed by Harley, Ellington and Day, was part of a post-World War II building boom that helped unite scattered student services and the central administration. It was until recently the home of the radio station WUOM. Today it houses the offices of the Registrar, and the Sociology and LS&A Departments. The original interior is of interest for its Art Moderne features, including the indirect lighting and stylized aluminum mailbox in the entry rotunda, figured marble and indirect lighting in the main light-filled room, and its terrazzo floors.

525 S. State
Alumni Memorial Hall/U-M Museum of Art   1910

222

This Classical stone building, designed by the Detroit architecture firm of Donaldson and Meier, was built as a monument to the University of Michigan men who had died in war and was the first building erected with funds from alumni. In 1868, a drive began to raise funds to memorialize the fallen of the Civil War and eventually the fallen from all wars. The foundation was laid in 1908 and the building opened in 1910, not only as a war memorial but as a home for the Alumni Association and the University's fledgling art collection.

In 1967, it became the University of Michigan Museum of Art (UMMA), though it had housed the Museum of Art since 1946. It is one of the largest university museums in the country. In 2009, while constructing the Frankel Wing, the memorials to the dead were refurbished and made more prominent, skylights were re-opened, and original moldings uncovered.

The building is in the Beaux Arts style, which revived classical models and is defined by paired columns with capitals, wreaths near the roofline, and dentils under the cornice line. The interior is mostly original with a large open two-story atrium framed by a balcony with iron railings. The side wings containing galleries originally were meeting rooms.

CCHD

223 530 S. State
Michigan Union
1919

The Michigan Union, a brick and limestone Collegiate Gothic building, was designed by the Chicago architecture firm of Pond and Pond and officially opened in 1919. Construction began in 1916, but was interrupted by World War I when the half-completed building served as a barracks for troops. Irving Kane Pond and Allen B. Pond were natives of Ann Arbor and their childhood home was actually on this site. Also demolished was the home of Law Professor and Judge Thomas M. Cooley, which had served as the first Michigan Union Clubhouse beginning in 1907. The Michigan Union still serves its original purpose as a central meeting hub for students, with rooms for organizations, restaurants and dining areas, bookstores, study rooms, a billiards hall, and a ballroom. Until the 1950s, women were denied entry except for special events.

Pond and Pond were known for their elegant brickwork with Gothic and Arts and Crafts detailing (see #231). The building is four stories with a central tower of seven stories that includes a three-story limestone bay window with small panes of colored glass (also seen throughout the building). At the base of the bay are two statues of "the student" and "the athlete." A wide set of terraced steps leads to four oak doors. Great Gothic windows outlined in stone flank the tower on the second floor. Two wings to the south were added in 1936 and 1938 and now house the International Center and offices. There is a marker on the steps where President (then candidate) John F. Kennedy stood in 1960 and proposed the Peace Corps.

The interior is done in an Arts and Crafts/Gothic kind of style with dark wood paneling in most of the rooms, and polychrome tile squares with stylized plant designs on the walls and columns. Just beyond the entry is an elaborately carved and pierced wooden staircase. Highly polished floors are done in various shades of slate. The building was renovated in 1994 and many pieces of original furniture were reinstalled on the main floor. Another renovation began in 2013.

625 S. State

Law Quadrangle

224

1923–1933

The Law Quadrangle, using mainly Tudor-Gothic models from Oxford and Cambridge in England, consists of several buildings built over a period of ten years. They are the result of a magnificent gift to the University by alumnus William W. Cook (see also #237), who was born in Hillsdale, Michigan, obtained his law degree from the University of Michigan in 1882, and moved to New York where he made his fame and fortune. He never visited Ann Arbor to view the results of his largesse.

Designed by the New York architecture firm York and Sawyer, all buildings were constructed of Weymouth granite trimmed with Indiana limestone. The Quadrangle consists of the Lawyers Club (1924), Hutchins Hall (1933), the W.W. Cook Legal Research Building (1931), and the John P. Cook Residence Hall (1930). The northwest entrance to the quadrangle is famous for its gargoyles, which represent former U-M presidents. The windows of Hutchins Hall have whimsical etchings on tinted glass satirizing legal terminology. The library (Research Building) is a stunning church-like space with stained glass, oak panels, and cork floors. The magnificent interior has heavy tie beams under the ceiling with lions, hawks, and griffins peering down on the hard-working students. Blue and gold plaster medallions decorate the spaces between the beams and bookcases of carved oak cover the walls. It is considered by many to be the most beautiful interior on campus. A major renovation of the Quadrangle began in 2012.

NR, CCHD

225 1000 S. State
Yost Field House

1922–1923

Yost Field House, a red brick and limestone building in the Italian Romanesque style designed by the Detroit firm of Smith, Hinchman and Grylls, was dedicated in 1923. It originally provided space for indoor track and field events, and was part of a three-building collection of structures that made the University of Michigan one of the finest college athletic campuses in the nation. Its huge dimensions were meant to provide year-round space for training, especially for football. It was used by the basketball team in the 1960s, and in 1973 became the home of the U-M hockey team, and renamed Yost Ice Arena. Fielding Yost was coach of the football teams from 1901–1924 and Director of Intercollegiate Athletics from 1921–1941.

The building, with its three-story tall windows along State Street, has been renovated many times—in 1992, 1996, 2001, and 2012 when the original windows were replaced. These renovations were for energy efficiency, updating mechanicals, adding a press box, a 300-seat balcony, lounge, and pro shop. The original trusses from 1923 are still visible, and the large round-topped Romanesque-style windows remain. The building resembles a basilica church in some respects, with the windows that face north reaching their maximum height at the peak of the gable and then descending in size. The arched entries on the north, obscured from the street by a brick wall, add to the Italian flavor of the building.

503 Thompson
Fleming Administration Building

226

1966

Begun in 1966 and completed in 1968, the Fleming Administration Building stands out with its cube-like form, minimalist ground floor entry arches, and the geometric placement of long, narrow windows and trim that resemble the art work of Piet Mondrian. The building was designed by Midland-based architect Alden Dow, who was responsible for a total of 18 buildings in the city of Ann Arbor, and who was a big fan of Mondrian's work.

The design followed Dow's architectural philosophy of "composed order" to promote harmony between people, ideas, and materials. However, this harmony was never really achieved, and the building has been unpopular because of its fortress-like feel, both inside and out.

Despite criticisms, the building has been seen by other architects as Dow's most original building in the city. The building was conceived in the early 1960s, years before the era of student unrest. Nevertheless, rumors persist that the building was designed to be "riot proof." This probably stems from the fact that it opened in 1968, at the height of campus protests surrounding the Vietnam War and the Civil Rights Movement. Robben Wright Fleming, after whom the building is named, was the ninth president of the University and served in that role for eleven turbulent years, from 1968 until 1979. He also served as interim president in 1988.

227 610 E. University
University Elementary and High School/
School of Education   1924/1930

The University of Michigan School of Education occupies two red brick, Collegiate Gothic buildings constructed as the University High School (1924) and University Elementary School (1930). The high school was designed by Perkins, Fellows and Hamilton of Chicago and fronted E. University. The Elementary School was designed by the Detroit architecture firm of Malcomson and Higginbotham and faced what was then Monroe Street. Both buildings were combined to form a quadrangle around a courtyard that was used as a children's play area and is still maintained. The impressive entry to the high school contains stone carvings on the Gothic columns that culminate in two pinnacles extending above the roofline. Old copper light fixtures still flank the doorway as do new windows with half-stone, half-brick dividers.

The 1930 building is less Gothic, with a plainer stone entry and tiles above the arches. The south entry leads to a foyer of Gothic carved-wood walls with multi-paned glass on both sides. To the right is a two-story vaulted study space with wood wainscoting, a balcony with iron railings, a mosaic shield over the stone fireplace, and original pendant lamps.

Up the steps and just beyond this foyer, however, is an exuberant Art Deco space filled with green tile walls, a green and orange tile fountain, and tile floors in colorful designs. An office on the first floor, a former children's library, has a charming fireplace with three nursery rhymes illustrated in colored tiles. Green tiles cover the walls of much of the first floor and some of the room openings on the upper floors as well. All were products of the Flint Faience Company, a by-product of General Motors' spark plugs production process.

The School of Education occupied one floor of these buildings and used the schools for practice and experimentation. The schools graduated their last classes in 1969 and 1970 and from then on the building was used solely by the U-M School of Education.

CCHD

264

825 N. University
Hill Auditorium

228

1913

This brick, limestone, and terra-cotta structure, designed by Albert Kahn with Ernst Wilby, was the first performance space built on campus and Kahn's second building on campus. Parabolic in shape, it is said to have among the best acoustics in the country. Regent Arthur Hill donated the funds for this 4,300-seat auditorium, designed in the spare Prairie style started by Louis Sullivan in Chicago. The facade, with its tapestry brick framing classical columns, resembles several of Sullivan's buildings. These brick patterns are almost the only exterior decoration. The name "Hill Auditorium" is spelled out in simple, almost invisible, copper lettering.

Kahn used a special reinforced concrete system developed by his brother Julius (who had two degrees from U-M) known as the "Kahn Bar." The building underwent a major renovation and was re-dedicated in 2004. The seven arcs of light bulbs that had framed the stage were restored as were lights in the ceiling and entry hall. New mechanical systems were installed, the windows were restored, and accessible bathrooms were added. Although capacity was reduced, a new space was created in the lower level for exhibits, refreshments, and gatherings during intermission.

Hill has been the centerpiece of the cultural scene in Ann Arbor since its opening in 1913. The University Musical Society (UMS) has actively programmed the space and ran an annual May Festival with the Philadelphia Orchestra from 1897–2005. Each year it produces some 75 performances and hundreds of educational events. Hill has also been important as a site for graduations, lectures, demonstrations during the 1960s, welcoming speeches by U-M presidents, and jazz and pop concerts produced by student groups. It is truly the central gathering spot for the University community.

NR, CCHD

229 830 N. University
Edward Kraus Natural Science Building   1914

This dark-red brick, stone, and terra-cotta building with large windows is another of the many buildings on campus designed by Albert Kahn. It features his characteristic tapestry brick designs that can also be seen at Hill Auditorium and the University Library. Kahn based the construction on that of his factory buildings, using evenly spaced steel and concrete piers for support to maximize the amount of light. The building, usually referred to as "Nat Sci," originally housed many science departments (zoology, botany, mineralogy, and biology) but now contains the Biology Department. It has a large auditorium and a greenhouse on the south side. Major changes in use are scheduled for 2015.

Despite its North University address, the building faces what was formerly Ingalls Street, where some original elm and oak trees remain. The arched limestone two-story entrances both here and on North University contain three stone shields, the central one with the lamp of learning, a sunburst, and the words "Artes, Scientas, Veritas." They are flanked by stone shields with the dates "1837" and "1914": the year the University was established in

Ann Arbor and the date of the building. At the roofline, terra-cotta bands look like frosting on a cake as they run across the top floor and top off each brick column. Below the North University cornice the name "Natural Science" is spelled out in copper lettering, similar to that on Hill Auditorium.

The building was renamed in 1973 for Edward Henry Kraus, who was a professor of mineralogy from 1904–1945 and Dean of the College of LS&A from 1933–1945. It is on the site of one of the original four professors' houses from 1840.

CCHD

881 N. University
Burton Memorial Tower

230

1936

It had long been the dream of U-M President Marion L. Burton (1920–25) to have a centrally located tower and carillon. He died before it became a reality but it now perpetuates his name. The carillon, a set of 55 bells cast in England, was the gift of Charles M. Baird, a lawyer and the U-M's first athletic director. The carillon marks every quarter hour with Westminster chimes, and during the noon hour and on special occasions tunes are played. It forms a unique part of Ann Arbor's ambiance and can be seen and heard far from Central Campus.

The 10-story limestone sheath, an obelisk in the Art Deco style with a pointed copper cap and clocks on each of its four sides, was designed by the Detroit architect Albert Kahn and begun in 1935. Burton Tower originally was going to be much taller and it's believed that Kahn's design was highly influenced by his friend Eliel Saarinen. The Depression affected the funding, which resulted in the building we see (and hear) today.

It houses the University Musical Society and offices for the School of Music. An iconic structure, it appears in many publications promoting the University.

CCHD

267

231 911 N. University
The Michigan League   1929

Despite its N. University address, the League's main entry is off the Ingalls Mall, opposite the water fountain by Swedish sculptor Carl Milles and Hill Auditorium. This beautiful Gothic soft-red brick and limestone building was designed by Pond and Pond and built as a meeting place for women, since the Michigan Union was off-limits. It has an elaborate

entry from the west that opens into a lobby of oak wood paneling, comfortable furniture, and floors of Pewabic tile and polished slate. The exterior has a three-story stone bay and tower with multi-paned, multicolored glass windows decorated with limestone, and a slate roof with

copper gutters. Above the main entry are statues representing "Character" and "Friendship," designed by one of the architects and sculpted by Chicago artist Nellie Verne Walker. The main staircase is of wood carved in a Gothic style, with a gorgeous three-panel stained glass window depicting Science, Inspiration, and the Arts on the landing. There are also "gay corners and secluded nooks," according to a 1929 pamphlet. One meeting room has murals of famous women of the world.

The architects, brothers Irving Kane and Allen B. Pond, who also designed the Michigan Union (see #223), were Ann Arbor natives who had a successful practice in Chicago. Their signature style is a mix of Arts and Crafts, Art Deco, and Gothic. A main design feature throughout the building is the use of stylized flowers: at the Ingalls entry (on the stone tower and wood entry doors), on the second floor in the ballroom, in the arched hallways of oak and walnut paneling lit by cove lighting, and on the two-story high meeting rooms (decorated in period furniture and lit by windows with small panes of colored glass). These flowers may also be seen at the Michigan Union. The League contains the Lydia Mendelssohn Theatre, restaurants, study alcoves, a charming garden with sculptures, and hotel rooms. It is a center of campus life, now welcoming both men and women.

CCHD

913 N. University
Harlan Hatcher Graduate Library

232

1919

When the 1883 library proved inadequate after only 12 years, plans were drawn up for an entirely new one by Detroit architect Albert Kahn. Interrupted by World War I, it was completed in 1919 and retained the original fireproof stacks from the old building. It was renamed the Harlan Hatcher Graduate Library in 1968 after the former president (1951–1967). An eight-story addition was added in 1970. It has over 3.5 million volumes, numerous special libraries, and since 2004 has collaborated with Google in a digitization of its holdings.

The library is in the Prairie and Arts and Crafts styles favored by Kahn at the time (see #228 and #229) and is of restrained design in red brick, with limestone medallions by Ulysses Ricci between the windows, brick diaper patterns below a cornice of copper, and a red tile roof. From the outside, a grand stair leads to a lobby decorated with Pompeii-like murals painted by the DiLorenzo Studios of New York. Two marble staircases that flank the lobby lead to the barrel-vaulted grand reading room on the second floor, which contains two murals by Detroit artist Gari Melchers. They had been displayed in 1893 at the Columbian Exposition in Chicago, and were purchased after the fair along with the Frieze Organ now at Hill Auditorium.

CCHD

233 930 N. University
Chemistry Buildings

1909/1948/1989

This distinctive orange brick building with its buff Indiana limestone trim was designed by the Detroit firm of Smith, Hinchman and Grylls and opened for a few classes in 1909. Its Classical entry faces the Natural Science Building across the former path of Ingalls Street. A few large oaks and elms from that era survive. The entry has a keystone arch supporting a balcony with balusters held up by Classical consoles. A large "C" is inscribed in the keystone. The entry foyer has a mosaic floor and an arched ceiling reminiscent of ancient Roman sites. The exterior walls of the 1909 building are of thinner Roman brick (popular in the early 20th century) with heavily incised mortar joints, topped by a terra-cotta cornice and parapet with a guilloche (rope) design.

The older building housed the Pharmacy and Chemical Engineering Departments. There have been three additions to the building: one added in 1948 in an Art Moderne style, another later addition in matching orange brick, and a third addition that was completed in 1989, known as the Dow Lab Building. This later addition replaced the Barbour-Waterman Gymnasium Complex, whose demolition in 1976 spurred the creation of the Central Campus Historic District in 1978. It is on the site of one of the original professors' houses from 1840 and is commemorated by a plaque from the University Committee on History and Traditions.

CCHD

1100 N. University
East Medical (C.C. Little) Building   1925

234

The former East Medical Building is a brick and limestone structure designed by Albert Kahn and completed in 1925. It is a V-shaped building at the juncture of old Washtenaw and E. University and complements the V-shaped Ruthven Museums Building across the street. The main entry off East University is marked by four attached Ionic columns that are

three stories high. There is a smaller entrance on the Washtenaw side. It now houses the Departments of Earth and Environmental Sciences (Geological Sciences), Biochemistry, and many labs. Huge rocks outside tell a partial story of what goes on inside.

Above the front doors are stone panels with mermen holding medical-related items, including a mortar and pestle and a caduceus. There are also eagles and heads of men in profile, decorative reliefs in the spandrels, and lion's head gargoyles along the cornice. They are similar to those on the Museums Building and created by sculptor Ulysses Ricci whose initials are carved into the mermen panels. He also sculpted the medallions on the Hatcher Library, the corbel figures in the Law Quad, and the bas-reliefs on Angell Hall.

The building became the third of the medical buildings on Central Campus (the second is now the Dana School of Natural Resources, see #208). It was used as the main teaching unit of the Medical School until the 1950s when the school moved closer to the University Hospital on Observatory. It was one of the many buildings that went up during the short presidency of President Burton. It was renamed in 1968 for Clarence Cook Little, University president from 1925–1929.

CCHD

235 815 S. University
University of Michigan President's House
1840/1864/1891/1920/1933

It is unusual for a university president to live directly on campus, but the University of Michigan's presidents have kept this tradition since the original house was completed in 1840. It is a stucco-over-brick house scored to resemble stone, and was one of four houses constructed for faculty when the university opened in 1841. When Henry Philip Tappan became the first president of the University in 1852, it became the President's House. During the 1860s, Italianate features were added, including a truncated hipped roof with double brackets under the eaves, and a balustrade which replaced the original cupola. Still remaining from the original house are four chimneys and the Doric columns and entablature at the entry. As part of a remodeling in 1871, and at the insistence of incoming President James B. Angell, indoor plumbing and a hot air furnace were installed.

At the beginning, the presidency at the U-M revolved among faculty members representing different religious affiliations. Much bickering ensued and it was decided to have a permanent president. The first was Henry Philip Tappan in 1852. He was ousted in 1863 by the Regents with the help of assorted faculty and the *Detroit Free Press,* due to politics and personal issues with Tappan's lifestyle (he drank wine with dinner!).

Under the third president, James Burrill Angell (1871–1909), a library wing was added on the west side. A sun porch, garage, and bigger kitchen were completed in 1920 for the fifth president, Marion Leroy Burton, and in 1933 a study was added for the seventh president, Alexander Grant Ruthven. The building still serves as the official residence of the president and is the oldest building on campus.

NR, CCHD

855 S. University
Tappan Hall

236

1893

This red brick and fieldstone building in the Romanesque style was designed by the Detroit firm of Spier and Rohns (see #137, #155, #208, and #219,) and was built in 1893. It is now the oldest classroom building on campus. It was designed originally for "recitation" and named in honor of the University of Michigan's first president, Henry Philip Tappan. It has had many uses over the years, but since 1948 it has been the home of the History of Art Department. In 1985, a sympathetic modern addition, designed by Luckenbach/Ziegelman, was added to the south.

The building has an above-ground fieldstone first floor, topped by two floors of unpainted red brick with an asymmetrical arrangement of windows varying by floor. The arched entry, in the Romanesque style with stone bases carved with vines, opens onto an outer staircase leading to a foyer facing a beautiful wooden stair. The red tile roof is hipped with dormers topped by finials, and two pairs of chimneys are at each end. Inside are classrooms, study rooms, a fine arts library, and in the lobby, a bronze bas-relief of Tappan by Karl Bitter.

CCHD

237 906 S. University
Martha Cook Building   1914

Considered one of the most beautiful buildings on campus, the Martha Cook Building was part of a large gift from alumnus William W. Cook ('82) who named it after his mother. Cook's future gifts included the Law Quadrangle that was built in the 1920s and 1930s. Cook never saw any of the finished products.

Cook, a resident of New York, hired the New York architectural firm of York and Sawyer to design the building in an English Gothic style with some Renaissance touches. It is of red brick with stone quoins around the leaded glass windows. An elaborate Gothic doorway is surrounded by carved stonework, and a statue of Portia, the heroine of Shakespeare's *Merchant of Venice*, stands in a carved niche above the door. A large garden on the east, surrounded by a decorative iron fence, completes the picture.

The interior is paneled in oak, with wondrous plaster ceilings in the large spaces on the main floor, which are patterned after English buildings. The Red Room is a copy of Castleton Manor House (1603) and has a "wagon head" ceiling, while the Gold Room has original castings from the ceiling of Sir Paul Pindar's house (16th century). Remaining from the original interior are Flemish tapestries, Jacobean furniture, Ming vases, and a replica of the Venus de Milo.

Residents of the residence hall (still all-female) refer to themselves as "Cookies" and are protective of their building and their old-fashioned traditions. They have formal teas and special dinners for events such as the singing of the "Messiah" and are required to dress accordingly.

CCHD

909 S. University
William L. Clements Library
238

1923

The Clements Library was a gift to the University from William L. Clements, a native of Ann Arbor (born on State Street just south of where the Michigan Union now stands), businessman from Bay City, alumnus, and Regent of the University. Clements had an immense collection of Americana (primarily on the discovery of America and the American Revolution) and instructed Detroit architect Albert Kahn to design the building as a "… library for advanced research…for scholars already well equipped rather than a library…not for undergraduates or the ordinary graduate student." Clements also chose the first director, Randolph Greenfield Adams, who served for 28 years.

This limestone building with its triple-arched entry is in the Italian Renaissance style and modeled after the 1587 Villa Farnese in Italy. Kahn said it was his favorite building. The exterior has relief sculptures of angels holding a panel bearing the name of Clements and quotations from University of Michigan Professor Ulrich Phillips.

The interior is gorgeously decorated in gilt, carved wood, and painted plaster full of neo-classical details. It has a vaulted ceiling over the main reading room, painted by Thomas DiLorenzo of New York City and restored in 2004. The reading room also has symmetrical alcoves and oak-paneled bookcases lining the walls. Persian rugs, chandeliers, and period furniture complete the scene of a "gentleman's library." One of its most valuable assets, Benjamin West's 1770 painting of "The Death of General Wolfe," hangs on the wall near the entry. The building was constructed like a bank vault with reinforced concrete behind the exterior stone skin. A major renovation, begun in 2013, closed the building and moved the collections offsite.

CCHD

239 1085 S. University
West Engineering/West Hall   1904/1910

This is Detroit architect Albert Kahn's first building on the U-M campus and was designed with George DeWitt Mason, another well-known Detroit architect. It has been a landmark for over 100 years and students entering the campus from the east must walk through its archway (the "Engine Arch"). The building was constructed with the most modern technical advances of the time, including an iron frame and poured concrete floors. The L-shaped building is decorated with copper cupolas and a red-tiled hipped roof over the entry with smaller tiled dormers on the two extensions. It is in the Arts and Crafts style with period additions from 1910. Kahn was a pioneer of American industrial architecture and this is one of the first examples in his long career.

The Engineering School moved to North Campus in the 1980s. The building now houses the Department of Anthropology and others in the College of LS&A, but still has a naval tank used by the Naval Architecture and Marine Engineering Department.

CCHD

1402 Washington Heights
Observatory Lodge
240

1930

This brick, stone, slate, and half-timber former apartment building is a tour de force of the Tudor Revival style. Steeply pitched slate roofs with asymmetrical angles cover a busy array of half-timber wood trim, copper eaves, and oriel, bay, and casement windows. Pewabic tiles are interspersed throughout the entry, which leads into a beautiful foyer with art tile floors, stucco walls with raised symbolic designs, a fireplace, a stairway with twisted iron railings, multi-paned and multicolored stained glass windows, and gargoyles near the ceiling. One of the few apartment buildings near the hospital, it was perfect for medical personnel who walked to work.

The University purchased the building in 1966 and maintained the apartments until 2001. In 2005 a complete restoration of the building for the Kinesiology Department was begun. New windows mimicking the old multi-paned ones were installed and many of the original details were refurbished. The University also repaired the slate roof, replicated the old sign, and restored the squirrel weather vane. In 2008, the building received a Rehabilitation Award from the Ann Arbor Historic District Commission.

241 1610 Washington Heights
Nathan Burnham House   1837

This center-entry, Colonial-style brick house has a symmetrical facade and a Palladian window over the porticoed entry, and is one of the rare surviving houses dating to the 1830s in Ann Arbor. It is believed to have been a speculative house built at 947 Wall Street by Nathan Burnham for Caleb Ormsby (see #17) during the fevered building boom (see #16) that accompanied the development of the neighborhood across the Huron River known as "Lower Town."

The house has a Georgian floor plan with a central hallway and four rooms on each floor. It sits on a high brick foundation with two fireplaces at each end. The beautiful entry is a fine example of the carpenter's craft, with carved pilasters and intricately mullioned sidelights. The doorway was salvaged in 1969 by Dr. Mark Hildebrandt from a nearby house being demolished on Broadway. His architect designed the portico with the Ionic columns. In the rear was a cobblestone smokehouse with brick quoins that Hildebrandt also preserved. Later this building became the office of Dr. Edward Pierce, a well-known health activist, who served as mayor of Ann Arbor (1985–1987).

In the 1990s, the U-M began to demolish houses on Wall Street for a parking structure, and this house was moved to its current location. A few others were also moved (see #190). The Burnham House is now the Reader Center at the U-M Arboretum, with a beautifully landscaped garden in the shade of trees from nearby Forest Hill Cemetery. The move in 1998 was noted as the "Preservation Project of the Year" by the Historic District Commission in 2000.

Former IHP

915 E. Washington

242

Horace H. Rackham School of Graduate Studies   1938

The Rackham building was a gift to the University and dedicated in 1938 to be a school of graduate studies. Thirty buildings were removed, as well as graves from the first Jewish cemetery in Michigan. It was designed by the Detroit firm of Smith, Hinchman and Grylls in an Art Deco interpretation of Classical design.

Constructed of Indiana limestone, it has two bas-reliefs by sculptor Corrado Parducci representing fine arts and museums in the flattened Egyptian Deco style, and five figures representing the social sciences, physical sciences, languages, literature, and biological sciences. Three massive pairs of bronze and glass doors lead to the foyer, which has walls painted Pompeian red with blue-green and gold stenciling on the ceiling. The adjoining performance space is also in Pompeian red with stenciling in polychrome and gold using an Egyptian Deco motif of overlapping bands in a radiating circle, and a lapis lazuli blue ceiling twinkling with gold stars. On the second floor is a magnificent reading room flanked on either side by study rooms graced with period furniture ranging from Duncan Phyfe to Chippendale and Queen Anne.

It was designed to define the north end of the space known as the Ingalls Mall and faces the Harlan Hatcher Graduate Library. The Graduate School celebrated its centennial in 2012.

CCHD

OLD WEST SIDE/ FAR WEST

I n 1972, the Old West Side became one of the first neighborhoods of primarily Vernacular late 19th- and early 20th-century buildings to be listed on the National Register of
Historic Places. Its houses are generally small to medium sized, with gable fronts facing
the streets. Victorian and Craftsman-style front porches grace most of the buildings, creating a particularly inviting streetscape. The neighborhood began in 1848, when the area was
subdivided, and quickly became the home of Ann Arbor's growing German population
who began settling in Washtenaw County in the late 1820s. Surprisingly, very little German
influence is found in the neighborhood's architecture beyond the solid, simple, and Vernacular character of the buildings. The earliest German immigrants quickly adopted the

prevailing architectural tastes of their Yankee neighbors, with many simple Greek Revivals being built prior to the Civil War (see #244, #266, and #281). The tiny cabin built around 1850 by William and Katherine Kuhn (see #269) is a rare survivor of the early, often one- or two-room homes built in Ann Arbor. Along W. Liberty and W. Huron, the architecture is more pretentious, with grand examples of the Greek Revival (see #275), Italianate (see #272), Gothic Revival (see #255), Second Empire (see #263), and Queen Anne (see #254) style homes built during the Victorian period.

Despite the presence of many high-style buildings, the dominant form of building in the Old West Side remains the Vernacular, gable-front homes that were built by working-class laborers between 1870 and 1920 (see #277, #283, and #284). In addition to the modest working-class homes, a number of large factories were built in the neighborhood (see #247, #249, and #250). Following the first World War, the neighborhood expanded to the west with many fine examples of the Craftsman, Tudor Revival, Colonial Revival, and modern styles being built in the neighborhoods around Virginia Park, Eberwhite School, Wildwood Park (see #276), and Wurster Park (see #278 and #285).

243 416 S. Ashley Street
Toledo, Ann Arbor, and
Northern Michigan Railway Depot
1889

This passenger depot for the Toledo, Ann Arbor, and Northern Michigan Railway is one of the few remnants of Ann Arbor's second railroad, which began in 1878 and ran from Toledo, Ohio to Frankfort, Michigan, where car ferries took passengers to Wisconsin. The railroad was organized by James Ashley (after whom Ashley Street is named), an energetic politician and astute businessman originally from Toledo. Affectionately known as the "Annie" when it became the Ann Arbor Railroad in 1895, this line also served to take families north to resorts at Zukey Lake and Whitmore Lake. Passenger service ended in 1950 and car service ended in 1982. The tracks that snake through town are now owned by the Tuscola and Saginaw Bay Railroad. Freight trains still come through town at night and their mournful whistles are heard and appreciated by many.

The building is a typical depot of the period, consisting of a clapboard structure with a long hipped roof forming a wide overhang supported by ornamental wooden brackets. Both interior and exterior have been remarkably preserved, including the original waiting room with its 15-foot ceilings and tiers of wall paneling. Deeply incised metal brackets accent the fireplace, and carved floral designs grace the wooden archways into the room. After uses as a restaurant, antique store, and music venue, it was purchased by the Law Montessori School and restored in 1985. Since 1987, it has been the home of the Doughty (or Doughty-Law) Montessori School. Lynn Law and James Marron received a Preservation Award from the Historic District Commission in 1988.

SR, Former IHP

1500 Dexter
Baldwin-Heimerdinger House

244

1850

This tiny (only 866 square feet) 1½-story Greek Revival was noticed by Professor Emil Lorch and drawn for the Historic American Buildings Survey (HABS)—a WPA project—in 1933. These drawings are at the Library of Congress in Washington, D.C. (labeled as the Covert House). It is a simple, wooden L-shaped clapboard structure, with two windows flanking a central doorway and a lean-to in the rear. The original windows have been replaced with inappropriate vinyl windows. The portico in the front, with turned posts and spindle work in the upper section, was added in the late 19th century. Its location at the fork of Jackson and Dexter Roads makes it a highly visible landmark in Ann Arbor.

The house is said to have been built with 12-by-12 timbers and has stone walls in the basement. It was built by carpenter Norman B. Covert for Eunice Baldwin, the mother of his new bride, on an 80-acre farm, then in the countryside. Covert's property was separated from the Baldwin estate by what is now Revena Boulevard (created in 1918). Lots sold off in the 20th century are filled with over 300 homes in the former backyard.

Baldwin died in 1868, and her children inherited her estate. Andrew Heimerdinger acquired the property in 1887 and it remained in his family for four generations until 1994. The 1891 biography of Norman Covert mentions that his wife taught two of the Heimerdinger children how to read English.

Former IHP

245 1730 Dexter
Schaffer Family House

1890s

It is believed that John L. Schaffer built this house shortly after his father's death in 1891. Schaffer's father was German pioneer John Jacob Schaffer, who owned farmland along Jackson and Dexter Roads. John L. Schaffer, brother Jacob, and sister Caroline farmed the surrounding land, specializing in growing fruit, which was common on the farms near downtown Ann Arbor. John and Caroline never married, and Jacob was a widower. Caroline and John L. died in 1912. Jacob continued to live at the house and was joined by his sister Maria Allmendinger, her husband Harvey, and their children. By 1915, the family's farmland had been sold off for development. Harvey Allmendinger died about 1921, and Marie and her daughters Edith and May continued to live in the house until 1929.

Hidden behind towering spruce trees, the house is a great example of a Vernacular take on the Queen Anne style. The hipped roof is flat on top, and featured a balustrade, long since removed. The home also features small Gothic-inspired peaks on the front and back of the house, as well as decorative brickwork. Windows of varying sizes dot the brick facade, including a miniature, arched, double-hung window that is centered in the front of the first story. The large wraparound porch features simple square columns with curved tops.

2961 Dexter
Frederick Kuehnle House

246

c. 1832–37

It is unclear exactly when this house was built. It could have been built by Jacob Steffy as early as 1832. The house is an interesting variation of the Greek Revival style and shows the adaptability of the style in the hands of local carpenters. Hipped roofs were not common in early Greek Revivals of the area, though the frieze band with narrow windows, six-over-six windows, an entry with sidelights, and a simple entablature are all hallmarks of the style. The uniqueness of the house led Emil Lorch to draw the property for the Historic American Buildings Survey in 1936.

Frederick Kuehnle bought the property in 1837. He was one of the early German pioneers in Washtenaw County and farmed both sides of Dexter Road with his sons Israel and Emmanuel until his death in 1875 at the age of 89. His son Israel had a large vineyard on the property, and had a successful career as a vintner and wine merchant. In the *Ann Arbor Argus* in 1888, he advertised "Pure Native Wines grown and prepared at the vineyard of Israel Kuehnle 1¾ miles west of Ann Arbor." The Kuehnle family continued to live in the house until 1927. Kuehnle Street perpetuates their name. Current owners Mr. and Mrs. William Kuhn received a Preservation Award from the Historic District Commission in 1996 to recognize their 40 years of stewardship.

Former IHP

247 315 S. First
King-Seeley Factory
1928/1939

Allen Creek and its tributaries, which once ran roughly along the railroad tracks between Ashley and Third (now in an underground pipe), was the center of a large amount of Ann Arbor's early industry. Machine shops, foundries, and tanneries used the creek's water in their operations. Henry Krause opened a tannery here in 1850, which was expanded in 1868 into a large 30-by-120 foot brick building.

In 1925, the old Krause Tannery became the home of King-Seeley Company, which used the facility to manufacture gas gauges. King-Seeley was founded by University of Michigan Civil Engineering Professor Horace King and auto parts entrepreneur Hal Seeley in 1919. King invented the first practical dashboard-mounted gas gauge for automobiles, and by 1922 the company was ready for production. The Krause Tannery building soon proved insufficient, so the company built a four-story reinforced concrete addition in 1928, seen today in the northernmost portion of the four-story building. Demand for the gas gauges grew and in 1939 the company added on toward William Street and built the large greenhouse addition on the north side. The factory was sold to Chrysler in 1968 and by 1982 it was owned by G.T. Products. From 1998–2003 Eaton Corporation used the building before moving operations to Mexico.

Not empty for long, the property was purchased two years after Eaton shuttered the facility by the Morningside Group, which redeveloped and restored the old factory as Liberty Lofts Condominiums. The greenhouse was restored for commercial space now occupied by the U-M Taubman College of Architecture and Urban Planning. Unfortunately, the 1868 Krause Tannery building could not be saved and was demolished, with the new western wing of Liberty Lofts built on the same footprint. The owners received an Adaptive Reuse Award from the Historic District Commission for this project in 2007.

OWSHD

632 S. First
Raab-Harlacher House

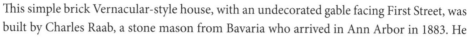

248

1885–1887

This simple brick Vernacular-style house, with an undecorated gable facing First Street, was built by Charles Raab, a stone mason from Bavaria who arrived in Ann Arbor in 1883. He

built it with the help of his wife and children and moved in when it was half-finished. A common shape in the Old West Side Historic District, it consists of two stories, with three bays on the first floor and two bays on the second, and an oculus window in the attic. A porch was added in the early 20th century. It is unusual because it is an un-remodeled version of the type and has its original shutters.

The Raab family occupied this house when their youngest daughter Matilda married William Harlacher in 1915. Matilda Harlacher still occupied the house in 1977 when the first edition of *Historic Buildings, Ann Arbor, Michigan* was published, and said the house was unchanged from her childhood except for the addition of indoor plumbing.

The house received a historic plaque from the Ann Arbor Sesquicentennial Committee in 1976.

OWSHD

249 400 Fourth

Argus Optical Manufacturing Building/
Argus II Building   1941/1944

The Argus Camera Company was founded in Ann Arbor in 1936 by Charles Verschoor and was known for its small, personal cameras (see #250). In 1941, with World War II raging around the world, Argus Camera won massive defense contracts which led to the construction of this building for defense-related orders.

Originally only one story, the building was designed by Ann Arbor architects Fry and Kasurin (see #317) and was finished and ready for production in April of 1942. In 1944, a second story was added to the building to provide space for the engineering department. The slight variation in the brick color from the two phases of construction is still visible. It was built with continuous banks of steel casement windows on the front elevation to make it easier to observe blackout conditions and it was outfitted with special air-filtration and air-conditioning systems to ensure proper air quality in the manufacturing areas. Another addition was added to the second floor in 1953. This otherwise spare industrial building features a large, simplified Art Moderne entrance with stepped brickwork, limestone pilasters, and a simple door canopy. The corners on the front facade are curved, with banks of windows that wrap around the building, another trademark of the Art Moderne style.

When the Argus Camera Company was bought out in 1963, the building was sold to the University of Michigan.

OWSHD

405 Fourth (525 W. William)
Keck Furniture Company/Argus Building   1868/1884

250

This group of three- and four-story red brick factory buildings was constructed in phases by John Keck, beginning in 1868, for the manufacture of furniture. Situated in the heart of the Old West Side Historic District, it reminds us of the 19th-century lifestyle of the German immigrant who walked to work. Keck began in a wooden building at the corner of William and Fourth (this portion is now brick-veneered) and was so successful he added a three-story brick portion in 1881 after he formed a stock company. In 1884, a four-story portion along William was built for the newly named Michigan Furniture Company.

Keck was an immigrant from Swabia, who apprenticed to Florian Muehlig in furniture and coffin making, striking out on his own in 1868 with three brothers. The rapid growth of the business was due to two things: a new technology—the steam engine, which replaced water-driven power—and a new market in the emerging middle class after the Civil War. As early as 1869 Keck also had a salesroom on Main Street selling furniture (bedroom and parlor suites), carpets, and curtains. He went bankrupt in 1886 and moved to Grand Rapids to work for the Berkey and Gay Furniture Company, whose records at the Grand Rapids Public Museum contain his drawings. He died there in 1908 and is buried in Ann Arbor at Forest Hill Cemetery.

The Michigan Furniture Company continued here until 1929, and in 1931 the building became the home of Charles Verschoor's Kadette tabletop radio company. Later he manufactured the Argus Camera and renamed the company (see #249). Argus received many contracts during World War II but after the war they were unable to compete with Japan and Germany. The University of Michigan purchased the building in 1963 and it has been called the Argus Building ever since.

The University sold the building in 1983 to C-3 Partners (Joe O'Neal and Bill Martin), who restored the building to be the headquarters of O'Neal Construction. They received a Rehabilitation Award from the Historic District Commission in 1993. O'Neal and Martin maintained an Argus Museum in the building with Argus cameras, memorabilia, and Keck Furniture Company artifacts which were transferred to the Washtenaw County Historical Society in 2013.

251 449 Fourth
Reuben and Emily Armbruster House   1892

Reuben and Emily Armbruster built this fine Queen Anne house in 1892. More elaborate than many of its Old West Side neighbors, the Armbruster house exhibits all of the characteristics of a classic Queen Anne: a hipped roof with front and back cross gables, a two-tiered porch with elaborate turned columns and spindles, windows of different sizes and pane configurations, and patterned shingle work in the front gable. The fine details of the house are likely due to its first owner, carpenter Reuben Armbruster. Armbruster and his wife Emily (Weitbrecht) were both natives of Washtenaw County and the children of German immigrants. He worked as a carpenter in Scio Township and Ann Arbor and then was a patrolman in the Ann Arbor Police Department from 1895 through about 1920, when he went to work at the Hoover Steel Ball Company. Descendants of the Armbrusters remained in the home until 1950. The current owners have done a wonderful job maintaining the beautiful home.

OWSHD

709 W. Huron
John N. Gott House

1861

This Italianate brick mansion with the characteristic cube shape (a widow's walk was removed in the 1950s), bracketed eaves, shutters, cast-iron grilles (see #53), and portico with grouped columns, was begun in the 1850s by William C. Voorheis and finished by his attorney, John N. Gott. Gott, a prominent lawyer and member of an early pioneer family, lived here for 30 years. In 1890, he sold it to Dr. William J. Herdman, a local physician and University of Michigan professor, who converted it to a hospital. Later the hospital was run by Dr. William Koch.

In 1941, Eugene Hannah and his wife purchased the place from Koch, converted it to lodgings for women, and named it the "Martha Washington House." In 1955, it was purchased by Jack and Marjorie Craven who kept it as a rooming house for working women. By 1960, it was listed as having 11 apartments. It was converted back to single-family use by Donald and Lorraine Haugen in 1971. In 1980 it was sold by the Haugens to Donald Shelton of the Bishop and Shelton Law Firm—back to its original roots in a sense. Shelton, his wife Marge, and others began the huge task of restoring the house, from the doorknobs to the wood floors. They even insisted that new electrical wiring be hidden within the walls. For this restoration, they received an award from the Historic District Commission in 1984.

NR, OWSHD

253 844 W. Huron
W.H. Mallory House 1872

This Old West Side landmark at the busy intersection of Huron and Seventh Streets is the fine work of William H. Mallory who built the house in 1872. The elaborate details, fine carpentry, and complicated design of the house reflect Mallory's profession as a carpenter and builder, and also his owner-ship of a wood planing mill that specialized in sashes, shutters, doors, and "gingerbread."

Mallory did not hold back when he constructed the house with its steep Gothic Revival gable front, double cross gables, and smaller back wing. The gables feature one of the earliest exam-ples of an "oculus" window in Ann Arbor. Two bay windows are highlighted by mansard roofs, Italianate brackets, and tall, narrow windows with rounded top sashes. The two porches feature similar mansard roofs and brackets, in addition to delicate jig-sawn spindle work. The tall windows all fea-ture rounded top sashes and fine eared trim with elaborate scroll details. Mallory built many of Ann Arbor's great buildings of the Victorian period, including Dr. Chase's Steam Printing House (see #90) and what was originally a twin of this house, located kitty-corner at 903 W. Huron.

The house has served as a rental for most of its history and was neglected until the 1970s. The large Victorian-style lamp posts date from the 1890s and were moved from their origi-nal location on Belle Isle in Detroit and installed during the 1970s restoration of the house.

OWSHD

921 W. Huron
Martin and Helene Noll House

1888

Martin Noll and his wife Helene built this clapboard house using the proceeds of a German lottery ticket shared with John Haarer (see #82). Noll, an immigrant shoemaker from Germany, built this fine example of the Queen Anne style in 1888. It shows the characteristic features of the early Queen Anne: multiple and inter-secting gables, symmetrically arranged windows, and a few embellishments such as the half-round windows with keystones, bay window, fish-scale shingles in the gable, and a porch with turned spindles, gingerbread decoration, and a Chinese Chippendale railing. After Martin died in 1890, Mrs. Noll occupied the house with her children until 1911. The Sherk family owned it from 1913 until 1975, when they sold it to Barbara White and Richard Green who undertook a massive renovation.

Green and White restored the house inside and out and landscaped it with period gardens. They used a three-color paint scheme typical for the 1880s, repaired the shutters and their hinges, and re-milled elements when necessary. Original interiors were refurbished as well. In 1985 they received a Rehabilitation Award from the Ann Arbor Historic District Commission. White helped organize the Old West Side Association and served as its president for several years.

OWSHD

255 | 1020 W. Huron
Wheeler-Breed House
1859

This Gothic Revival stucco-over-brick home was designed by English architect Gordon Lloyd the year after he arrived in Detroit (see also #145, #149, and #173). It was built in 1859 by John M. Wheeler, a lawyer from Indiana by way of upstate New York. It has the long and narrow double-hung windows (which once had shutters), and the steep gables with bargeboards characteristic of the style. Old photographs show it was more elaborate at one point and had wooden porches with lavishly carved Gothic arches on slender columns on both the east and west sides of the main house. Famed architectural historian Fiske Kimball noted in 1919 that it was a "Victorian estate in its perfection with a Gothic cottage nestling among trees, the long terraces of garden roses…a brook meandering through the meadow with willows and a rustic spring reached by winding paths." It had a beautiful picket fence and a windmill nearby that was torn down in 1940.

Wheeler arrived in Ann Arbor in 1858, and established a legal practice and a reputation as a prudent financier. He was active with the First National Bank and was treasurer of the University of Michigan from 1872–1878. He was active until his death in St. Andrew's Episcopal Church and served on the Ann Arbor School Board from 1859–1871. The house later became the property of Catherine Breed, a descendant of Wheeler.

It has been featured in many architecture books as a fine example of the Gothic Revival. U-M Architecture Professor Emil Lorch noted in 1935 that it had been remodeled by U-M Architecture Professor Louis Boynton around 1900. In the 1930s, it was divided into apartments.

OWSHD

1203 W. Huron
Traver-Bycraft House

256

1870

This home is often called the "Icicle House" after its icicle-like bargeboards, which are thought to be the only surviving examples in Washtenaw County. The house shows the great adaptability of the front-gabled Folk house form that was popular in Ann Arbor from 1865–1920. It features multiple architectural influences, from the Gothic Revival bargeboards and fascia, to the original Italianate front door and four-over-four windows. There are remnants of the earlier Greek Revival style in the door surround and "eared" window trim. The Colonial Revival porch dates to the early 1900s, when similar porches were added to many 19th-century houses in the city.

The house was built in 1870 by Jane Traver, the daughter of Ann Arbor pioneer Absalom Traver (see #8). Traver only lived in the house until 1873 when it was sold to Civil War veteran Edward Bycraft and his wife Harriet (Marsh). Shortly after the Bycrafts bought the house, Edward and three other relatives were charged with the murder of Martin Briettenbach. Briettenbach was hit in the head with a rock by 14-year-old Ezra Marsh in what may have been self-defense after Briettenbach had shot at the men. Bycraft and two other family members were fined and Ezra Marsh spent one year in prison. Harriet Bycraft, after divorcing Edward, continued to reside in the house with her children until her death in 1909. It passed to her son Edward and his wife Mary, who lived here and ran a farm outside the city.

OWSHD

257 1217 W. Huron
Seth and Frances Otis House   1870

This fine Italianate residence was built in 1870 as the retirement home of Major Seth T. Otis and his wife Frances, the daughter of Hon. Charles H. Kellogg (see #190). Otis, according to a family history, "retired from business and bought a country place of twelve acres just outside the west city limits of Ann Arbor, Michigan. Here he passed his last days playing at farming while his youngest son attended the schools and State University. Here also he died…he and his wife are buried…on a knoll in the beautiful cemetery overlooking the charming valley of the Huron River [Fair View]." Prior to his life in Ann Arbor, Otis made a name for himself in Chicago and New York. He served as director of the Chicago Branch of the Illinois State Bank and founded the Young Men's Association, which later became the Chicago Public Library. He was appointed by President Tyler to be the United States consul in Basel, Switzerland and served from 1844–1846.

The home he built in 1870 is one of Ann Arbor's finest wood-clad Italianates. The house sports tall four-over-four windows topped with decorative milled pediments, and a cornice with an unusual curved frieze board that highlights the paired brackets and dentils. Otis lived in the house until his death in 1882.

The family sold the farm to Rev. Samuel H. Adams in 1884. In 1887, when it was incorporated into the city of Ann Arbor, it was purchased by Benjamin and Mary Crookston who lived here into the 20th century. Crookston was president of the Peninsular Soap Co. In 1912 the farm was subdivided into the Huron Crest Subdivision. The first gathering of the re-organized (Quaker) Ann Arbor Friends Meeting took place in this house in 1935 when it was the home of Esther and Arthur Dunham. It was divided into apartments after World War II. Avalon Housing, which restored and maintains it as affordable housing, received an Historic District Commission award for their restoration work in 2000.

OWSHD

298

1319 W. Huron

258

John A. and Fredericka Wedemeyer House   1887

The Wedemeyer house is a spectacular example of the type of Vernacular houses German immigrants were building on the Old West Side in the 1880s and 1890s. The only hints of

any particular architectural style are the Queen Anne cross gable and the arched Italianate two-over-two windows. The front doors are not original nor is the tasteful Italianate portico which was taken from another house in the area. It may have originally had a small wraparound porch. The small oculus window in the front gable was another popular feature of Old West Side buildings between 1870 and 1890.

The house was built by John A. Wedemeyer and his wife Fredericka (Rehfuss), both natives of Germany. John and Fredericka bought this property in 1887 from the estate of Seth Otis (see #257). The Wedemeyers operated a small farm on the property and on a lot they owned across the street. Mr. Wedemeyer also worked as a wagon maker in town. John Wedemeyer died in 1909 and Fredericka continued to live in the house until her death in 1915. It was the home of realtors Mary Stuhrberg and her son Carl from 1919 into the 1950s. In the 1960s, it housed apartments but was converted back to single-family use in the 1990s. Owner Scott Koll received an award for his restoration of the property in 1996.

OWSHD

259 420 W. Jefferson
John Frederick Schaeberle House   1895

This wonderful example of the carpenter's art appears first in the *City Directory* of 1895 as #30, occupied by William Stoll, a clerk at Staebler's Grocery. By 1897, however, it was the home of John Frederick Schaeberle, and it remained in his family until the 1930s. The house is a typical turn-of-the-century Queen Anne wooden structure, notable for its ornamental porch, intersecting gables with cut bargeboards, and decorative fish-scale shingles in alternating squares in the front gable. It has the original porch with turned posts and spindles in both the balustrade and the upper portion. The house has an unusual four-car garage that probably dates to the 1940s when the house was converted to four apartments.

The Schaeberle family came to Ann Arbor from Germany in 1843 when John Frederick was nine. They were saddlers and harness makers. One son went on to become a famous professor of astronomy at the Lick Observatory in California and John Frederick opened a fine music store at 114 W. Liberty, which moved to 110 S. Main in 1907.

OWSHD

520 W. Jefferson
First German Methodist Church

260

1896

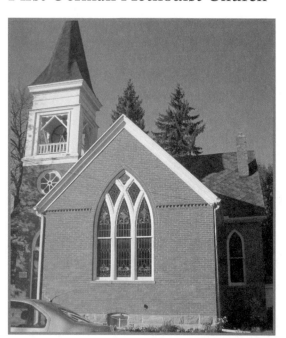

This charming small brick church, with a wooden bell tower at the crook of the "L" shape, was built in 1896 for the German Methodists, a small group amongst the mostly Lutheran Germans who lived in this neighborhood. They were a German-speaking church and wanted to separate themselves from the other Methodists in town. Later, after services changed to English, it changed its name to West Side Methodist Church. When this congregation moved to larger quarters on Seventh Street in 1951, they sold it to the Reorganized Church of Latter Day Saints. It continues almost unchanged in appearance save for a handicap ramp.

It has a simplified Gothic Revival style with the characteristic pointed arch on the large stained glass windows and the entry doors. It was the second building for the German Methodists, who built their first church in 1847 at Liberty and Division. It was then known by its German name, Die Erste Deutsche Methodisten Kirche.

OWSHD

261 609 W. Jefferson
Schneeberger's Grocery Building 1920

In the 19th and early 20th century, when home refrigeration was unknown and the automobile was rare, neighborhood markets such as this were common, as shopping was done daily and within walking distance. This restrained brick commercial building was erected in 1920 by Swiss native Ernest Schneeberger Sr. and his wife Elizabeth, who lived in the back of the building. The building did not extend all the way to the sidewalk at first, but was bumped out early in its history.

Ernest Schneeberger worked at the Ann Arbor post office while Elizabeth ran the market. Schneeberger's carried a large variety of staple goods, and were known for their fresh meats and sausages, cut by butcher Emil Frey. Schneeberger died in 1934, and the family kept the store open until 1940 when it was sold to Gene Towner, later the owner of the renowned Big Ten Party Store on Packard. John Komosinski ran the market as a convenience store for Towner until 1981, selling candy and beer.

It continued in this vein until 2000, when the building was restored and revitalized as the Jefferson Market, serving homemade sandwiches and baked goods, as well as candy and refreshments. Now known as the Jefferson Market and Cakery, it is a focal point of the Old West Side neighborhood.

OWSHD

112 Koch
William A. and Catherine Benedict House   Late 1850s

262

This well-preserved Greek Revival looks quite out of place on a street filled with 1910s and '20s Folk houses, bungalows, and colonials. The home was moved to the site by brothers John and Christian Koch, who subdivided the neighborhood as the John Koch Subdivision in 1914. The home originally stood on the west side of S. Main Street, where Koch Street ends. Christian Koch lived in the home for a number of years beginning in 1905 before moving the home onto the newly platted lot 4 of the Koch Subdivision. John and Christian Koch, natives of Wurttemberg, Germany, were the owners of the Koch Brothers Construction Company, which built many of Ann Arbor's landmark buildings of the late 19th and early 20th century (see #12, #51, #55, #122, #155, #301, and #351).

The home was built in the late 1850s by farmer, businessman, and real estate speculator William A. Benedict and his wife Catherine. Benedict was co-founder and director of the brief and unsuccessful Mozart Watch Company, which was founded by the mad-genius watchmaker Don J. Mozart. Mozart watches are among the most unusual and rarest watches ever made in the United States. The Benedicts lived in the house until the late 1860s, when it became the home of Delevan and Fannie (Nash) Doane and their children. Delevan Doane was a retired farmer from the Dexter area, who later moved to El Paso, Texas in the early 1880s where he was in the cattle and dairy business. The home stood vacant for a number of years, and had a series of revolving tenants until Christian Koch's purchase in 1905.

The home is a rare form of the Greek Revival style in Ann Arbor, with a front porch that wraps around three sides of the building, as in the J.S. Henderson farmhouse (see #329). The cornice and broken pediment are particularly muscular, as are the corner pilasters. The home features a fine classical entrance and sidelights, as well as two sets of French doors that exit onto the large front porch. William A. Benedict was proud enough of his large Greek Revival home to have it prominently featured on the 1866 Birdseye Map of the City of Ann Arbor.

OWSHD

263 326 W. Liberty
Peter Brehm House   1870

The steep mansard roof, with flares at the corners that resemble East Asian architecture, sets off this Second Empire house built in 1870 for Peter Brehm. He was the owner of the nearby Western Brewery and probably chose this style to advertise his success in business and in America. It is rare, since most of Ann Arbor's Second Empire-style houses have been demolished. This very solid brick house features other aspects of the style, including brackets under the eaves, a bay window, and heavy hoods over all of the windows. The 1870s witnessed a post-Civil War building boom that abruptly ended in the Panic of 1873.

Brehm founded the Western Brewery in 1861, the year he arrived in Ann Arbor. By the 1880s, under different ownership it was the largest brewery in town. Wealthy from his beer

business, Brehm demolished another home on this site to build his. He committed suicide in the wake of his business failures in 1873. His wife and son continued living here until 1896. It became the property of the Arnold family, well-known jewelers in town, who used it for a summer residence.

Later occupiers of the building included the IOOF, or Odd Fellows, after 1952, and the Moveable Feast restaurant in the 1980s and '90s. The restaurant showcased a major restoration of the interior, which included repairing the interior shutters. It has seen a number of uses since 2000, and at this time the building is undergoing a major restoration, including a replication of the front porch and long-missing Italianate brackets.

OWSHD

408 W. Liberty
Albert Mann House

1891

Built at the height of the Queen Anne period, this brick version has unusual features such as a second-story porch complete with original posts and balusters, and a conical tower atop a two-story round brick base. It has an irregular and steeply pitched roof and projecting bays on both sides of the house. The original double entrance doors with stained glass remain, as do the sunbursts on the gables.

This area was subdivided from the David Lord estate in the 1880s and pharmacists Albert and Henry Mann purchased it in 1891 from the builder John Koch. Albert's family occupied the "castle" for more than 40 years. The Mann family were early German pioneers, arriving in the 1830s. Albert's father Emmanuel went into the drug business with Christian Eberbach (see #325) and later opened his own shop which Albert continued to run. Descendants of the Mann family lived here until the 1940s. In 1958 the house was converted to four apartments, which have been kept in fine condition by the Wessinger family who has owned it for many decades.

OWSHD

265 420 W. Liberty
St. Paul's Lutheran Church   1928

St. Paul's Lutheran Church was founded in 1906 and first met in 1907 in a church building at the corner of Chapin and Huron Streets. Reverend Herman Brauer led the services, which in the early days catered primarily to University of Michigan students. The congregation soon outgrew that facility, and in 1919, the old Krause family home on the corner of Third and Liberty was purchased to serve as school and parsonage. In 1928, the home was demolished to make way for this church building, which was completed in March of 1929.

The church is built in the Neo-Gothic style, extremely popular for religious buildings of the 1920s. The brick with limestone accents, particularly on the entrance, front parapet and pinnacles, and bell tower are hallmarks of the style. The front elevation features delicate stone window tracery with leaded glass that lights the main sanctuary. In 1957, a gymnasium and classroom space was added to the east side of the building.

OWSHD

509 W. Liberty
Hirth-Jenter House
1855/c. 1871

266

This home was raised in two distinct stages, with the side-gabled portion built in 1855 by Wurttemberg native and wagon maker John Hirth and his wife Elizabeth. That home was a typical one and one-half story Greek Revival, featuring six-over-six windows, a center entry with simple pilasters and entablature, and small windows in the frieze band.

In 1856, Hirth sold the small home to cabinet maker and carpenter Christian Jenter and his wife Anna Marie. Jenter added the front-gabled portion of the home in about 1871. Also in the Greek Revival style, the newer addition shows Jenter's carpentry skills in the window pediments, more delicate gable returns, and in the extensive use of dentils in the cornice. The two parts of the house were unified with a small porch. Anna Marie Jenter died in 1894, and Christian died in 1910. Since the Jenters, the exterior of the home has been preserved in almost original condition. Cedric Richner restored it and received a Preservation Award from the Historic District Commission in 1996.

OWSHD

267 ## 523 W. Liberty
George and Elizabeth Visel House   1885

George Visel married Elizabeth Kern in 1883, the same year that he arrived in America from his native Germany. Two years later the couple built this well-preserved Queen Anne on Liberty Street. Like his neighbor Christian Jenter (see #266), George Visel worked as a cabinet maker and carpenter, and is thought to be responsible for the construction of his home.

Though more restrained than many of the other Queen Anne houses of the era, the Visel House is much grander than most of its Vernacular Old West Side neighbors. Built on a high, cut-stone foundation, the highlights of the home are the four porches with turned columns and spindle work, including a double porch sheltered under the west elevation's cross gable.

For part of his career Visel worked at the Allmendinger Organ Factory (see #63). Visel was proud of his German heritage and active in the German-American community in Ann Arbor. He served on the building committee for Bethlehem Church (see #68), was a member of the Arbeiterverein (a German working man's club), and helped organize the festivities of Ann Arbor's German-American Day, first held in 1890.

The home remained in the Visel family until 1963. In recent years, a small studio was built on the lot, with the owners taking special care to match many of the home's fine details on the new building. Hugh McPherson restored it and received a Rehabilitation Award from the Historic District Commission in 1999.

OWSHD

603 W. Liberty
Jackson-Weitbrecht House

268

1847/1863

Shortly after William S. Maynard platted this area in 1846, John and Andrew Jackson purchased this lot at the southeast corner of Fourth Street and Liberty. They built their two-story clapboard house with the classic features of an I-House: two stories high, with two rooms up and two rooms down, flanking a central hallway. Note the Greek Revival-style doorway with sidelights and transom. A one-story addition with a brick foundation was added in the rear by John M. Weitbrecht, who purchased the property in 1862. The Weitbrechts occupied the house for another 40 years.

In 1930, it was partly commercialized with the south portion becoming Lunsford's Bakery. They served famous cinnamon rolls until 1970. In 1986, the house was purchased by Susan and William Johnson, who removed the asphalt siding and corrugated canopy and restored the clapboard. They received a Rehabilitation Award from the Historic District Commission in 1991. They have since added a small addition on the south side.

OWSHD

269 626 W. Liberty
William and Katherine Kuhn House   c. 1850

The front portion of this complex of buildings is a tiny 1½-story Greek Revival cottage built around 1850 for William and Katherine Kuhn. William died in 1879 and willed his dwelling and land to his wife and eight children. The house is a great reminder of how some people

lived in the mid-19th century, with a sleeping loft upstairs and two rooms below for living and eating.

The house has its original clapboard and windows, and an unusual nine-over-six window facing the road. The only stylistic flourishes are the returns at the side gables.

The house faced demolition in 1985, but was rescued by Doug Trubey who bought it in 1986 and restored it. Later he and his partner Michael Milliken added several buildings in the rear, which complement the tiny structure and let it stand on its own. Two awards from the Historic District Commission were given in 1989 and 2004 in recognition of both projects.

OWSHD

706 W. Liberty
Christian Burkhardt House

270

1867

This cube-shaped, hip-roofed, center entry, Vernacular-Italianate house was built in 1867 by Christian Burkhardt, a harness and trunk dealer. He was the son of J. Christian Bur-khardt, a German immigrant carpenter and cabinet maker, who came to Ann Arbor in 1845. Oral tradition has it that he also built the house at 707 W. Liberty (across the street) in 1849 and died that same year while building the first Bethlehem Church at Washington and First. His son was born in 1848, died in 1880, and is buried at Forest Hill Cemetery.

In 1987, Charles Rieckhoff purchased the house from Casper Enkemann—a former chief of police and Burkhardt's grandson—and restored it, removing aluminum siding and repairing the wood clapboard. The outlines of an old porch were revealed, which he then rebuilt. He received an award from the Historic District Commission in 1990. Since 1993, owners Carolyn and Gregory Smith have kept it in pristine condition and have also been rewarded for their work by the Historic District Commission.

OWSHD

271 818 W. Liberty
Haas-Hagen House
1860s/1888

This imposing castle-like brick building at the important corner of Liberty and Seventh has all the hallmarks of the Queen Anne style—a turret with conical roof topped by a decorative metal ornament, and an arched Richardsonian Romanesque entry with a repeated arch on the open sleeping porch above, fronted by a railing in the Chinese Chippendale style. Multiple gables intersect, and the windows are different sizes and shapes, which completes the picture.

Jacob Haas, a harness maker, is listed as living at this address as early as 1868. He continued to live here throughout the 1870s. The property was occupied by 1894 by John Hagen, a successful farmer in Salem and Ann Arbor Townships, who arrived in Washtenaw County in 1844 with a band of Germans from Prussia. Many children from his two wives lived with him, including daughter Mary Hagen Haas. Cora Haas, who died in 1977, was the last of the line living in this house. It was converted into four apartments in the 1940s.

OWSHD

902 W. Liberty
Christian Walker House

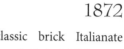

1872

This classic brick Italianate house was built in 1872 by carriage maker Christian Walker (see #83). It has the typical cube shape, hipped roof, bracketed eaves, and round-topped four-over-four windows with heavy brick hoods that define the style. It was converted into apartments in the 1930s and painted white, typical of the fate of these houses in the mid-20th century.

In 1979, it was purchased by Dr. John Hatch, a dentist who refurbished the interior. The Hatch family were early Ann Arbor pioneers and built many houses in the 19th century. Hatch received an award from the Historic District Commission in 1986. The house remains in the family.

OWSHD

273 1048 W. Liberty
Mathias and Barbara Lutz House   1868

The Lutz house is a well-preserved, 1½-story transitional building, bridging the Greek Revival style popular before the Civil War and the simple Vernacular style that characterized the Old West Side between 1870 and 1900. The symmetrical facade, center entry, window pediments, and frieze band windows are all taken from the Greek Revival style, though gone are the Classical cornice returns and heavy frieze board. The result is a rather charming Vernacular building that is set apart by its side-gabled form. The original four-over-four windows remain, as does the Italianate front door with the rounded glass windows so popular in the late 1860s.

Mathias Lutz came to the United States from Wurttemberg, Germany in 1866 and in 1868 married Barbara Rarsle. Two months later the young couple purchased land on Liberty Street in what was then Ann Arbor Township and built this house. Mathias is believed to have built the house himself. He worked with wood for most of his life as a cooper, carpenter, cabinet maker, and partner in T. Rauschenberger and Co., "manufacturers of fine furniture and chamber suites." "Cylinder" book cases were a specialty of the company, which appears to have been housed here or next door. Later in life Lutz became a liquor dealer in the city. Barbara Lutz passed away in 1897, and Mathias remained in the home until about 1920. Their daughter Mary Lutz lived in the house until 1962.

OWSHD

1422 W. Liberty

MacKenzie House/Anna Botsford Bach Home   1916/1927

274

This wonderful brick and stucco example of a three-story Italian villa in a Neoclassical design was originally built in 1916 as a home for physician and University of Michigan Obstetrics Dean Dr. Robert MacKenzie. Unlike most of his peers, he and his wife preferred to be in what was then the "country" and to have more acreage. Dr. MacKenzie was fluent in German which made him popular with his neighbors.

The house is characterized by large rooms, high ceilings, verandas, a huge central hallway, and fieldstone fireplaces. In 1926, illness forced them to move to Frankfort, Michigan, where the doctor died in 1930.

In 1927, the house was purchased by St. Joseph Mercy Hospital for an Old Ladies Home. The third floor was added then and later it was renamed to honor Anna Botsford Bach, who had worked so tirelessly to have a home for elderly women.

After 75 years of service, the home closed in 2002. It was purchased by the Community Supported Anthroposophical Medicine Inc. group in 2003 and is now a health center and community resource.

Former IHP

275 1444 W. Liberty
Jacob Beck House   1864

Hidden away behind shrubbery off Liberty Street sits this brick Greek Revival house built for Jacob Beck and his wife for their retirement after farming in Scio Township since 1832.

It has the classic features of the Greek Revival: an entry with sidelights and transom, gable returns with dentils in the eaves, four-over-four windows with shutters, and frieze windows in the upper portion. Originally a 1½-story house, the roof was raised in the 1880s to accommodate higher ceilings. The bay window on the west is a modern addition.

The house has been well maintained and furnished with period antiques. It was the home for years of Dr. L. Dell Henry and Elizabeth Robinson. In the 1980s it was purchased by John and Laura Baur, who have won awards for their preservation efforts.

Former IHP

1904 Linwood
Clarence and Charlotte Newman House

1932

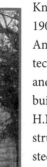

Known as "The Castle," 1904 Linwood is one of Ann Arbor's true architectural oddities. Built and designed in 1932 by builder and civil engineer H.N. Hariton, the house's structure is composed of steel-reinforced concrete, which was sold as being "fire proof and weather proof." The first owners were Mack School teacher Clarence Newman and his wife Charlotte who lived in the house until 1936.

"Build well, build once and provide a structure that will last through the generations to which maintenance bills will be relics of the past," were the words of Hariton in a 1932 article on the dwelling. Hariton's ideas never really caught on, perhaps because of the high upfront cost of using steel-reinforced concrete and other "maintenance free" building materials. Behind the faux-stone facade and castellated parapet is a basic front-gabled house form—the only thing that is conventional. A round turret on the front of the house contains a large cedar closet and the interior sports a mission-style fireplace with colored tiles, stucco walls, and expensive and rare terrazzo floors in the kitchen and bath.

Though the quirky architecture is marred by the unfortunate use of white vinyl replacement windows, the house remains a neighborhood landmark from an era of experimentation in building.

Mulholland and Murray Streets 277   1911–1924

Mulholland and Murray Streets represent a unique and pleasingly uniform collection of working-class houses from the early 20th century. With a few exceptions, the narrow streets are lined with simple, front-gabled, post-Victorian Folk houses, nearly all with welcoming front porches. This was the most common type of Folk house built in the city of Ann Arbor from 1900 to the early 1920s.

The buildings generally have the same floor plan, but differ in detailing. This is especially noticeable in the porches, which range from Colonial Revival Doric columns, square Craftsman-style columns, and, on Murray Street, more delicate, Victorian-style, turned porch columns. It's interesting to note that while the buildings look nearly identical, there are variations in square footage (between 900 and 1,100 sq ft), floor plan, building height, chimney placement, dormer type (gabled or shed), and roof pitch, indicating that they were not actually built from identical plans but perhaps from the builder's memory.

In 1909, Judge William Murray married Julia Allmendinger, and built an imposing Tudor Revival house (see #289) next door to his in-laws (see #290). In 1911, he subdivided the land behind his house and began building the houses on Murray Street, originally a footpath through the James Mulholland farm. In 1913, Murray subdivided Sixth Street (which became Mulholland Street in the 1920s), and in 1916 began building similar houses on these lots. The Mulholland farmhouse, built in the early 1900s, still stands at 714 W. Liberty.

In 1924, the city built a brick water-pumping station at 245–251 Mulholland. It was converted into condos in the 1980s, and received awards from the Historic District Commission. Murray Street residents have also won awards from the Historic District Commission and Mulholland Street received a Preservation Award in 2010.

OWSHD

814 Pauline
Chester and Sophie Stackhouse House
278

1940

814 Pauline is an extremely rare house, designed in an Art Moderne style that was never very popular here, especially for modest homes such as this. The home is purported to have been designed by its first owner, University of Michigan Track and Field Coach Chester Stackhouse. The Stackhouses' daughter, who lived here as a child, is the noted true crime author Ann Rule. The Stackhouse family only lived in the house until 1945.

The house is built of cinder block painted white—an uncommon building material except in the years immediately before and after World War II. The blocks were laid with four bands that run nearly the entire perimeter of the house, a common feature in Art Moderne and Art Deco buildings, which emphasize the horizontal. The non-original front door is flanked by curved, glass-block sidelights. Glass block is used again for two of the windows on the west side of the house, while the remaining windows are metal casements. The attached garage on the front of the house is an unusual feature of this period. The area above the garage was once an open air porch.

Before this house was built, the lot was the site of a garage where the first meetings of Ann Arbor's Greek Orthodox Church were held.

279 102 S. Revena
Frederick Staebler House   1864

This solid brick Vernacular farmhouse is often admired for its charming simplicity and its many original shutters, including those on a tiny pair of arched attic windows on the north elevation. The symmetrical design of the original brick house, with its matching end chimneys, was somewhat marred in the early 20th century by a small front portico, bay window, and two-story frame addition on the south side. This farmhouse is a reminder that this busy and densely populated neighborhood on the city's west side was once made up of small farms, many of which survived well into the 20th century.

The home was built by Frederick Staebler in 1864, and its simple architecture speaks to the German heritage of its builder. Staebler arrived from Wurttemberg at age six in 1831 and was a member of one of Washtenaw County's oldest German families. He grew up on his parents' farm in Lodi Township and owned his own farm in Scio Township before moving his family to this location, which was outside the city limits. He died in 1910 at the age of 85 and the farm passed to his son Jacob. The land was subdivided by David and Ray Killins in 1918 as the Killins Heights Subdivision.

328 Second
John and Anna Pfisterer House

280

1885

John Pfisterer came to the U.S. from Wurttemberg, Germany in 1866, first settling in Wisconsin before moving to Ann Arbor. He operated a hardware store under the name Hepfer and Pfisterer, which allowed him and his wife Anna (Schlenker) the resources to build this fine Italianate-Queen Anne home in 1885.

The building is solid brick and features arched Italianate windows with segmental window hoods and a hipped roof with balustrade. The home's cross gable is highlighted by a wrap-around Queen Anne-style porch with turned columns and decorative brackets, and a side "coffin door." The Pfisterers built, owned, and lived in a number of other residences in town, including the old North District Public School building (see #183). Later in life, John Pfisterer owned a men's clothing store on West Liberty.

In 1891, the Pfisterers sold this home to Henry and Catherine Wesch. Henry Wesch (sometime spelled Waesch) came from Germany in 1855 and made his living as a carpenter. He also served as trustee of Zion Lutheran Church. The Wesch family lived in the house until 1941.

OWSHD

281

448 and 454 Second
John Christian Walz Houses   1862/c. 1888

These two houses offer a wonderful contrast in the change in architectural styles and tastes that occurred in Ann Arbor between 1860 and 1890. 448 Second was built in the Greek Revival style by carpenter John Christian Walz and his wife Catherine (Burkhardt) in 1862. Exceedingly simple, gable-front Greek Revivals such as this were the dominant form of house constructed throughout the city from the late 1820s through the mid-1860s. The only hints of architectural style are found in the Classical entry with sidelights, Doric pilasters and entablature, and the Greek Revival gable returns. The porch, dormer window, and foundation are early 20th-century changes. Walz and his wife lived in this house until about 1888 when they built a larger, highly detailed Queen Anne next door at 454 Second. At this time they gave their old house to their daughter Catherine and her new husband William Stoll.

The grander Walz house at 454 Second exhibits detailing that was made possible by advances in the manufacturing of house parts that was taking place at steam-powered planing mills in the 1860s and 1870s. The mechanization and mass production of house parts made elaborate "gingerbread" affordable to middle-class families. In addition, the changeover from heavy timber frames to lighter, more versatile

balloon frames allowed more complicated shapes and rooflines, which made the Queen Anne style possible. The later Walz home is heavy on ornamentation, particularly in the gables and bay windows, which exhibit elaborate bargeboards with recessed panels and bull's eyes, decorative brackets, and unusual lace-like carvings. An upper window on the Jefferson Street side features an interesting double window with excessively ornamental trim. The multicolored "Queen Anne" windows were a popular feature of the time. The porches were added in the early 20th century when classical columns and fieldstone foundations were becoming popular in Colonial Revival and Craftsman-style buildings.

OWSHD

631 Second

Wiegant-Hochrein House

c. 1885

This Vernacular brick house, with three bays on the first floor, two on the second, and an oculus window in the gable, represents a type found all over the Old West Side area. With its long overhanging but undecorated eaves, it could be from the 1850s or the 1880s, since the form persisted over many decades. This is a pristine example of the type, and the four-over-four windows are arranged in an asymmetrical fashion.

It was first occupied by cabinet maker Christian Wiegant and his family, and was built by Wiegant's wife's brother-in-law Charles Raab. Raab had an identical house (see #248) and the two back up to each other.

Their cousins, the Michael Hochrein family, arrived from Germany in 1884, and had the house to themselves when the Wiegants moved around the corner. In the 1890s, Ferdinand Hochrein apprenticed to Wiegant, became a cabinet maker, and later worked for the gas company. Ferdinand's siblings made their names in construction and plumbing. A descendant, Miss B.M. Hochrein, was an informant for the first edition of *Historic Buildings, Ann Arbor, Michigan* in 1977.

The brickwork had already been painted by 1956 when University of Michigan Math Professor Fred Gehring bought the house. He replaced dirt floors with concrete in the basement and made other improvements. In 1959, Ruth and Clarence Roy created a stunning modern interior and landscaped the house. They were activists in establishing the Old West Side Association and the historic district designation.

OWSHD

283 # 202 S. Seventh
Beck-Stollsteimer House

1881

This sturdy Vernacular home is a fine example of the types of houses German-Americans were building on the Old West Side during the last quarter of the 19th century. Like other homes of the period, the house features a front-gabled roof, pedimented two-over-two windows, and a front porch. The oculus window in the attic is a feature that appears on many Vernacular buildings of the time period, almost exclusively on the Old West Side. The original functional shutters are another common feature on German-American homes of the time, when they were fast becoming obsolete elsewhere. The Doric porch columns are an early 20th-century addition, and the decorative millwork on the window pediments, while typical of the time period, was added in the late 20th century.

The house was built by retired farmer Jacob Beck (see #275) in 1881. Beck lived in the house until 1885, when it was sold to Reuben and Julia (Armbruster) Stollsteimer. The Stollsteimers were both born in Saline to German parents. Reuben worked as a laborer and farmhand. Following the Stollsteimers, the house was purchased by widow Catherine Koch, who lived there with five of her children. The Koch family owned the home until 1975. During the 1960s, mechanic Oscar Koch operated an automotive repair business in the large garage on the property.

OWSHD

217 S. Seventh
Philip and Elizabeth Gauss House
284
c. 1901

Built in either 1901 or 1902, this home was occupied by renters George and Alice Rustine until 1909. From 1913 to 1947, it was the residence of Philip and Elizabeth Gauss. He worked a number of odd jobs including stock worker, bartender, and foreman for the Motor Products Corporation.

The Old West Side Historic District is filled with simple, gable-front Folk houses such as this, most of which do not necessarily stand out historically or architecturally on their own. Recent history makes this property unique. In 2006, the home was purchased by Matt and Kelly Grocoff, who have made it the oldest "net zero" house in America and the first "net zero" house to be located in a historic district. A "net zero" house produces more energy than it consumes. The Grocoffs began their project by removing the asbestos siding and restoring the wood siding and front porch. The original windows were weather-stripped and restored. In 2010, rooftop solar panels were installed. The work was done with the greatest respect for the historic details of the house, and shows that historic preservation and environmentalism can work hand-in-hand. In 2011, the Grocoffs received the Preservation Project of the Year Award from the Historic District Commission.

The home has been featured in a number of local and national publications, and was named one of *USA Today*'s "Best Green Homes of 2010."

OWSHD

285 1200 S. Seventh
Robert and Rose Nichols House   1950

For a short period from 1948 to 1950, Lustron homes offered a serious alternative to traditional wood-framed houses. A total of nine were built in Ann Arbor during their brief popularity. Built entirely of steel, including the framing, roofing, interior and exterior walls, and built-in appliances, Lustron homes were the idea of engineer Carl Strandlund. The exterior was constructed of enamel-coated steel panels, which were similar to those in the prefabricated gas stations designed by Lustron's parent company, the Chicago Vitreous Enamel Corporation. The buildings were designed by Chicago architect Morris Beckman. Ann Arbor businessman and Democratic Party activist Neil Staebler had the local Lustron franchise. The buildings were shipped as a 3,300-part kit, and all but one of Ann Arbor's Lustron houses was assembled by local carpenter Clarence Kollewehr. Though the houses cost roughly twenty-five percent less than a conventional home, the idea of an all-steel home never caught on, and the Lustron Corporation went bankrupt in 1950.

Built in 1950, the first owners of this home were Robert L. and Rose I. Nichols. Robert Nichols was a salesman at Kouhn's Menswear and was city alderman from the First Ward in 1949 and 1950. Rose Nichols was a longtime teacher in Pittsfield Township and Ypsilanti.

In addition to the Nichols House on S. Seventh, other Lustron homes in Ann Arbor can be found at 800 Starwick, 1711 Chandler, 605 Linda Vista, 3060 Lakewood, and at 1121, 1125, and 1129 Bydding. Despite the naysayers of the late 1940s, Carl Strandlund's Lustron homes have held up well over time and offer an interesting window into an era when people were willing to experiment with and bend the idea of what a house could be.

502 Sixth
John Lucas House

1883

286

This brick Queen Anne with intersecting gables, arched limestone lintels over the windows, an oculus window below the gable, and decorative carved ornament at the gable peak defines the style. The one-over-one windows were a new design and an element in this perfect, unremodeled example of the Queen Anne structures built in the 1880s. The only modern element is the fiberglass canopy over the entry stairs on Sixth.

John Lucas, an immigrant brick mason from Hesse-Darmstadt, Germany via Canada, was like many of the Germans living in this neighborhood, the son of a brick mason who trained him in the craft. He moved to Ann Arbor in 1870, married his second wife, Elizabeth Wagner, and used his expertise to build this handsome house for his family. He also built several buildings for the University of Michigan Hospitals on Catherine, which are now gone. He died in 1891 and his wife lived here until 1908 when she sold it to the Koch family. The Kochs were also builders and masons. Descendants of the family lived here until the 1990s when the Gilbert family purchased it.

OWSHD

287 544 Sixth
Christian and Caroline Roth House   1885

Christian and Caroline Roth built this Old West Side favorite in 1885. The use of masonry on such a small dwelling is unique in this part of town and can be attributed to the fact that Christian Roth was a mason. The small Italianate/gable front and wing-style home is built of solid masonry (not a veneer). Part of its charm comes from the tall and narrow appearance of the two-story part of the house, built on a high cut-stone foundation, with an interestingly positioned chimney on the front of the building. The four-over-four windows, which still feature their original louvered shutters, are topped with brick window hoods, common in Italianate buildings made of brick. The side wing features a fine Italianate porch with elaborate brackets. A small, brick, shed roof addition was added to the back of this side wing early in the home's history.

In addition to working as a mason, Christian Roth owned a saloon on East Liberty. During the 19th century, most of Ann Arbor's saloons were run by German immigrants. Caroline and son Christian Roth Jr. also worked in the family's saloon, with Christian Jr. serving as bartender. Following Christian Sr.'s death in 1891, they continued to run the saloon until the early 1900s. Christian Jr. later worked as a tinsmith and sheet-metal worker. Son George J. Roth remained in the home until 1929, when it became the home of Alfred Pepper.

OWSHD

536 Third
Louis and Lydia Betz House
1889

This wonderful example of the Queen Anne style was built in 1889 by Louis and Lydia Betz on land owned by Lydia's parents, Emil and Christine Osiander. The home features double front gables with sunburst designs and late period working shutters, still common in Ger-

man-American homes of the era. Also of note are the two "dummy" windows with shutters on the front facade, which give the appearance of a window for the sake of symmetry. The wonderful Arts and Crafts-style stone porch is a later addition from the 1910s, as is the unique gambrel-roof garage in the back which was built in about 1929.

Louis Betz was a clerk for Eberbach and Co., and later owned his own saloon and grocery before a series of financial hardships that may have led to his bizarre disappearance. In July of 1893, he went to Whitmore Lake and was never heard from again. It's unclear whether he killed himself, drowned, or fled the state by railroad, as was reported at the time. Louis' financial problems and disappearance led to a number of court cases, though Lydia Betz and her mother Christine Osiander were able to remain in the home until 1910. It then became the home of plumber Otto Koch and his wife Lydia.

The home has been lovingly maintained by Scott Kunst and Jane Raymond, who run the internationally famous Old House Gardens from here, a mail-order business that specializes in historic bulbs. Their adaptive reuse of the barn as a business space received an award from the Historic District Commission in 2011.

OWSHD

289 711 W. Washington
William H. and Julia Murray House   1909

This wonderful brick Tudor Revival-style home was built in 1909 by Judge William Murray on property of his wife's father, David Frederich Allmendinger, who had lived at 719 W. Washington since 1890 (see #290). Allmendinger owned the organ and piano factory nearby at the northwest corner of First and Washington (see #63). When his daughter married Judge Murray, Allmendinger gave them his side yard to build their home. A huge oak tree needed to be cut down and tables were made from it and given to members of the family.

Note the steeply pitched roofs, half-timbering and stucco, stone front porch with patterned columns, and original multi-paned windows that are of many sizes and shapes. There is a wonderful back porch covered in grape vines from the Murray era.

Murray was responsible for developing Murray and Mulholland Streets (see #277) on property of his father-in-law and other landowners. He didn't live in this house long, however, because after Allmendinger died they moved into 719 W. Washington to live with his widow in 1916.

In the 1970s, the Haas family purchased the house and members of that family still live there today. The home

has been featured on the Old West Side Homes Tour, and the Haas family was awarded a Preservation Award from the Historic District Commission in 2012 for their care of the home.

OWSHD

719 W. Washington
David F. and Marie Allmendinger House

290

1890

This clapboard Queen Anne structure, with carved king-post gable decoration and original windows and shutters, is a restrained version of this usually exuberant late 19th-century style, with a symmetrical arrangement of windows and doors and a white and green color scheme. It has a newer porch with stone walls and square tapered columns, probably dating to c. 1910. An old photograph of the family in front of a massive burr oak tree shows the house with its original wraparound porch.

The house was built by local businessman David F. Allmendinger, who began building parlor organs under Gottlob F. Gartner in 1867 and later married Gartner's daughter. When Gartner retired, he established the Allmendinger Organ Works in 1872. It was located in a house at the northwest corner of Washington and First. From this "factory," Allmendinger expanded several times, building three brick factories that now take up an entire block on First between Washington and Huron (see #63). As it expanded, the name of the company changed to the Ann Arbor Organ Co. and later to the Ann Arbor Piano Co.

Arriving from Wurttemberg in 1851, his was a true German immigrant success story. He focused his wealth on creating a large home and garden for his family of 13 children. Lying close to Allen Creek, his 1½-acre property was his own "Belle Isle" that included a grape arbor, goldfish and carp ponds, a croquet lawn, fruit trees, and a gazebo. Allmendinger died in 1916 and his daughter Julia and her husband Judge William Murray (see #277 and #289) moved in after selling their house next door in 1916. Descendants lived here until 1991.

The Mouat family have been custodians of the house for many years and received a Preservation Award from the Historic District Commission in 2013.

OWS

BURNS PARK/
WASHTENAW/HILL/
IVES WOODS/
SCOTTWOOD

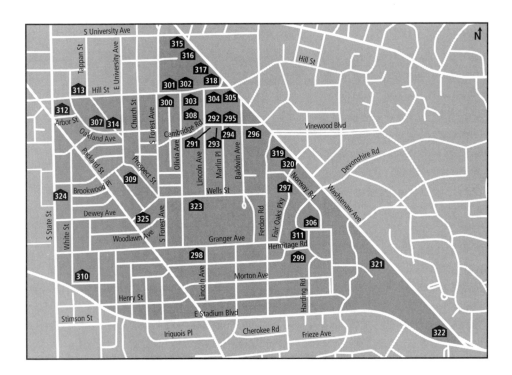

The Washtenaw/Hill, Ives Woods, and Burns Park area has long been the home of Ann Arbor's well-to-do, with many of the early residents associated with the University of Michigan. In the mid-19th century, this land was dominated by the J.D. Baldwin farm (see #305) and the Christian Eberbach house and farm (see #325). Professors began building grand Victorian homes along Washtenaw Avenue in the late 1850s and 1860s, a few of which survive, including the Henry Simmons Frieze home (see #353). Hill Street (see #303), Oakland (see #307), Tappan, and E. University (see #314) were also lined with the homes of distinguished University of Michigan faculty, many of which were designed by prominent architects of the day.

Burns Park (see #323) was the site of the Ann Arbor fairgrounds, which featured a race track and trolley barns for the street cars that began running to this part of town in the 1890s. Olivia Hall subdivided portions of the Baldwin Farm (current Burns Park neighborhood) beginning in 1891, with many high-style homes being built on Olivia (see #308), Lincoln, and Cambridge Road (see #291–#296), which was originally named Israel Street after Hall's late husband Israel Hall.

During the 1910s and 1920s the Burns Park neighborhood flourished, with large homes being built on Cambridge, Olivia, Lincoln, Baldwin, and Martin Place. The homes are more modest south of Wells, and the architecture is more conservative, though there are still many fine examples of the Colonial Revival, Craftsman, Tudor Revival, and Italian Renaissance style (see #298), and an interesting group of Art Moderne-style homes along Morton, Shadford, and Stadium. West of Packard, in the area often called "Lower Burns Park," the architecture is slightly later and a bit more playful with a wide variety of styles of the era being present (see #310).

In 1914, Marvin Ives built a massive Georgian Revival mansion (see #299). The expansive grounds were later subdivided as Ives Woods in 1923. Also in 1914, Charles Spooner platted the nearby Scottwood neighborhood, with a series of winding streets lined with large Colonial Revival and Tudor Revival homes (see #306 and #311). University of Michigan professor Fiske Kimball designed six homes in Scottwood, including the James Petrie Home in 1916 (see #297).

291 1502 Cambridge
Jacob and Katherine Reighard House   1901

This imposing Queen Anne is a superb example of the simplification of the style that was occurring in the early years of the 20th century when the Burns Park neighborhood was being developed. Gone are the fish-scale shingles, turrets, and other ostentatious ornamentation that was being replaced by simpler Colonial Revival detailing. Highlights include the massive wraparound porch supported by simple Doric columns, and double third-story windows on the front facade with their entablature and four Doric columns.

The home was built by zoology professor Jacob Reighard and his wife Katherine (Farrand). Reighard came to Ann Arbor in 1886 to study medicine (see #204), but soon became acting Assistant Professor of Zoology. From 1895 to 1925, he was director of the Zoological Laboratory at the University of Michigan. Prominent in his field, Reighard was active in the American Society of Zoologists, the American Society of Naturalists, and in charge of the Michigan Fish Commission, leading a large survey of the Great Lakes' fisheries from 1898 to 1901. The home became the Delta Sigma Pi fraternity house from 1925 to 1940.

In the 1960s and 1970s, the house was owned by U-M Architecture Professor Joseph Wehrer and his wife Anne who founded the ONCE Group, a collection of artists, musicians, filmmakers, and architects that created the ONCE Festival and the Ann Arbor Film Festival. The Wehrer's home was a gathering place for many of the most influential creative people of the era, including Andy Warhol, John Cage, Robert Rauschenberg, and Claes Oldenburg. It was a frequent hangout for Anne Wehrer's friend James Osterberg, later famous as Iggy Pop, singer of the seminal Ann Arbor punk band The Stooges.

1503 Cambridge
Daniel and Frances Zimmerman House

292

1901

Eugene Hall, the son of Israel and Olivia Hall, who subdivided this portion of Burns Park, built this stately brick Colonial in 1901. The symmetrical Colonial, built of common brick with matching end chimneys and a classical entry, is an interesting contrast to its neighbor across the street (see #291) that was built in the same year but in the older Queen Anne style. Hall built it as a speculative venture and never lived in the house.

In 1903, Hall sold the property to Daniel and Frances (Farr) Zimmerman. After serving in World War I, Daniel Zimmerman returned home to Ann Arbor, where he became a director of the State Bank of Ann Arbor and later its president. Zimmerman's accomplishments and business achievements were vast, including his becoming president of the Washtenaw Gas Company, the Washtenaw Abstract Company, and the Artificial Ice Company (see #7).

From 1916 to 1934, the house was owned by Professor Samuel Moore and his wife Rebecca. Sometime after their purchase in 1935, the house was significantly altered by owners James and Bess Edmonds. The Edmonds family added the side kitchen wing and garage, perfectly matching the brick and stonework of the original house. During the renovation, the interior was extensively "Colonialized," with some more modern Art Deco touches. The home has been lovingly maintained for years by preservationists Steve and Ellen Ramsburgh, who received a Preservation Award from the Historic District Commission in 2007.

293 1520 Cambridge
Max and Clemence Winkler House   1911

Born in Kraków, Poland (then part of Austria) in 1866, Max Winkler came to America at the age of 16, first settling in Cincinnati. He graduated first in his class at Harvard in 1889 and by 1890 had arrived at the University of Michigan to teach in the German Department. Along with Moritz Levi and Louis Strauss (see #295), Winkler was among the first Jewish faculty members at the U-M. In 1902, he became Professor of German Language and Literature. By 1906, Winkler had married Clemence Hamilton, and in 1911 the couple built this center-entry Georgian Revival with parapeted gables.

The home is said to be modeled after Max Winkler's grandparents' home in Cincinnati, where parapeted gables and Federal-style architecture are common. The yellow brick is a stark, yet pleasant contrast with the red tile roof, both rare in Ann Arbor. The third-floor gabled dormers feature delicate, semicircular fanlight windows and pilasters. The frieze board and gable returns are highlighted by large modillions, a feature repeated on the large side porch. Leaded glass sidelights and fanlight surround the front entrance, which is sheltered by an oversized front portico supported by delicate Doric columns. The side features a two-story bay window, and the back of the home features a two-story screened porch. Professor Winkler died in 1930, and in 1948 the home was inherited by Winkler's nephew Stephen Atwood. Current owners Martin and Susan Hurwitz have done major restoration work and received an award from the Historic District Commission in 2014.

1606 Cambridge
J. Karl and Clara Malcolm House

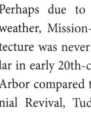

294

1909

Perhaps due to the winter weather, Mission-style architecture was never very popular in early 20th-century Ann Arbor compared to the Colonial Revival, Tudor Revival, and Arts and Crafts styles. J. Karl Malcolm, though, looked to Spain and the American Southwest for inspiration in the design of his home. The defining features of the home are the Spanish-style front parapet, stucco wall cladding, and orange-tiled hipped roof. Influences from Moorish Spain include the center window on the second story which is flanked by Moorish, spiraled or "Solomonic" pilasters and fan. The entrance is traditional, with entablature and fluted Ionic columns. The separate garage matches the house with stucco walls and Mission-style parapets.

Born in Canada in 1878, John Karl Malcolm came to Ann Arbor in 1902 and worked as a tailor before buying the Consumers Clothing Company, which he operated for 10 years on E. Liberty. He later made a small fortune as manager of the Ypsi-Ann Land Company (see #107) which developed vacant land in the area, including the College Heights Subdivision in Ypsilanti. In 1909 J. Karl and Clara (Laing) built this home at 1600 Israel, now called Cambridge Road. The Malcolms lived in the home until 1960.

295 1601 Cambridge
Louis and Elsa Strauss House   1912

Louis Strauss was born in Chicago and came to Ann Arbor to attend the University of Michigan, where he graduated in 1893. By 1895, he was teaching in the English Department, and by 1904, he was assistant professor. Strauss taught at the University for 46 years, including service as chair of the English Department and was among the first Jewish members of the faculty.

Strauss' distinctive 1912 Arts and Crafts home was designed by his cousin, architect Albert Kahn, and is one of the few private residences that Kahn designed in the city (see #301 and #340). The home was designed in the Arts and Crafts style, with different materials used on each story, in this case brick and stucco. The large overhangs feature exposed decorative rafter tails. Kahn makes a bold statement in the massive front bay and the dormers with rounded tops. The absence of a front porch is uncommon in Arts and Crafts homes, though Kahn compensates with a hanging door canopy and a side porch (common in Colonial Revival buildings). The building's most unique feature is the stunning green tile roof. Often found in grand Detroit homes of the period, this type of roof is extremely rare in Ann Arbor. Louis Strauss lived in the home until 1938. Current owners Barbara and David Copi received a Preservation Award from the Historic District Commission in 2009.

1710 Cambridge
Clement and Alice Gill House

296

1915

Clement W. Gill and his wife Alice built this home in 1915. The large and stately Georgian Revival was designed by Samuel Stanton, a local architect. Built with brick veneer and a slate roof, the home features a fine front entrance with a delicate elliptical fanlight and sidelights, sheltered by a large porch with Doric columns. Decorative modillions wrap around the cornice, which is topped with an elaborate balustrade. Two side porches have identical detailing. Those details are likely due to Gill being in the lumber business. The front roof features three pedimented dormers, the center one containing a three-part window and fanlight. The side gables each feature a three-part Palladian window. The gables, gable returns, and frieze all feature dentiled trim, and the cornice conceals a built-in gutter system. At the back of the home sits a porte-cochère with a sleeping porch above, a popular feature in the days before air conditioning.

Gill was owner of the C.W. Gill Lumber Company on S. Main, which became Arbor City Lumber that later merged with Fingerle Lumber. He was also treasurer of the Board of Education and sat on the board of the State Bank and the German-American Savings Bank. The home remained in the Gill family until 2006. New owners received a Rehabilitation Award in 2010.

297 1111 Fair Oaks
James and Clara Petrie House   1916

In 1914, developer Charles Spooner planned a subdivision called "Scottwood" that promised to be "a group of handsome residences...amid a landscape setting not hitherto attempted...with winding roads, a large garden space...indeed each house stands on a little knoll commanding a pleasing view." This was the setting for the home of James Petrie, Esq., his wife Clara, and sons Warren and Floy.

Many houses in Scottwood were designed by Dr. Fiske Kimball, Assistant Professor of Architecture at the University of Michigan, who later served as director of the Philadelphia Museum of Art. Kimball was a historic preservation pioneer who oversaw the preservation of Monticello and the re-creation of Williamsburg in Virginia. Kimball created an unusual Classical Revival house with a circular floor plan in the center flanked by rectangular wings. The round portico with two-story columns exhibits Kimball's fondness for Classical detailing. As stated in the brochure for the development, these designs were to have the "quiet unobtrusiveness of good taste. Each completely individual, they nevertheless harmonize in charm of design and refinement of detail." The house was described in detail by Kimball in a 1918 issue of *Architecture* magazine.

In 1918, the Petries sold the house to osteopaths Thomas and Dorothy Sellards. Mrs. Sellards lived in the home until 1940. After a succession of occupants, Dr. Norman Maier, professor of psychology, purchased the house in 1944. In 1979, it became the home of Bob and Carol Mull who have owned the house for over thirty years and have received awards for their preservation efforts.

Former IHP

1430 Granger
Arthur and Etta Arnold House

1916

Like the Mission Revival style (see #294), Renaissance Revival-style homes like this are rare in Ann Arbor. Built in 1916 by Arthur and Etta Arnold, this sturdy and stately home's most striking feature is the hipped red tile roof supported by decorative rafter tails in the eaves. The Corinthian columns and pilasters that support the small entry portico are rare, as are the oval windows that flank the front entrance. In a nod to the popular Craftsman style of the day, the first story is done in veneer brick, laid in an English bond pattern, while the second floor is stuccoed. Massive sun parlors built on the east side of the house feature large banks of multi-light casement windows. The garage is in the same style and material as the house.

Arthur Hugo Arnold was born in Ann Arbor in 1881, the son of William Arnold (see #263), a jeweler and owner of the German-American Savings Bank and the State Savings Bank. Arthur Arnold was a watchmaker, and with his brothers Emil and William owned Arnold & Co. Jewelers at 220 S. Main Street, which made him wealthy enough to construct this grand home in one of the city's most fashionable neighborhoods.

Former IHP

299 1808 Hermitage
Marvin A. Ives House/The Hermitage   1914

This over 8,000-square-foot, 28-room stuccoed brick mansion set on a hilltop in 1.3 acres of large trees exemplifies the estate of a country gentleman. This Georgian Revival house (with some Beaux Arts features) exhibits the rigid symmetry, imposing mass, symmetrically arranged windows and doors, corner quoins, Palladian windows, and pedimented entry that characterize the style. It was built for Marvin Ives, a soap manufacturer from Detroit. "I built this house about 1914," is written across the back of an old photograph of this house by local builder Levi D. Wines. Wines was famous for building houses for Ann Arbor's elite, going back to the 19th century. He was a professor of mathematics at Ann Arbor High School, a founder of the University Musical Society, and an early member of the Ann Arbor Parks Commission.

The creation of the subdivision of 20 lots known as Ives Woods in 1923 coincided with the death of Ives' wife. Ives sold the home to the Hermitage fraternity that year and the new street took its name. The fraternity remained in the house until 1934. It was then home to several other fraternities, including Sigma Delta (1949–1970). Professor Jesse and Anitra Gordon purchased it in 1970.

The Gordons attempted to restore the house to some semblance of its former grandeur after rough years as a fraternity house. In 1972, they held a reception here for feminist writer Gloria Steinem to benefit the Ann Arbor Feminist House. They had apartments in the house, one of which housed Joseph Brodsky, later Poet Laureate of the United States, who had a stamp issued in his honor in 2012. The restoration of the massive house proved too much for the Gordons and they put it up for sale in 1981. In 1982, a Designer Showcase was held in the house while it was empty to help raise scholarship money for the University of Michigan School of Art. It is again a single-family residence.

Former IHP

1310 Hill
Campbell-Lydecker House

300

1890

This spacious and attractive home is perhaps the earliest remaining home in the city designed in the Colonial Revival style. The Colonial Revival was inspired by the U.S. Centennial of 1876, and the interest in earlier design led to adaptations of the styles of the 18th century. The center entry projects from the base rectangle in a two-story fully pedimented design, with a Palladian window on the second story. The windows with shutters are arranged symmetrically around the entry and have spool designs on the interior resembling chemical elements, in honor of the chemist owner. The house is bookended by chimneys and is sided in clapboard with a design that was very restrained for the 1890s.

The first occupant was Edward DeMille Campbell, a junior professor of chemistry and metallurgy at the University of Michigan who became head of the Chemistry Department. Five of the six Campbell children were born in this house and a tree was planted to honor the birth of each child. The massive copper beech in the front lawn, named Cornelia, is the only survivor today.

In 1901, the family moved down the street (see #354) and Margaret Lydecker, recently widowed, purchased it and ran it as a boarding house, famous for having the best food in Ann Arbor. Her daughter Margaret Lydecker married Professor Earl D. "Doc" Wolaver and they raised their family in this house. Margaret sold the house in 1971 to University of Michigan basketball coach David Strack, who was called to Arizona and sold it in 1972 to Haskell and Janet Newman. Janet's development of a board game about historic buildings used this house as an example of the Classical Revival.

WHHD

301 1331 Hill
Delta Upsilon Fraternity

1903/2012

Albert Kahn, noted Detroit architect, designed this building for the men of ΔY in 1903. It is the oldest fraternity house in Ann Arbor still being used by the same organization and is one of the few examples of Kahn's non-commercial, non-industrial work in Ann Arbor (see #295 and #354). It was almost completely destroyed by fire in 2008. It re-opened in 2012 with much of the first floor interior restored, down to the tiled fireplaces and light fixtures. One burnt light fixture was kept as a memento of the fire. This won the Historic District Commission Project of the Year Award in 2013.

It was built in the Tudor Revival style, with a brick base, stuccoed second floor, and multi-paned windows. It has multiple gables with half-timbering in the portion above the main entry, a bowed window on the second floor, and four multi-paned windows on the third. It was built by the Koch Brothers, who used it in their advertisement in the 1905 *Michiganensian* yearbook.

Delta Upsilon was founded in 1834 at Williams College as a non-secret fraternity. The University of Michigan chapter was established in 1876, renting places before they were able to raise enough money to build this home. Old photographs show that the house has changed little since it was built. The reconstruction will probably have a few details missing that only specialists could discern.

NR, WHHD

1335 Hill
Wilson-Johnson House

1894

This beautiful Queen Anne with irregular roof gables, a tower with conical roof and finial, alternating bands of clapboard and fish-scale shingles, a decorative porch with turned posts and unusual railings and foundation screening of decorative lumber, was built in 1894 for Farwell Wilson, a lumber dealer. The elaborate two-story porch with mansard roof and Chinese Chippendale railing is a testament to the woodworking skills of the time.

Mrs. Wilson was active in the Equal Suffrage Club in 1912 and held meetings here to promote equal rights for women. Widowed in 1914, she sold the house to Clarence and Bessie Johnson who made it their home for over 50 years. Johnson was the director of Davis Engineering Company.

In 1970, the Delta Upsilon fraternity purchased it for an annex. It was sold to the congregation of Machon L'Torah in 1994, who share the building with the Jewish Resource Center. Machon L'Torah, the Jewish Learning Network of Michigan, was founded in Detroit in 1980 by an Israeli rabbi to increase Jewish awareness in America and to educate Jewish college students about their heritage and values. Today it serves as a Jewish Education Center, just a few doors from the Hillel Center.

WHHD

303 1410 Hill
Freer-Shearer House   1898

This house was designed in 1898 by the prestigious Chicago firm of Pond and Pond for Paul C. Freer, professor of chemistry. It exhibits the unique Shingle style of the Pond brothers,

including intentional asymmetry, a half gable interrupted by a turret with no tower, many different-sized windows in odd relationships to each other (some with their trademark diamond panes), and a two-story side porch. Ralph Latimer, a writer for *The Inlander* in 1901, commented that it was a "good

example of houses in quite a different style (than the colonial) and are particularly pleasing in their air of solidity and competence to meet the climatic conditions…"

The Pond brothers were natives of Ann Arbor and their family home stood on the site of the Michigan Union. They were, in fact, the architects of the Union (see #223), the Michigan League (see #231), the Student Publications Building (see #212), and the first YMCA (see #164). This is one of the few residences they designed in Ann Arbor.

Professor Freer stayed four years and advertised it as having 10 rooms, hardwood floors, laundry in the basement, 30′ × 15′ living room, large fireplace, 20′ × 20′ veranda off the living room, and a dining room in the Alt Deutsch style. He sold to Professor Albert Stanley of the Music School, who sold it in 1907 to insurance agent Chauncey Shearer and wife Louise, who made it their home until the 1970s.

Since 1972, it has been the home of Frank and Julie Casa. The Casas have often opened their home for tours and have won awards from the Historic District Commission. The interior is intact, with original woodwork and quirky items from 1898 in the kitchen. One feature is "October 1897 Hutzel's Plumbing," written in a beautiful 19th-century script on a wall behind the wall-mounted toilet tank. There are beautiful gardens in the front and back of the house.

WHHD

1508–1522 Hill
Bogle and Cutting/White Panther Houses   1892/1897

304

These grand Victorians near the corner of Washtenaw and Hill were the homes of some of Ann Arbor's most well-known radicals in the turbulent era of the late 1960s and early 1970s. In 1968, John Sinclair and his wife Leni moved to Ann Arbor and created a commune in the two houses for the White Panther and Rainbow People's Party. They advocated communal living, drug legalization, the end of the Vietnam War, racial equality, environmental protection, and the complete overthrow of the United States government. Many prominent radicals of the era lived at the houses, including the Sinclairs, White Panther co-founder Pun Plamondon, and The MC5, the legendary hard rock/proto-punk band. By 1969, the MC5 had left the party and moved out, and in 1971 Plamondon and John Sinclair were sentenced to long prison terms for possession of minor amounts of marijuana. Sinclair's harsh nine and one-half year prison sentence led to one of the most famous concerts in Ann Arbor's history, the John Sinclair Freedom Rally, featuring performances by Stevie Wonder, Bob Seger, Phil Ochs, Allen Ginsberg, John Lennon, and Yoko Ono.

The homes didn't always have such an anti-establishment history. 1508–1510 Hill, the older of the two houses, was built in 1892 by Thomas Bogle, attorney and law professor at the University of Michigan. 1520–1522 Hill was built by John and Fannie Cutting in 1897. John Cutting was a wealthy man, president of Cutting, Reyer and Company. The Cuttings only lived in the house for four years, when it was sold to chemistry professor S. Lawrence Bigelow and his wife Mary, who remained in the house until 1936.

Both buildings were designed by Ann Arbor architect George Scott, and feature a variety of intersecting and complicated rooflines, large front bays and porches, and various-sized windows. The spirit of communal living is still alive in the homes, which are owned by the Inter-Cooperative Council and operated as the Luther Buchele Cooperative.

WHHD

305 | 1530 Hill
Baldwin-Hall/Hayden House   1848/1885

Located at the intersection of Hill and Washtenaw, this flat-roofed, stucco-over-brick house, scored to resemble stone, is an unusual form of the Greek Revival, more Roman in character. It is believed to have been built by Daniel Wines (see #98). Originally painted pink with green shutters, it was a bright landmark on the Ypsilanti Road (later renamed Washtenaw).

It was built for J.D. Baldwin, a fruit farmer from Baldwinsville, New York. He purchased 154 acres of land outside the city and became prosperous growing fruit and berries. His farm in New York was the home of the Baldwin apple. An expert on peaches, strawberries, and apples, Baldwin was an active member of the Washtenaw Agricultural Society and a leader in the Washtenaw Pomological Society.

In 1876, he sold the home and 78 acres to Olivia and Israel Hall. Excepting the house and three acres, Olivia later platted the area bounded by what is now Baldwin, Wells, Forest, and Hill Streets, requiring the 60-foot setback that gives this area so much character. The house was a wedding present to the Halls' son Louis and his bride Elizabeth in 1885. Elizabeth changed the color of the exterior, replaced the stoves with fireplaces (a retro act then), and added the sloped-roof porches with their copper roofs. Louis Hall became a prominent member of the Dental School at the University of Michigan, and resided here until his death in 1948. His daughter, Mrs. J.F. (Betty) Hayden resided in the home until the 1980s with her niece Winifred Favreau, keeping it in this family for over 100 years.

The house was studied and drawn in 1958 as part of the Historic American Buildings Survey (HABS) at the Library of Congress.

The interior of the home was radically altered in a 1986 renovation. In 2008, Dr. Timothy Wang restored the stucco and received an award from the Historic District Commission.

WHHD

2038 Norway
George and Genevieve Moe House
306

1932

George J. Moe founded Moe's Sports Shop at 711 N. University in 1915 as a full-service sporting goods store, selling everything from golf clubs to baseball bats and ice skates. It is said that the "zebra-striped" shirts worn by referees were invented by Dr. Lloyd Olds of Ypsilanti and were first made at Moe's in 1948.

Moe's Sports Shop was successful enough to allow George and Genevieve Moe to build this splendid Tudor Revival house on Norway during the bleakest years of the Great Depression. The exceptional details of the house were likely made possible by the abundance of under- and unemployed carpenters and craftsman, and low-cost building materials of the time. The home is clad in rustic "clinker" bricks, with a steeply pitched slate roof and matching Medieval-styled chimneys. The windows are leaded glass casements with an unusual pane configuration. The sandstone Gothic-arched entry features acorn and oak leaf carvings which contribute to the romantic and charming appearance of this particularly fine Tudor residence.

Moe's Sports Shop passed out of the family in 1971, though it remains in business today. The house stayed in the Moe family until 1980 when it was purchased by Kenneth and Casey Wilhelm who remained until 2007.

307 915 Oakland
Alviso and Amoretta Stevens House   1893

The Stevens House is one of the more picturesque Queen Annes in the city. The flared gables and round corner turret give the home the look of a fairytale European castle. Adding to the effect are Gothic Revival elements in the square front bay with lancet windows. It is built of brick, unusual in the era when Michigan's white pine was king and most Queen Annes were executed in wood. Built on a slight rise, the imposing stature of the home is enhanced by the high stone foundation and tall central chimney. The porch is a sympathetic later addition of the 1990s.

This fine home was built for Professor of Pharmacy Alviso Stevens and his wife Amoretta. Stevens was renowned in his day for his knowledge of pharmacology, running a pharmacy in Detroit and teaching at the Detroit Medical College. He came back to his alma mater, the University of Michigan, in 1886 to teach in the College of Pharmacy, becoming Dean of the College. In the 1910s, he served as president and vice president of the American Pharmaceutical Association. Alviso and Amoretta lived in the house until 1904. By 1918, they had moved to Escondido, California to become citrus farmers. Converted to a fraternity like many of the large houses in the neighborhood, it became the home of Sigma Nu in 1904.

In 1919, Kappa Beta Psi occupied the house and in 1930, Delta Phi called it home. Today, the grand Victorian is divided into student apartments. Duane Black won awards from the Historic District Commission for his careful preservation of this house in 1997.

Former IHP

923 Olivia
Fred and Myra Jordan House

1893

Frederick P. and Myra (Beach) Jordan were noted members of the staff of the University of Michigan in the late 19th and early 20th century. Frederick Jordan graduated from the University in 1879 and from 1889 until his retirement in 1922 he served as assistant librarian, responsible for cataloging the entire University library. Myra Jordan was Dean of Women at the University from 1902 to 1922, and was noted for her care and attention to the living conditions of women on and off campus. The Mosher-Jordan Residence Hall at U-M is named after her and Eliza Mosher.

The Jordans built this grand Dutch Colonial Revival on Olivia Street in 1893. It is one of the oldest Colonial Revival buildings remaining in the city. Gone are the asymmetry and multiple textures of the Queen Anne style that grace many of this home's neighbors. While classically inspired and more restrained, the home exhibits plenty of ornamentation, including a three-part Palladian window and pedimented dormers on the third floor, large modillions and rows of dentils in the frieze band, and a grand front entrance with leaded glass sidelights. The home's most striking feature is the two-story full-width front porch with fluted Doric columns and muscular turned spindles.

Frederick and Myra Jordan lived here until 1914 when it became the home of Professor of Political Science Robert Treat Crane and his wife Maria (Riggs) who lived here until 1934.

1136 Prospect
Samuel and Harriet Miller House   1893

Neighbors know this red brick house as "the castle" because of its tall curved chimney, which envelopes a large arched window on the first floor. It was designed for Samuel and

Harriet Miller on land given to them by Christian Eberbach (see #325), Harriet's brother. The design was #27 in a pattern book entitled *The Cottage Souvenir, Revised and Enlarged* (1892) by the architect George F. Barber. Adding to the effect of grandness is the conical tower to the right of the entry and the elaborate side dormer. The use of different materials, varying window shapes and sizes, and multiple gables are from the Queen Anne playbook and extravagance was the overall effect.

Christian Eberbach's vast estate of orchards and gardens east of Packard was created in the 1860s. In 1892, Samuel and Harriet opened Prospect Ave. for access to Wells, East University, and Forest, and platted the Miller's Addition Subdivision. Their romantic villa was built on a hilltop at the edge of the orchard on two lots. The home remained in the Miller family until 1936.

Despite some unsympathetic additions done when it was converted to apartments, the house is considered a major landmark in the Burns Park neighborhood. In 1972, neighbors were successful in blocking the building of a large apartment building next door. It has appeared on covers of the *Ann Arbor Observer* several times and in local artist Milt Kemnitz's book *Michigan Memories*.

Former IHP

801 Rose
Ferdinand N. and Lucile Menefee House   1928

310

This modest Tudor Revival house looks like many of its 1920s and '30s neighbors, but is unique. Built of rammed earth (compressed adobe), the Menefee house along with the home of Roswell Franklin (see #15) are the only known examples of this construction technique in 20th-century Ann Arbor. Like the Franklin house, the Menefee house used the clay from the digging of the basement. The clay was put into oak forms and compressed using pneumatic tampers. The large adobe bricks were then laid up and covered in a coat of protective stucco. Though the primary construction materials were taken from the site, the labor-intensive technique raised the cost above a conventional frame house, though it was cheaper to heat and stayed cool in the summer.

The home was built by Professor of Engineering Ferdinand N. Menefee and his wife Lucile (Cull) in 1928. He likely got the idea of using rammed earth construction from Roswell Franklin, also in the Engineering Department in the 1920s. F.N. Menefee was an author, president of the Board of Public Works, director of the American Concrete Institute, and active in the Students' Christian Association. The original casement windows have been replaced, but the home retains much of its historic character and is an example of the alternative building techniques being explored in early 20th-century Ann Arbor.

311 1920 Scottwood
Raphael-Gehring House   1926

This particularly charming Tudor Revival home was built by Theophile and Mary (Malcomson) Raphael in 1926. The home maintains a quaint storybook appearance thanks to its multiple dormers and steeply pitched rooflines that terminate low to the ground at the small front-entry vestibule. The home's massing is broken up by a variety of textures, from stucco and half-timbering to brick and stone. It is all topped with a slate roof.

Theophile Raphael was a student and later professor of psychology at the University of Michigan, who started a mental health and counseling program for students at the University. Mary Raphael's father, Alexander Malcomson, was Detroit's largest coal dealer and one of Henry Ford's original financial backers. The Raphaels lived in the house for about a year, until Theophile went to work in Detroit for the State and City Courts of Detroit and the Wayne State Medical School. He eventually returned to the University of Michigan.

By 1928, composer and writer Carl Ernest Gehring and his wife Hester (Reed) had bought the house and made it their home until 1946. Gehring was a music critic for the *Ann Arbor News* from 1925 through 1962, and served as the state editor for the paper from 1941 through 1962. He also composed over sixty songs and was a member of the Michigan Composer's Guild. The home's Medieval architecture was a perfect fit for Hester Gehring, a student of Medieval German mysticism who wrote a book on the subject in 1957. For many years the home has been owned by Karen (Koykka) and Joe O'Neal, who received a Preservation Award from the Historic District Commission in 1998.

819 S. State
Eugene J. and Mary Helber House

1899

312

By the late 19th century, residents of German birth or background made up about fifty percent of Ann Arbor's population and were generally accepted in the community, serving in important public offices and operating many of the city's prominent businesses. Eugene J. Helber began publishing *The Neue Washtenaw Post*, a German-language newspaper in 1894. He was successful enough to build this spectacular Queen Anne home in 1899.

During World War I, antipathy to the German population reached its zenith, and Helber was charged with sedition. *The Neue Washtenaw Post* drew suspicion for its strong pro-German editorials in the early years of the war. The U.S. Postal Service refused to mail his papers and Helber was called to Washington to appear before Congress. The paper was allowed to continue after Helber transferred the publishing to his son, and changed the text to English. The paper became *The Washtenaw Post-Tribune* and later *The Ann Arbor Tribune* (see #72).

The Helbers lived in the house until 1914 when it became the home of the Apostles Club, a group of bachelor faculty members at the University of Michigan. In the 1950s, it was converted into apartments. In 1989, the home was restored and renovated inside and out by Marvin and Susan Carlson of Carlson Properties, who took great care in restoring the interior woodwork, and brought the exterior back to life, including the three-story corner turret, the simplified Colonial Revival porches, and the south side bay and dormer. They received an award from the Historic District Commission in recognition of their rehabilitation efforts.

Former IHP

313 730 Tappan
Memorial Christian Church/
Disciples of Christ Church   1891

This unusual church with a beautiful rose window, a tall tower with a four-sided cap, and a round tower with a conical cap was designed by Malcolmson and Higginbotham of Detroit and originally stood on South University Avenue at Tappan. The construction was undertaken by the Church of Christ, Disciples of Christ Church, and the Christian Women's Missionary Society and funded by Mrs. Sarah Hawley Scott of Detroit. At its dedication in 1891, Ann Arbor church leaders eloquently pleaded for Christian unity.

In 1923, when University of Michigan needed land for the law school, the church was moved to the corner of Tappan and Hill Streets. The University paid to put it on a high foundation (to ensure enough lighting in the basement) and the numbered original materials were reassembled, but in a mirror image of the original building. In 1924, the Christian Women's Board of Missions deeded the building to the Church of Christ. Despite building a school in 1945 and purchasing a parsonage in 1951, by 1955 the congregation seriously considered moving, but in 1958 they approved a plan for remodeling and held a rededication in 1959.

The church is a mix of the Queen Anne and Shingle styles. Features include varying roof heights and shapes, varying window sizes and shapes, an asymmetrical floor plan, and shingles of red slate.

In 2012, the church sold the property to the Sigma Phi Epsilon fraternity and moved to 5141 Platt Road. The Sig Eps remodeled the church to fit 45 beds, while preserving the historic features of the building.

Before moving, the church opened a time capsule that contained a Bible, a map of Ann Arbor, a history of the Church, and an American flag. Photographs, drawings, and notes by members of Emil Lorch's class in the 1930s are on file at the Bentley Library.

Former IHP

848 E. University
Emma Lowry House

c. 1911

Built in 1910 or 1911, the Emma Lowry House is one of the more interesting variations on the Arts and Crafts style in the city. The home features a variety of materials, including randomly laid cut granite on the lower story, brick on the second story, and a clay tile roof with large overhangs. The front porch features a rounded roof and stucco face, and the back porch also features stucco but with half-timbering. The variety of the materials works well with the unusual architectural details. The small entrance porch is very much of the era, but above the porch is a strange, somewhat Tudor-style bay window. To the right the home features a single round-arch window sandwiched between the porch and an interesting stone bay with three-part window. The overall asymmetry of the house implies the Queen Anne era, while the home is predominantly Arts and Crafts with some Tudor Revival detailing.

The home was built by a Mrs. Emma Lowry, an elderly widow by the time she moved into the house in 1911. Little is known about her except that she was originally from New York, and was the widow of Henry R. Lowry. She lived in the house until 1920 and by 1923 it became the residence of realtor James A. Rose and his wife Frances. From the late 1950s through 1970, Austin Warren, a renowned literary critic, professor of English at U-M, and biographer, lived here with his wife Antonia.

315 1414 Washtenaw
Kappa Alpha Theta Sorority
1867/1916

Inside what appears to be a large 20th-century Colonial Revival sorority house is a much earlier home built by physician Silas Pratt in 1867. In 1868, it was the home of dentist Charles B. Porter, and by the mid-1890s, Burke A. and Mary Hinsdale were living here. Burke A. Hinsdale was the former president of Hiram College and superintendent of the Cleveland Public Schools. He later became Professor of Education at the University of Michigan, and is recognized as a pioneer in the methods of the teaching of educators. He died in 1900, and his widow Mary lived in the house until 1916 when the home was purchased by the Kappa Alpha Theta sorority. Founded in 1879, Kappa Alpha Theta was the first Greek letter sorority at the University of Michigan.

The sorority hired James Boynton of the University of Michigan Architecture School to remodel the older home in the Colonial Revival style, which totally obscured the original building. Boynton designed a large two-story veranda, likely modeled after George Washington's Mount Vernon. The front roof is Dutch Colonial inspired, topped with six round-topped dormers. The exterior is finished in smooth stucco. The interesting front entrance projects out, forming a small entry vestibule topped with a detailed balustrade. The interior has butternut woodwork in the living room and a Pewabic tile fireplace. It was added to the State Register of Historic Places in 1982.

SR

1432 Washtenaw
First Presbyterian Church

316

1937

The First Presbyterian Church was organized in Ann Arbor in 1826, later building a church at the corner of Huron and Division. By the 1920s, it had outgrown the older building and plans were made for a new building on the site of the Isaac Newton Demmon house on Washtenaw Avenue. The Great Depression delayed construction until 1935.

Ready for services in January of 1938, the First Presbyterian Church is a wonderful example of Neo-Gothic church architecture. Designed by New York architects Mayers, Murray, and

Phillip, a firm known for its church designs, it is built with a steel and clay tile masonry frame faced with an Indiana limestone ashlar veneer. The steeply pitched Gothic Revival roofs are slate. The original building was L-shaped, with the sanctuary in one wing and the student activities wing, or "Lemon Wing," in the other.

A modern back addition known as the "Kuizenga Wing" was added to the church in 1956 to house classrooms. Another addition in the Neo-Gothic style was added to the back in 1998. As the congregation had limited funds during construction, the church had very few stained glass windows. English stained glass windows were installed in the 1960s. The building sits on beautiful lush grounds with many ancient trees, some of which date to the era of the Demmon house.

317 1530 Washtenaw
Chi Phi Fraternity   1929

First established at the University of Michigan in 1883, the Alpha Tau chapter of the Chi Phi fraternity built this house in 1929. Constructed of a subdued tan brick with limestone trimmings and a steeply pitched hipped slate roof with shed roof dormers, the fraternity house features very little of the half-timbering typical of Tudor Revival buildings. It is essentially a long hipped roof structure, though the central portion of the building's front facade projects out at a diagonal, adding to the architectural interest. The unique diagonal projection also features a two-story bay, an arched entrance door, a tall masonry chimney, and half-timbering above the small side porch.

The interesting design was drawn by Ann Arbor architects Paul Fry and Lynn Kasurin. The firm of Fry and Kasurin are notable for their designs of other Ann Arbor landmarks, including the First United Methodist Church, the First National Bank Building (see #94), and the Tuomy Hills Gas Station (see #322).

1550 Washtenaw
Phi Kappa Psi (Zeta Tau Alpha) 1920

318

This brick Tudor Revival with its mature trees and deep setback off Washtenaw was built in 1920 for the Phi Kappa Psi fraternity, replacing their earlier building on the site which had been the home of Chauncey Millen, a local clothier. Millen shared a driveway with his neighbor to the west, Jerome C. Knowlton, and six brick pillars lined the borders of the drive. When the house was demolished, Knowlton's initials (JCK) were carved in the westernmost pillar to honor his memory and the others were inscribed with the initials of the fraternity (unfortunately these pillars remain targets of graffiti).

A textbook example of the Tudor Revival, it has steeply pitched gables and a second story with many panels of stucco and half-timbering, some carved with quatrefoil designs. Flattened Tudor arches grace the entry and a row of windows in the sunroom, formerly a garage.

Since 1971, it has been the home of the Zeta Tau Alpha sorority which renovated the house for its 50 residents. The interior of the house they call "The ZTA Castle" has some original features, including many-paned leaded glass casement windows, mahogany woodwork (al-

though painted white), some fixtures, and parts of the original floors. They won Preservation Awards in 1992 and 2013.

WHHD

319 1830 Washtenaw

Scott-Canfield House/Women's City Club 1886/1917/1962

More than most of the houses on Washtenaw, this one has had three very different lives. When Evart Scott built his farmhouse here in 1886, Washtenaw was a dirt road. Scott ran a nursery and orchard on a 30-acre plot just outside the city limits, planted elm trees along the Washtenaw frontage, and called his spread the "Elm Fruit Farm."

Scott arrived in Ann Arbor from Ohio in 1868 to attend the University of Michigan and after two years of school left to become a successful farmer, businessman, and community activist. He ran a flour mill at Argo Dam, was a member of the school and public works boards, was president of the Ann Arbor Agricultural Company, and on the board of Forest Hill Cemetery.

When the city annexed this area in 1915, Scott sold most of his land to Charles Spooner who, with architect Fiske Kimball, developed what is now known as Scottwood. In 1917, Scott moved to 1930 Washtenaw and sold this house and three acres of land to Dr. R. Bishop Canfield, a University of Michigan Professor of Medicine. Canfield hired University of Michigan Architecture Professor Lewis J. Boynton to remodel the farmhouse into something grander and more colonial. The current Dutch Colonial is the result. A wraparound porch was removed and two wings were added on the north and south. A steeply sloped roof extended over the wings and a new entry was graced with slender Ionic columns. The interior was remodeled into a Colonial style as well and remains so today.

After Mrs. Canfield's death in 1950, a group of women banded together to buy the house so that various womens' organizations could meet in a comfortable and congenial atmosphere. It was known as the Ann Arbor Women's City Club (AAWCC). Since 2008, it serves both men and women and was renamed the Ann Arbor City Club. Ralph Hammett was engaged in 1962 to design a modern addition, which includes a dining room, auditorium, office, lobby, and member lounge. In 2008, a capital campaign was begun to renovate the ballroom, add more restrooms, and improve the dining facilities and the interior décor.

1850 Washtenaw

320

Edward L. and Sarah Adams House

1917

Built in 1917 for University of Michigan Professor of French Edward L. Adams, this brick Georgian Colonial Revival was designed by local architect Samuel McCoskry Stanton. Stanton wanted it to resemble an 18th-century Colonial and gave it a central, double-columned porticoed entry, with a Palladian window above and a Chinese Chippendale balustrade. Somewhat unusual are the eyebrow dormers on either side of the gabled one, and an off-kilter plan with five bays on the first floor and three bays on the second. End chimneys complete the look.

Stanton, the grandson of the first Episcopal bishop of Michigan, was born and raised in Detroit and studied in Paris and Stuttgart. He came to Ann Arbor around 1900 and had

an established practice by the time he designed this house. His other well-known buildings include the Hobbs house at the corner of Hill and Oxford, and his own homes at 1705 Washtenaw, 1710 Cambridge (see #296), and 501 Onondaga. He practiced in Ann Arbor for over 40 years.

Edward Adams lived in the house until his death in 1958. His son, Edward L. Adams Jr., a psychologist, lived here with his wife until 1986. He and his brother perpetuate their father's name through a scholarship in the Romance Language Department. Due to their long ownership, the house has remained in almost pristine condition. Current owners Gregory and Margene Henry received a Preservation Award from the Historic District Commission in 2013 for their long stewardship.

Former IHP

321 2200 Washtenaw
Hildene Manor   1926

Set back on a wide expanse of lawn, this Tudor Revival building resembles an English country estate but holds eight six-room apartments that have been converted to condos. They were the epitome of apartment living with large roomy spaces, air conditioning, and maid's quarters. There are also a caretaker's flat and common areas. In the early 20th century, apartment living was chic and appealed to the wealthy who were selling their large estates after the establishment of an income tax in 1913. Hildene Manor residents have always been a "who's who" of Ann Arbor. The first occupants included George Millen and Luther L. James (see #146).

The Tudor Revival style was chosen by the builders, Group Homes Apartments, to signify refinement and good taste. There is half-timbering on the front facade with symmetrical stone Tudor-arch entries, a steeply pitched roof punctuated by chimneys, and groups of double-hung nine-over-nine and six-over-six windows. Asymmetry adds to the effect of one building with varying bump-outs in front. Since it is a cooperative, owners share responsibility for the grounds, the exterior, water, and heating. They received a Preservation Award in 1990.

The name Hildene Manor was adopted in 1927 so the post office could find it (they were then in the country). Hildene is an Old English word meaning "hill and valley" and was the name of Abraham Lincoln's son's 1905 estate in Manchester, Vermont (now a museum).

Former IHP

2460 Washtenaw
Tuomy Hills Gas Station

1928

322

Local developers Kathryn and Bill Tuomy (see #368) were savvy enough to build this tiny gas station when the "cut off" (now Stadium Blvd.) was opened in 1927. They hired local

architects Fry and Kasurin to design something that would blend with the residential neighborhood. The result is this charming fieldstone building, which has become a beloved Ann Arbor landmark. When Amoco proposed demolition in the 1980s, the citizens arose in protest and the building was protected as an Individual Historic Property in 1988.

The structure resembles an English toll gate, with sixteen-inch-thick stone walls, a slate roof, and hand-hewn oak posts with knee braces supporting the roofs of the two gabled porches. The porch facing Washtenaw has a stucco and half-timber facade. The Stadium-facing one has a clipped gable with horizontal siding.

In 1995, it was purchased and restored by University Bank, which used the porches for drive-through ATMs. They received a Rehabilitation Award in 1998. Today the porches serve as drive-throughs for the Bearclaw Coffee Company which leases the space. It is a great example of the adaptive reuse of a small commercial building and is a landmark at the gateway to Ann Arbor.

NR, Former IHP

1414 Wells

323 ## Tappan Intermediate/
Burns Park Elementary School   1926

Named after University of Michigan president and educational innovator Henry Tappan, the Tappan Intermediate School was built during the post-World War I school building boom. It served as an elementary and junior high until 1951, when it became Burns Park Elementary.

Unlike other public school buildings which were built in the Collegiate Gothic style during this period, the Tappan School was designed in the Colonial Revival style. One of the building's highlights is the elaborate Georgian Revival entrance, with scrolled broken pediment, dentils, transom windows, and pilasters. The double windows are trimmed in stone. The second-floor windows have arches above with Colonial-style reliefs executed in stone. The red brick building stands three stories tall with a shallow hipped roof topped with an ornate cupola and weather vane. The cornice is stone and is lined with delicately carved stone modillions that run the perimeter of the building. Though the windows are not original, the building retains much of its historic character and remains the most picturesque of Ann Arbor's public schools.

1220 White
Stephen Hedges House

324

Early 1860s

Along with its Italianate neighbor at 1212 White Street, this home stands out in a neighborhood of 1920s and '30s Colonials, Tudors, and bungalows. In the years immediately following World War II, the University of Michigan was expanding in all directions due to the large influx of former soldiers enrolling under the G.I. Bill. Originally at 701 Tappan, this Italianate home stood in the way of the expanding Business School. The building was saved from demolition and "reused" when C.A. Johnson and Son moved it on July 20, 1946.

The home was built by carpenter and joiner Stephen Hedges and his wife Sarah in the early 1860s. "Joiners" were highly skilled tradesmen, dating back to the Middle Ages, who specialized in the intricate and difficult task of building with heavy timber frames. These frames were hand-hewn from raw, freshly cut logs, and the sills, posts, plates, and girts were carefully mortised together and fastened with wood pegs. The home originally had a front gabled roof, but sometime before 1880, it was reconfigured into the hipped, Italianate roof seen today.

Rev. David H. Taylor and his wife Martha followed Hedges. After the Reverend's death in the 1880s, the widowed Martha Taylor lived here into the 1920s. A student rental, the home is remarkably intact—retaining its original windows, fine Italianate door and sidelights, and original bracketed portico.

325 1115 Woodlawn
Christian and Margaretha Eberbach House   1863

When this textbook example of a brick Italianate villa-style house was built in the 1860s on what was then Packard, it was in the country. It was built by Christian Eberbach who ran a successful drugstore and laboratory equipment factory which he established in 1843 (it still exists as the Eberbach Corp.). The main body is L-shaped with a four-story tower where the two sides join at the entry. A 1½-story wing is attached at the rear and has a covered porch that faces Woodlawn. The windows are four-over-four and have corbeled brick crowns with segmental arches. A bay window, paired sets of windows on the ground floor, bracketed eaves, brick corbels at the roofline, an oculus in the gabled arch of the upright portion, a high fieldstone foundation, slate roof, and shutters complete the picture. The tower has varying shapes of arched windows separated by horizontal bands of contrasting brick, and a balcony by one window. Underground there are vaulted brick storerooms for grains and fruits, and a brick smoker for curing hams and bacon.

Eberbach and his wife Margaretha (Laubengayer) were from Stuttgart, and were concerned about giving their five children a good education. They located near town where they could send them to the University of Michigan and still enjoy the country air. Christian Eberbach presided over his businesses and this farm, and co-founded Hutzel Plumbing Company (still in business) and Ann Arbor Savings Bank. He was active in the Republican Party and participated in the election of Lincoln. He was mayor of Ann Arbor from 1868–69.

Like many large houses built in this era, it was empty after Eberbach's death in 1901. The land was subdivided in 1907, providing for 81 home sites. Eventually the house was occupied by State Senator and Mrs. George McCallum Sr., and then other families who turned some of the spaces into apartments. Since 1987, it has been owned by Krista and John Williams who have restored it inside and out. The house has been featured on numerous tours and articles about Ann Arbor architecture. The interior woodwork shows the fine craftsmanship of the 1860s. The Williams received a Preservation Award in 2013 for their over 25 years of stewardship.

Former IHP

FAR SOUTH SIDE

The area south of Stadium Boulevard is generally lacking in historic character, with a vast majority of the homes built during the 1950s through 1980s. Winding and pleasant tree-lined streets are primarily filled with Cape Cods and ranches, with a few Mid-Century Modern-style houses mixed in. The area was predominantly farmland prior to World War II, though some of the residences off Packard, Baldwin, and South Industrial date to the 1920s. Arts and Crafts-style gems can be found on Jewett and Rosewood, and the neighborhood northeast of Packard and Platt Roads. Also off Packard and Platt on Terhune Road lies one of the city's oldest cemetery, the Terhune Pioneer Cemetery.

South State Street is primarily commercial and light industrial, though the 1866 J.S. Henderson farmhouse (see #329) survives as office space. Other landmark farmhouses still survive on Packard, including the Benajah Ticknor farmhouse (see #328) from 1844, which is a choice example of cobblestone construction, owned by the City of Ann Arbor as the Cobblestone Farm Museum. The dining room of Cobblestone Farm is the Maynard cabin from the late 1820s, which may be the oldest remaining building in the city of Ann Arbor. The William Anderson farmhouse (see #326) is another survivor from Ann Arbor's earliest days. Built in 1846, it is a unique take on the Greek Revival style, reminiscent of a small Greek temple.

326 2301 Packard
William Anderson House/Wisdom Chapel   1846/1941

This wonderful example of a "temple cottage" Greek Revival house with its pillared portico, board and batten siding, pedimented front, frieze windows, and ornamental cast-iron grilles, was built in 1846 by Sheriff John Anderson and his son William. At the time it was in Pittsfield Township. Three generations of this family lived here until it was sold to Dr. Inez Wisdom in 1937 who used it as her home and office.

Dr. Wisdom was a pioneering female physician who served as president of the Washtenaw County Medical Society and the St. Joseph Mercy Hospital Medical Society. A very religious woman, she built her own chapel for private prayer patterned after those she had seen in Europe. Patients who could not pay helped her build it and University of Michigan art student John Maxon painted the unique fresco of the Transfiguration behind the altar. In 1953, she and her companion, Miss Gertrude Griffith, gave the chapel and part of the grounds to the Episcopal Diocese of Michigan, establishing the St. Clare of Assisi parish. In 1968, Miss Griffith obtained the house and later gave it to the church. St. Clare's eventually built a larger building next door, joining forces with the Temple Beth Emeth in 1975. The two formed a group known as Genesis, which now owns the property. This unique combination of church and synagogue received accolades from the Huron Land Use Alliance in 1997.

The house was drawn for the Historic American Buildings Survey (HABS) in 1934, and has often been featured in books on the Greek Revival in Michigan. It received a Preservation Award from the Historic District Commission in 1988.

NR, Former IHP

2600 Packard
Stone School

1911 **327**

A landmark at the intersection of Packard and Platt Roads, this picturesque rural school-house of fieldstone with a tile roof topped by a four-gabled belfry was constructed in 1911. It replaced an earlier fieldstone school built in 1853 for Pittsfield District #7, which had

replaced the Mallett's Settlement School, built in 1827. The white boxed cornices vividly contrast with the multicolored stone and red tile. The school features oculus (circular) air vents at each gable.

With a growing student popula-tion, additional wooden build-ings were added. From 1918–1927 Michigan State Normal College (now EMU) used it for teach-er training. An "ultra-modern" cinder block school was built across the street in 1949 to accommodate more growth and this school was boarded up.

In 1955, the Pittsfield District was absorbed into the Ann Arbor school system. Parents petitioned to use the old school as a nursery and the Stone School Cooperative Nursery was born, led by Millie Seltzer and Jane Herrin. The school rented the building until it went up for sale in 1994. A community effort led by Barbara Loomis bought and restored the decay-ing structure, for which they received a Preservation Award in 1995. Children still ring the bell to mark the end of the morning and afternoon sessions.

NR, Former IHP, SR

328 2781 Packard
Ticknor-Campbell House (Cobblestone Farm)   1828/1844

Cobblestone Farm is a city-owned facility used to interpret farm life of the 19th century. It was built in 1844 for Dr. Benajah Ticknor by Stephen Mills, a mason trained in New York. Mills laid the front facade cobblestones in a delightful herringbone pattern with quoins at

the corners. The sides and rear are of cobblestones laid in a regular manner. A beautiful recessed doorway with side-lights, six-over-six windows, and green shutters complete the restrained elegance of this Federal/Greek Revival house.

The interior has a wide central hall with staircase and "grained" woodwork. A parlor and library, sitting room, and bedrooms complete the stone portion of the house. The dining room portion at the rear of the house is older, dating to the initial time of settlement by the Maynard family in the 1820s, and was attached to the house in 1845 when the kitchen wing was constructed. The wing also housed a hired man's room, milk room, pantry, and toilets. Heman Ticknor purchased this property for his brother Benajah, a U.S. Navy surgeon who traveled to the Far East and South America for years and wanted to invest in Michigan property. Benajah was a noted scholar who participated in University of Michigan life. He died in 1858 and his papers are now housed at the University and at Yale.

In 1860, Ticknor's widow sold the farm to Horace Booth, who enlarged it by 183 acres and added barns and an Italianate front porch. It was passed to his son Nelson Booth and in 1881 the farm was purchased by Scottish immigrant William Campbell, an Ypsilanti merchant soon renowned for his purebred cattle. Three generations of the family worked the farm until the City of Ann Arbor purchased the house and the last 4.5 acres from Mary and George Campbell for Buhr Park in 1972.

A dedicated group of citizens began raising money to restore and establish the cobblestone house as Cobblestone Farm and create a working farm museum. The Cobblestone Farm Association works with the Ann Arbor Parks Department and oversees these activities. They recently restored the pioneer log cabin that was moved to the site in 1981, maintain a historic garden, partner with the Eastern Michigan University Preservation Program, and run special events at holiday time. A new barn was built in 1988 to accommodate events. Several awards have been given to this project, including one for the restoration of the shutters.

NR, SR, HABS, CFHD

2190 S. State

329

John S. and Louise Henderson House   1866

This house looks nearly the same as it looked in 1874, when it was featured in the *Atlas and Map of Washtenaw County* as the "Res. of J.S. Henderson, Sec. 5 Pittsfield Twp. MI." This well-preserved home was built in 1866 by John S. and Louise (Roye) Henderson in the Greek Revival style. Unlike many of the other late period Greek Revivals in town, which often featured more contemporary Italianate or Gothic detailing, the Henderson house shows that old habits die hard, looking more like an 1846 house than an 1866 house. The porch is particularly old fashioned, with its square columns and low hipped roof, when one might expect slender chamfered columns and Italianate or Gothic Revival gingerbread.

J.S. Henderson came to Washtenaw County in 1835 and for many years was a partner in a hardware and stove business on Main Street known as Risdon and Henderson. He was a man of many talents and served as president of the Washtenaw County Agricultural and Horticultural Society, as alderman in the city of Ann Arbor, and manager at the All-mendinger Organ Company (see #63). He also worked installing water and sewer systems in Illinois. Henderson ran a farm on his State Street property from 1866 until his death in 1890. Soon after John Henderson's death the farm was sold to A.S. Hammond. Though surrounded by and used as a commercial building, the home is the last remaining intact farmhouse in this part of town.

GEDDES/OXBRIDGE/ ORCHARD HILLS

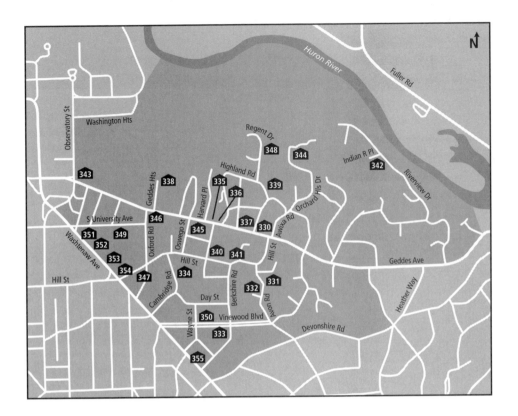

During the 19th century, the Geddes and Oxbridge area was lined with small- to medium-sized farms, many of which specialized in growing fruit. Several of these early farmhouses can still be found (see #336 and #337). Change came slowly to the area, which accounts for the continued existence of many of the early homes. In 1858, Forest Hill Cemetery (see #343) was opened and by 1867 its Gordon Lloyd-designed Gothic Revival gatehouse was built.

Along Hill Street fraternities and sororities built large Tudor Revival and Colonial buildings (see #347). In 1907, fruit farmer Walter Nichols (see #338) donated his farm to the University of Michigan, which became Nichols Arboretum, one of the most popular parks in the city. By the early 20th century, with the advent of the automobile, many of the farms were subdivided and split into small subdivisions. Hill Street became a street of many grand houses built on large lots (see #340 and #341). Craftsman style, Tudor Revival, and Colonial Revival homes were built by University professors and upper-middle-class professionals along Geddes, Geddes Heights, Harvard Place, Ridgeway, Berkshire, Oswego, Devonshire, and Awixa (see #330). Professor Albert J.J. Rousseau designed his unique Prairie-style house on Vinewood in 1928 (see #350) and architect Alden Dow designed a Mid-Century Modern home on Berkshire for his sister Margaret Towsley in 1932 (see #333).

The Great Depression and World War II put an end to much of the construction in the area, but the post-war years brought a new wave of building and many fine examples of the Mid-Century Modern style were constructed in the area. The most famous and striking is the Frank Lloyd Wright-designed Palmer House (see #344), which remained in the Palmer family until recently. Other notable buildings of this era were built on Oxford Road (see #346), Geddes (see #335), Regent Drive (see #348), and Indian River Place (see #342). The grand historic homes, rolling terrain, and winding tree-lined roads make the Geddes area one of the most beautiful, well maintained, and expensive of Ann Arbor.

330 408 Awixa
Eli and Blanche Gallup House   1926

The City of Ann Arbor is blessed with 157 parks covering over 2,000 acres of land. Eli Gallup, Superintendent of Parks from 1919 to 1961, deserves much of the credit for making the city parks what they are today. A native of New York, Gallup first came to Ann Arbor to attend the University of Michigan where he earned an M.S. in forestry in 1916. During his tenure as Superintendent of Parks, Gallup was responsible for direct-ing the maintenance and purchase of park land in the city as well as overseeing the city airport and cemeteries. He added Buhr Park, Frisinger Park, Fritz Park, Gallup Park (named in his honor), Allmendinger Park, Hunt Park, Veterans Park, and the Huron Hills Golf Course. Ann Arborites today will recognize "The Rock" at the corner of Hill and Washt-enaw, which Gallup had placed on the site in 1932 in honor of the 200th anniversary of George Washington's birth, and the stone walls he had built on Fuller Road in the 1930s.

For their own house the Gallups chose a beautiful site on the corner of Geddes and Awixa. The Colonial Revival house was designed by F.C. Odell and completed in 1926. For the time period, it is a fairly authentic take on an early New England colonial, complete with saltbox shape and central front cross gable and an overhanging second story, or "jetty," featuring carved, decorative pendants. The Gallups owned the house until 1975, when it was purchased by local preservationists Al and Louisa Pieper. Louisa Pieper was voted Pres-ervationist of the Year in 2003 by the Historic District Commission for her many years of preservation work in Ann Arbor and the State of Michigan.

819 Avon
Leslie and Mary White House 1950

331

This Mid-Century Modern home was designed by architect George Brigham in 1950, and built by Albert Duckek. Following Brigham's ideas of "organic architecture," all superficial details were removed from the design and natural materials were used—in this case, red brick, redwood, cedar beams, and tinted concrete floors. The home features a cross-shaped floor plan with open space in the middle. Professor White's office was in the far end of one wing for complete quiet and privacy. Massive glass panels allow for large amounts of light and some solar heat in the winter, while the four-foot overhangs shade the interior in the summer.

The building was designed for professor and founder of the Anthropology Department at the University of Michigan Leslie White and his wife Mary (Pattison). White was an influential and well-known anthropologist who taught at the University for 40 years. He often ran afoul of the school's administrators and even the local Catholic church, who tried to get him dismissed for his radical socialist and atheist views. White is remembered for his contributions to the theories of social evolution, cultural evolution, and neoevolutionism, which ran contrary to the general thinking in the academic world of his day, though generally favored and viewed as correct today. White studied the culture of the Keresan Pueblo Indians, and served as president of the American Association for the Advancement of Science and president of the American Anthropological Association. Leslie White lived in the home until 1971, when he moved to California. He is buried at Forest Hill Cemetery with his wife.

Owned by local preservationists Nancy and David Deromedi, the Leslie and Mary White house has been returned to its former glory by the removal of unfortunate renovations. The Deromedis hired architect Robert Metcalf (see #356) to restore the "remuddled" garage, and had Metcalf add a large overhang with skylights over the front door. Nancy Deromedi is one of the founders of A2 Modern, a group organized to foster appreciation for Ann Arbor's Mid-Century Modern buildings. They were recognized for their advocacy work by the Historic District Commission in 2012.

332

830 Avon
H. Richard and Florence Crane House   1954

The Crane house was the first private commission of the modern architect Robert Metcalf (see #356). Metcalf's design paid attention to the Cranes' needs as a family. The home featured no formal dining room (as the Crane's usually dined buffet-style), easy access from the entry to the children's recreation area on the lower level, and the master bedroom and children's bedrooms were placed in separate wings of the house. The exterior of the home's lower level is brick, with vertical cedar above. Large banks of windows, including corner windows, bathe the interior in light.

H. Richard Crane was a member of the University of Michigan Physics Department from 1934 through 1978, and was chair of the department from 1964 until 1972. His work in nuclear physics led to the invention of the race track synchrotron, which has been used in nearly every particle accelerator since. Crane was a member of the National Academy of Science and in 1986 was awarded the National Medal of Science by President Reagan.

Florence (Rohmer Le-Baron) Crane was also a distinguished member of the community. She served on the Ann Arbor City Council for two terms, served 17 years on the Michigan State Corrections Commission, and was the first woman on the board of the National Bank and Trust Company. The Cranes were both active in the Ann Arbor Hands-On Museum and the Ann Arbor Community Foundation. Prominent guests to the Cranes' Avon Road home include Congressman and later President Gerald Ford, Defense Secretary Robert McNamara, and University of Michigan President Robben Wright Fleming. The home was owned by the Crane family until 2004.

1000 Berkshire

Harry and Margaret Towsley House

333

1932

Famed Michigan architect Alden Dow (son of Herbert Dow, the founder of Dow Chemical in Midland) designed this home for his sister Margaret Dow Towsley and her husband Harry in 1932. It was his first domestic commission. According to the *AIA Guide to Detroit*, it was the first residence in the U.S. with an attached garage facing the street. Typical of Dow, who studied with Frank Lloyd Wright, the structure is a long and low brick house with

sharp verticals in the chimney and brick piers supporting the overhanging standing seam copper roof. It marks the beginning of the "modern" movement in architecture in Ann Arbor and retains a remarkably fresh look today.

Dow was named Architect Laureate of Michigan in 1983, shortly before he died. His home and studio in Midland are now open to the public as a museum. Dow designed over 300 buildings during his lifetime and many are in Ann Arbor, including City Hall (see #57), the Ann Arbor Public Library (see #58), the ISR building on Division Street, the Fleming Administration Building (see #226), the Matthaei Botanical Gardens, Greenhills School, the Morris House (see #348), and many more.

The house is large (over 4,000 square feet) due to additions in 1934, 1940, and 1950. Dr. Towsley was a well-known pediatrician, and the Towsleys were generous philanthropists. The family has endowed many buildings and scholarships that carry their name. Mrs. Towsley spent 60 years in this comfortable home.

Former IHP

334 | 1930 Cambridge
Rebec-Hildebrandt House   1907

In 1906, following his studies at Harvard, architect Emil Lorch came to Ann Arbor to head the Architecture Program at the University of Michigan's Engineering School. This home was one of his first commissions in Ann Arbor, and was built for Professor of Philosophy

George Rebec. Lorch's design for Rebec's home is an interesting early take on the Craftsman style with hints of the Prairie style. The hipped roof building with exposed rafter tails is sided in stucco and features a thin belt course that delineates the lower and upper stories and emphasizes the horizontal. The front facade is asymmetrical, with a projecting bay and arched overhang sheltering the front entrance. The back features a recessed two-story open porch. The home is identical to its next door neighbor at 1942 Cambridge, also Lorch-designed, which was built in 1908 for Professor of History Claude Van Tyne. Lorch designed a number of similar houses within a few blocks of Rebec and Van Tyne.

George Rebec sold the house in 1911 to Physics Professor Karl Guthe, and Guthe's widow Belle sold the home in 1927 to her niece Dora (Ware) and her husband Theophil Hildebrandt, chairman of the Mathematics Department. Dora Hildebrandt, an avid botanist and gardener, planted a wildflower garden in the forested front yard, which can still be appreciated today. Their son H. Mark Hildebrandt, a retired pediatrician, has done a remarkable job of restoring his old family home, including the fine interior woodwork and his mother's forest wildflower garden. Dr. Hildebrandt received the Preservationist of the Year Award in 2006 from the Historic District Commission.

Former IHP

2037 Geddes
Tole and Elizabeth McDivitt House
1866

Despite what books on American architecture may tell you about the waning popularity of the Greek Revival style by 1860, it continued to be very popular in Ann Arbor and Washtenaw County until at least the late 1860s (see #329). The front-gabled portion of this house is believed to be the original 1866 farmhouse, and the tall four-over-four windows hint at its late date in the Greek Revival period. The side wing is said to have been moved from elsewhere on the lot and attached in the early 20th century when the entire building was stuccoed and "modernized" to the Arts and Crafts and Colonial Revival tastes of the day.

Tole and Elizabeth McDivitt built this farmhouse shortly after they bought 11 acres on Geddes Road in late 1865. The McDivitts came from Ireland and operated a small farm here until 1881. Following the McDivitts, the house changed hands many times, and was occupied by Minister Edwin Spence from 1881 to 1882, Charles Nichols from 1882 to 1886, physician Charles Howell and his wife Sarah from 1886 to about 1905, and Professor John Langley and his wife Martica from 1906 until 1918. An old carriage barn on the northeast corner of the property is where the Psi Upsilon fraternity held their meetings during the late 1920s.

David Huntington, renowned professor of history and art and Dean at U-M in the 1980s, helped save Frederic Edwin Church's estate, "Olana" in New York, which is now a museum. He lived here with his wife Gertrude from 1968–1993.

336 2045 Geddes
Wells and Sybil Bennett House   1953

Wells Bennett served as Dean of the University of Michigan College of Architecture and Design from 1937. An early proponent of modern architecture in the state, one of Bennett's main interests was efficient, low-cost housing, which explains the construction of this home built in 1953.

Set into a hill on the former O'Kane-Smith Farm (see #337), the Bennett house is devoid of ornamentation. His focus was on simple geometric forms. The house is a box, the only pro-

jections being a side entrance porch, a narrow side deck on the east elevation, and a small bump-out on the front. The front bump-out features an unusual triangular "butterfly roof" and clerestory windows on the back side. Its site on a hill allowed the garage to be built under the house, and the home to blend into the landscape.

Bennett's earlier Colonial Revival house, built in 1921, stands behind this home at 500 Highland. Though the two buildings were built only 32 years apart, they offer a wonderful contrast between the "Revival" architecture of the early 20th century and modern architecture, which abandoned earlier stylistic and architectural precedents altogether. Current owner Barbara Levin Bergman received a Preservation Award from the Historic District Commission in 2007.

2103 Geddes
O'Kane-Smith House

337

1869

This Vernacular farmhouse was built in 1869 by fruit grower Hugh O'Kane and his wife Catherine. The house still boasts its original windows, shutters, and fine door surround with transom and sidelight windows. The porches appear to have been added in the early 20th century. Little is known about the O'Kanes except that they were from Ireland and quite well off. They settled in New York City before coming to Ann Arbor in the 1860s. Hugh O'Kane planted an extensive orchard on the property and farmed the land until his death in 1893.

The farm passed through a number of hands until it was purchased by Andrew Franklin Smith and his wife Kate (Inglis) in 1895. The Smiths were natives of Detroit where Andrew's family had a shoe manufacturing business and Kate's father was a successful physician. Andrew Franklin Smith farmed the land on Geddes and continued to grow fruit in O'Kane's orchard, but also began raising animals for research purposes at the University of Michigan, earning him the nickname "Guinea Pig Smith."

In 1923, the Smiths subdivided their farm as the Andrew Franklin Smith Subdivision, and a large 8.5-acre parcel was sold to Kate Smith's brother James Inglis. Inglis and his wife Elizabeth built their grand French/English-styled estate there in 1927 (see #339). The Smiths lived in the house on Geddes until their deaths. While the orchard is long gone and houses have been built in its place, the farmhouse remains as a reminder of the area's agricultural past.

338 9 Geddes Heights
Walter and Esther Nichols House   1894

On January 29, 1907, Walter Hammond Nichols and his wife Esther (Conner) made one of the great and lasting contributions to the University of Michigan and the City of Ann Arbor by donating 27 acres of land to the University for a botanical garden. It was Professors of

Botany George P. Burns and Frederick C. New-combe who conceived of creating botanical gardens at the U-M, and it was Burns who convinced the Nichols to donate their farm to the University. Named Nichols Arboretum in 1923, it was designed by Professor O.C. Simmons with Professor Aubrey Tealdi planting many of the trees and shrubs seen today. With additional land from the City of Ann Arbor and Detroit Edison, the park and botanical garden has become the crown jewel of the city known for its parks and natural areas.

Walter Hammond Nichols and his new bride Esther Conner Nichols started a fruit farm on the property in 1894 and built this imposing Queen Anne home. By 1898, they moved to Boulder, Colorado and later on to Palo Alto, California where Walter Nichols became a highly regarded principal and educator.

The home is a restrained take on the Queen Anne style that was coming into fashion in the later 19th century. The facade retains the typical asymmetry, multiple bay windows, rooflines, and porches. The attached garage and windows are more recent additions.

Vacant for many years, the home was eventually sold to Botany Professor Frederick C. Newcombe and his wife Susan (Eastman) in May of 1907. The Newcombes lived in the home until 1923, when Newcombe left the University of Michigan.

2301 Highland

James Inglis House

339

1927

Near the Nichols Arboretum, this imposing residence once known as "The Highlands" was built for Detroit industrialist James Inglis in 1927 as part of an exclusive subdivision on the eastern edge of town. It was at the rear of farmland his sister Kate Smith and her husband Frank had purchased in 1895 as a retreat from urban life (see #337).

"Inglis House" reportedly cost $250,000 and is designed to resemble a French château with some English Country elements. Nestled away from the bustle of Ann Arbor since 1950 it has been owned by the University of Michigan, which uses it as a guest house and reception center for visiting dignitaries, including President Gerald Ford, the king of Thailand, and the Dalai Lama.

The residence was designed by Lilburn "Woody" Woodworth, a friend of the family. It has 12 rooms with servants' quarters, a caretaker's cottage, a three-car garage, a greenhouse, workshop, and pump house. Unusual features at the time of construction included electrically operated garage doors, separate wash bowls, a golf course, and tennis courts. The lush gardens were often open for public tours when Mrs. Inglis was president of the Ann Arbor Garden Club.

Typical of the French Château style, it has a steeply pitched roof of slate pierced by small dormers, tall chimneys, and an asymmetrical floor plan. The interior has English touches, as in the striking paneled library.

Former IHP

2101 Hill

George W. and Merib Patterson House   1913

The Patterson house is one of the few residential commissions in the city of Ann Arbor designed by architect Albert Kahn (see #295, #301, and #354). Kahn designed it in the stately Georgian Revival style. Built in 1913 of red brick, the home features an unusual copper-shingled roof with five round-topped dormers. The symmetrical front facade features large porches fronting the recessed side wings. The home has a deep setback from Hill Street and sits on an unusually large 2.15-acre lot.

George W. Patterson was a distinguished physics and electrical engineering professor who held degrees from Yale and MIT. In 1888 he came to the University of Michigan to teach physics, later becoming head of the Department of Engineering Mechanics and Assistant Dean of the Department of Engineering and Architecture. He was the director of the Erie and Kalamazoo Railroad, and in 1921 he became president of the First National Bank of Ann Arbor.

Merib Patterson was also highly educated and accomplished, with a degree from the University of Michigan in 1890. Merib helped her husband with a number of his important research projects, including the translation of Palaz's *Photometry*. She was a member of the Colonial Dames, the Daughters of the American Revolution, and the Indoor Women's Athletic Club of Detroit. An active suffragette, she was president of the Equal Suffrage Association. The Pattersons owned the home until 1943.

2107 Hill
Joseph and Marguerite Bursley House

341

1918

Like his next-door neighbor George W. Patterson (see #340), Joseph Bursley was professor of mechanical engineering at the University of Michigan from 1904 until 1947. He is better remembered for his tenure as Dean of Students and Director of Housing at the University from 1921 to 1947. Bursley is reported to have been somewhat paternalistic in this role, which covered a broad swath of student life, including financial aid, housing, fraternities, and student discipline. Due to his long and distinguished career, Bursley Hall on North Campus is named in his honor.

Bursley and his wife Marguerite (Knowlton) built this large Tudor Revival house in 1918 on a large lot set far back from Hill Street. The home is built of interesting coursed brick with a slate roof. The steep front peaks project from a central hipped roof and the home differs from most Tudor Revivals of the period with a balanced and symmetrical facade. In addition, the home is built from a single, uniform material (brick), with none of the usual half-timbering.

Poet Robert Frost was friends with the Bursleys and stayed with them at this home for several weeks in 1921. Professor Bursley lived in the home until his death in 1950.

342 276 Indian River Place
Keeve Siegel House   1967

Keeve "Kip" Siegel was a giant in the field of nuclear physics in the 1950s, '60s, and '70s. Born in New York City in 1924, Siegel came to Ann Arbor in 1951 to head up the University of Michigan Radiation Lab. From 1957 through 1967 he was a professor in the Department of Electrical Engineering at Michigan. In 1960, he formed the Conductron Corporation, a

multimillion dollar business and a large employer in Ann Arbor. He left the University of Michigan in 1967, and after a disagreement with Conductron's primary financial backer McDonnell-Douglas, Siegel formed KMS Industries in 1969. In May of 1974, KMS Industries was the first company in the world to achieve controlled thermonuclear fusion. Siegel's success as a private entity experimenting with nuclear fusion ran afoul of the Atomic Energy Commission, and he died of a stroke on March 14, 1975 while testifying before Congress.

Besides his legacy in the world of nuclear physics, Siegel left this fantastic Mid-Century Modern home, designed by Robert Metcalf in 1967. Metcalf designed four houses on Indian River Place, and two on neighboring Riverview Drive. Siegel's wealth allowed this home (over 7,000 square feet) to be the largest that Metcalf had ever designed. The home's large plate-glass windows and balconies take advantage of spectacular views of the Huron River and Furstenberg Park.

415 Observatory
Forest Hill Cemetery

343

1858/1874

In the mid-19th century, cemeteries were moving away from churchyards to the outskirts of town where mourners could find peace and solitude in nature. Before 1859, Ann Arbor burials were mainly at what is now Felch Park by the Power Center, too close to the expanding town and University, or at the Fifth Ward Cemetery (see #32) in less fashionable Lower Town. In 1856, a cemetery company chose the Taylor farm in a hilly part of town, and in 1857 hired Col. J.L. Glen of Niles to design the grounds in the new picturesque or "Romantic" style. The cemetery was dedicated in 1859 with a huge parade of marching bands, military companies, and speechmakers. The first burial was that of Benajah Ticknor (see #328).

Forest Hill was inspired by Mt. Auburn Cemetery in Boston, the first Romantic cemetery in the U.S. Like Mt. Auburn, Forest Hill features curved paths that follow the slopes. The popularity of these cemeteries led to the establishment of America's public parks.

In 1874, the well-known Detroit architect Gordon Lloyd designed the office and the sexton's residence as well as the tripartite gates between. James Morwick was the builder and Walker Bros. did the stonework (their names are carved into the stones flanking the entry).

The office and sexton's cottage were built in the Gothic Revival style with lancet windows, a slate roof of many colorful lozenges and diamond patterns, trefoil and quatrefoil designs in the decorative woodwork, and wavy bargeboards curving under the eaves of each gable. The entry and buildings are an interesting melding of the religious and cottage Gothic styles. Note the original roof cresting on the sexton's cottage, some of the last remaining in Ann Arbor. The outbuildings along Geddes also have interesting lozenge roof patterns in asphalt.

After 1859, burials from other cemeteries were moved here and it now holds some 20,000 remains, including cremains and a columbarium. Many of Ann Arbor's 19th- and 20th-century elite can be found here, and ordinary citizens as well. At the entrance is a Civil War Memorial, moved from the front of the Washtenaw County Courthouse in 1954 when the new courthouse was built.

Former IHP

344 227 Orchard Hills
William and Mary Palmer House   1952

William and Mary Palmer asked Frank Lloyd Wright to design a house to fit their newly acquired hilltop property. The Palmers moved in on Christmas of 1952, and 60 years later the home and its surrounding garden are more or less as Wright designed them. Palmer, a professor of economics, said that Wright was not only a great architect but a wonderful human being and a joy to be around.

This house is from Wright's Usonian period when he designed small (2,000 square foot) houses for mass consumption. Begun in 1950, it was built in a pattern of equilateral triangles by local builder Erwin Niethammer.

The triangle shapes are repeated in the interior in furniture, beds, tables, chairs, dishes, and cutlery. The exterior required a lot of unusual materials: "claycraft" brick, perforated ceramic block, and red tidewater cypress. Cantilevered roofs of cedar shingles shelter the house with deep overhangs. The door is hidden from view, a typical feature of Wright houses. It had radiant heat built into the concrete floors which are scored with triangles. Most of the trim was painted "Cherokee Red," Wright's color of choice.

In 2009, it was sold to a San Francisco-based family of University of Michigan alumni. It is meticulously maintained and the only Frank Lloyd Wright house in Ann Arbor is available for short-term rental.

NR, Former IHP

515 Oswego
Burt-Greene House

345

1938

This classic Art Moderne home was designed in 1938 by architect George Brigham as a duplex. Brigham, considered the father of modern architecture in the city of Ann Arbor, designed many spectacular modern homes in the city beginning in 1936, and taught many of the city's future architects at the University of Michigan. He lived in the building's unit 517, while Ms. Anna Burt lived at 515. Brigham only stayed in the building until 1940, when he constructed his home and studio on Oxford Road (see #346). The home was briefly occupied by two generations of the Burt family, who converted the home to single-family use, with George and Ilma Burt living on the first floor.

It became the home of civil engineer and Professor Albert E. Greene and his wife Anna in 1947. Greene was raised in Ann Arbor, where his father was the head of the Engineering Department at the University of Michigan. Albert Greene was a professor and later acting chair of the department until 1912 when he returned to the private sector. He was retired by the time he moved to 515 Oswego.

Despite its original duplex configuration, the home is classic Art Moderne. It is built of cinder block, which, thanks to Brigham, was gaining acceptance as a building material at the time, and features a characteristic upper porch with metal handrail. The asymmetrical facade, front-facing garage, and recessed doorway with masonry screening contribute to its modern appearance. The use of glass block and corner windows were common features of the style and were used extensively in Brigham's other designs, including his own home and studio. It is now owned by Ann Arbor architect Carl Luckenbach and his wife Carol.

346 | 515 Oxford
George Brigham House and Studio 1940

George Brigham is considered Ann Arbor's first modern architect and his home and studio offer an insight into his architectural ideas and vision. Arriving in 1930 to teach at the University of Michigan, he designed over 40 notable modern houses between 1936 and the early 1960s (see #18 and #345). He also made a huge contribution through the students he taught, including the great modern architect Robert Metcalf.

His home and studio were begun in 1940, but by 1941 war-time rationing made building materials scarce; consequently, doors were made on site and trim and interior and exterior details were kept to a minimum, in the spirit of the simplicity and functionality he embraced as an architect. Brigham used exposed concrete block in the interior which was unheard of at the time. Large plate-glass windows and windows that wrapped around the corners of the building let lots of light into the interior. Brigham was also an early proponent of using glass block to increase the amount of interior light. The angled carport and flat rooflines show a debt to Frank Lloyd Wright. The home originally had a large trellis in the front.

Though the property has suffered in recent years as student housing, it retains much of its architectural integrity and is a reminder of Brigham's influence on the post-World War II era.

700 Oxford
Charles and Albertine Lockwood House/Sigma Nu   1910

347

Charles and Albertine Lockwood of Yonkers, New York had two sons, Samuel and Albert, who were on the U-M School of Music faculty after 1907 and 1900 respectively. Once established, their parents joined them and in 1909, began to build this spectacular 10,000-square-foot house, a magnificent example of the Tudor Revival style. Everywhere there are projecting gables with flared tile roofs, half-timber beams both vertical and cross gabled, forming cross and loop patterns on the front facade, emphasized by the brown and white paint scheme. The original windows have been replaced.

Albert built his own house at 1 Hillside Court and Samuel built his house at 800 Oxford (a shingle-style Dutch Colonial radically altered to a Colonial style with pillars in the 1960s). Charles died in 1913 and Albertine in 1919 so they didn't get to enjoy the house for long, but what they could enjoy was astonishing. The interior was filled with ceramic fireplaces, there was a music room with a winding stair to a performance balcony, and a second-floor balcony featuring hammer beams with hanging pendils and pierced quatrefoil designs, looking like a medieval church. Here Albert, a pianist and later Dean of the School of Music, and Samuel, a violinist and composer, could play to their parents' hearts' content, as well as perform with students. It was a real conservatory. According to a descendant in 1999, Albertine was a wonderful gardener, and her sundial still stands at Albert's house on Hillside Court.

The house was sold in 1919 to the Gamma Nu chapter of the Sigma Nu fraternity, and it is still their home. The fraternity was formed in 1869 at the Virginia Military Institute in opposition to the hazing and obedience policies of the time. They emphasized brotherhood and replaced fear with fellowship. The Ann Arbor chapter was founded in 1902 and first occupied 915 Oakland (see #307).

Former IHP

348 7 Regent
Joseph and Julia Morris House   1965

Dr. Joseph Morris was a cardiologist and pioneer in the field of cardiac surgery. Morris, along with Dick Sarns, developed many of the tools and techniques that make heart surgeries safe and possible. His wife Julia was a nursing instructor at the University of Michigan, an active environmentalist, and longtime member of the Ecology Center. The Morrises left the 240-acre Morris-Reichert preserve in Livingston County to the Southeast Michigan Land Conservancy.

The Morrises waited two years for a plan from the Midland architect Alden Dow. Dow designed a total of 18 buildings in Ann Arbor, including the Fleming Administration Building (see #226) and the much-altered Larcom Municipal Building (City Hall) (see #57). The Morris House is one of only three residential commissions in the city, which include a home he designed for his sister Margaret Towsley in 1932 (see #333) and the 1950 Hoobler House at 2228 Belmont. This house exhibits Dow's characteristically heavy fascia, softened by tapering in toward the house. The south elevation features an interesting porch structure, screened from the street by a brick wall, and supported in the back by two-story columns. As with the porch structure, the entire front of the building offers complete privacy from the street. Dow also designed much of the furniture for the home, including built-ins in the kitchen. The current owner, Howard Shapiro, is an active member of A2 Modern and opened his home for a fundraiser in 2013.

1608 S. University
Angell School

1922

349

In 1920 and 1922, Ann Arbor taxpayers passed bond issues to build new school buildings in the rapidly expanding town. Built as an elementary and junior high school in 1922 at a cost of $280,000, Angell School was the smallest of the new school buildings, with a capacity of 250 students. Originally called the South University Elementary, the building was renamed for former University of Michigan President James Burill Angell.

Built in the Collegiate Gothic style, extremely popular for academic buildings of the era, it features brick with stone trimmings around the windows, doors, and cornice. The school has a central Gothic entrance flanked by side wings highlighted by large bay windows with stone trimmings, and Mission-style parapets. The school features a central auditorium and originally housed a cooperative nursery school and a "fresh air room." "Fresh air rooms" were a popular experiment in education at the time, when it was thought that fresh and cold air benefited students who were ill. The building was added onto in 1976 and 2007, but retains its historic character.

350 2001 Vinewood
Albert J.J. and Blanche Rousseau House   1928

This home is another one of Ann Arbor's fine 20th-century residences designed and inhabited by a professor of architecture at the University of Michigan. A native of Quebec, Albert J.J. Rousseau was trained at the École Nationale et Speciale des Beaux-Arts in Paris, and came to the U.S. to teach at the University of Michigan in 1917. Rousseau designed many

landmark buildings during the 1920s, including the Phi Kappa Sigma fraternity (see #352), the facade of the Land Title Building (see #163), St. Mary's Student Chapel (see #106), the recently demolished Anberay Apartments that stood at 619 E. University, and the fabulous Art Deco Masonic Temple, demolished in 1976.

For his own home, Rousseau chose the same light-colored brick he used on many of his other local commissions, punctuated by bands and window lintels of darker brick. This is a late incarnation of the Prairie style, which was popular from 1900 to 1920, and owes much to Frank Lloyd Wright's early buildings. The nearly flat roof, bands of dark brick, and large overhangs are all characteristic and are used to emphasize a low, horizontal aspect. Albert J.J. Rousseau died in 1931 and his wife Blanche (Towne) remained in the home until 1937.

Following the Rousseaus, the highly regarded Cuban-born Professor of Romance Languages Julio Del Toro and his wife Marguerite (Skipper) lived in the home for many years. Beautifully restored and maintained, it is one of the few examples of the Prairie style in the city. Later owners Carolyn Burk and Richard Cicone received a Preservation Award from the Historic District Commission in 1989.

Former IHP

1437 Washtenaw
Phi Delta Theta Fraternity

351

1903

This 8,000-square-foot Georgian Revival was built by the Phi Delta Theta fraternity as their first permanent residence at the University of Michigan. Founded in 1864, the chapter was the seventh fraternity on campus. Distinguished members of the fraternity included football star Tom Harmon, General Motors president Roger Smith, and football announcer Bob Ufer.

The fine 1860s home of Professor Andrew Ten Brook stood on this site until demolished for the construction of this building. Built by the Koch Brothers (see #55, #122, #155, and #301) in 1903, the imposing residence rests on a high stone foundation. The building is clad in red brick with corner quoins, a hallmark of the Georgian Revival style. Other Georgian features are the round windows with keystones above and below the porch. The wood cornice features carved modillions and a built-in gutter system. The symmetrical facade is broken into three parts, with the recessed central portion featuring a large porch, with flared Doric columns and a small central pediment.

SR

352 1443 Washtenaw
Phi Kappa Sigma/
Trotter Multicultural Center   1924

"When this brick Prairie Style fraternity was built, it cost a staggering $125,000," wrote alumnus Edmund G. Love in a 1988 article in the *Ann Arbor Observer*. Love also noted that by 1932, in the midst of the Depression, they were so financially strapped that they gave him paying work only after he recruited a dozen new members. He reminisced that "…no matter how broke I was…I spent the day in a very posh atmosphere. The Phi Kappa Sigma house… sat on a huge plot of land…on Michigan's fraternity row, and had sweeping lawns, front and back, with a stand of great trees surrounding it."

The house was designed by local architect and University of Michigan Professor of Architecture Albert J.J. Rousseau (see #106, #163, #350). Its style references Frank Lloyd Wright with its full front porch with brick piers and low sloping hipped roof. Much of the interior has been altered but the original fireplace remains in the lounge and some original fixtures flank the entry.

In 1971, the University of Michigan purchased it for use as a center for African-American students following years of unrest on campus. It was named the Trotter House in honor of William Monroe Trotter, the first African-American to receive a Phi Beta Kappa key at Harvard. Trotter dedicated his life to battling oppression as a newspaper editor and businessman. He was one of the founders of the NAACP in 1909.

In 1981, the house was renamed the Trotter Multicultural Center and became a center for diversity as part of MESA, the Multi-Ethnic Student Affairs unit of the LSA College. In 2005, after more student protests, over $1 million was spent on upgrades to the infrastructure and exterior.

Former IHP

1547 Washtenaw
Frieze-Wilgus-Dodge House

353

1860

This fine example of the Italianate villa style, with its arched windows, bracketed eaves, and widow's walk on the hipped roof, was built for Professor Frieze in 1860. This was the country then and seven acres came with the property. Frieze had stonemasons from Guelph, Ontario (Canada) work the local fieldstone. It was highly unusual to build a house completely of fieldstone and no other example exists in Ann Arbor. Butternut and walnut were used on the interior, which had eleven-foot ceilings.

Frieze was a professor of Latin at the University of Michigan after 1854 and served three times as acting president. He and his wife lived here until 1870, when they moved to Cornwell and Ingalls. Evart Scott purchased the property and added the cupola. In 1898, it was sold to Horace Wilgus, a professor of law. He and his descendants (Caroline Wilgus Dodge) lived in the house until 1958 when it was subdivided into two apartments.

In 1969, Geoff and Theo Shepherd purchased it and restored it to single-family use. They were instrumental in establishing the Washtenaw/Hill Historic District and were recognized with a Bicentennial Award in 1976. Later owners Fred and Edith Bookstein received a Preservation Award in 2003.

NR, WHHD

354 1555 Washtenaw
Campbell-Hays House   1899

This textbook example of a Georgian Revival house, with its Palladian window over a central entry, symmetry of windows and doors, end chimneys, and gabled dormers was built for University of Michigan Professor of Chemistry Edward DeMille Campbell and designed by Detroit architect Albert Kahn. Campbell was part of Ann Arbor's elite—his father had been Dean of the Law School and on the Michigan Supreme Court and his wife was the sister of industrialist Marvin Ives (see #299). Campbell had been blinded in an accident and instructed Kahn to design his house for his ease in the same way he had altered his previous residence (see #300). According to Professor Emil Lorch, this was Kahn's first residence after organizing the firm of Nettleton, Kahn and Trowbridge.

It is a wood frame structure with a brick veneer, a popular construction technique in the early 20th century. It has fine interior woodwork, wide and spacious stairways, and a wood-paneled study. The porcelain keyholes, door handles, and marble fixtures in the bathroom are original.

When Campbell died, the house was left to his six children. A daughter, Mary Lavinia Ives Campbell, remained in Ann Arbor and purchased it with her husband, James Griffith Hays, in 1929 and remained until her death in 1978. In 1979, Holde and Robert Borcherts purchased the home and restored it, for which they have received several awards from the Historic District Commission, including one in 2013.

SR, WHHD

1917 Washtenaw

355

Dean Myers House/Unitarian Church   1917/1948/1955

This property consists of three distinct but attached buildings. The first was a private home, built in the Swiss Chalet style for physician Dean Myers, his daughter, and his mother-in-law. This cut fieldstone building was constructed by local contractors Weinberg and Kurtz who were so proud of it that they featured it on their checks. In 1923, Myers, a widower, married Eleanor Sheldon. In 1946, they sold the house and moved into Hildene Manor (see #321).

The house is a landmark on Washtenaw Avenue with its broad sloping roofline facing the street, its carved wooden balustrade on the second-floor balcony with columns attaching it to the carved woodwork in the attic area (the Swiss Chalet part). A broad band runs across the building above the first floor, simulating a porch line and giving it a Craftsman look, as

do the exposed rafters under the roof eaves. It still has some of the earliest metal casement windows in town.

The Unitarian Church, formerly located at State and Huron, had a dwindling membership when they moved here in 1946, but later expanded with two new buildings. In 1948 they added a parsonage on the rear (at an angle to the house—one floor at a time) and in 1955 hired George Brigham to design the addition to the south side of the building. It has a glass wall that faces Washtenaw, in sharp contrast to the stone house, and it is a wide expansive space with exposed wood beams under the porch roof and a sunken garden on the Berkshire side. Brigham (see #346), often called Ann Arbor's first modern architect, was a member of the congregation and a University of Michigan Professor of Architecture influenced by Frank Lloyd Wright.

After more growth, the church sold the buildings in 1999 to Kei and Christian Constantinov who opened a bed and breakfast that year named the Vitosha Guest Haus. It is now the Stone Chalet Bed and Breakfast.

Former IHP

407

ANN ARBOR HILLS

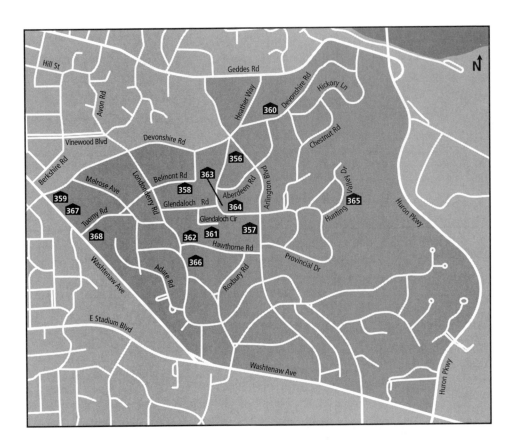

The Ann Arbor Hills neighborhood is a disorientating maze of streets, and a quiet and private oasis within the city. The neighborhood contains one of the finest collections of Mid-Century Modern buildings in the state. Historically, the area made up the farm of the Tuomy family (see #368), who ran a successful dairy and bred racehorses, sheep, and cows. Development began during the 1910s, when Leander Hoover built his imposing mansion on Washtenaw (see #367). By the 1920s, houses were being built along Devonshire (see #359) and a few others were constructed on Arlington, including the interesting Art Moderne-style home built by W. Carl and Maude Rufus in 1938 (see #357).

The post-World War II building boom transformed the neighborhood. Land continued to be subdivided into smaller parcels and subdivisions into the 1970s, and Mid-Century Modern-style houses were built for professors and wealthy citizens seeking to get away from the noise of the city. A who's who of Mid-Century Modern architects, most connected to the University of Michigan, designed homes in the neighborhood.

The internationally known architect William Muschenheim designed his own home in Ann Arbor Hills in 1954 (see #363). Edward Olencki and Joseph Albano, students of Mies van der Rohe, also designed a home on Heather Way (see #364). Noted architects George Brigham, David Osler (see #360 and #365), Walter Sanders (see #358), and Herb Johe (see #361) all designed distinctive Mid-Century Modern residences in the neighborhood. Robert Metcalf, Ann Arbor architect and professor at the University of Michigan, designed numerous homes in the neighborhood, including his own home in 1952 (see #356), as well as a home for world-famous physicist David Dennison (see #362).

A rash of demolitions have occurred in Ann Arbor Hills in the past decade, where smaller ranches are being torn down to build large mansions. These demolitions and a new appreciation for the Mid-Century Modern style has led to the creation of A2 Modern, a group which seeks to educate and foster an appreciation for these innovative post-war buildings.

356 1052 Arlington
Robert and Bettie Metcalf House · 1952

Robert Metcalf is one of Ann Arbor's premier Mid-Century Modern architects, having designed 68 residences in the city, including some of the city's Mid-Century Modern landmarks. Metcalf served as Dean of the University of Michigan School of Architecture from 1974 to 1986. He first came to Ann Arbor in 1941 to study architecture, but his studies were delayed by his distinguished service in the Army during World War II. Following the war, Metcalf began an internship with pioneering modern architect George Brigham (see #346), and served as Brigham's chief draftsman.

Begun in 1952, the house took 13 months to complete, and was only 1,080 square feet. Additions in 1972 and 1987 doubled the size of the house. The building served as a showcase for Metcalf's architectural practice, which began in 1953. Robert and his wife Bettie (Sponseller) Metcalf built most of the house themselves, working on the project in the evenings following their day jobs. Bettie was later the bookkeeper and secretary for Robert's architectural practice.

The low flat roof, massive plate-glass sidelight and windows were typical of the post-War modern architecture of Ann Arbor, in which Metcalf was hugely influential. The clerestory windows that wrap around the main block of the house allow large amounts of light into the house, while retaining privacy. Robert Metcalf still resides in the home, and has recently designed a larger garage addition. He received an award in 2008 from the Historic District Commission for 50 years of preservation.

1334 Arlington
W. Carl and Maude Rufus House

357

1938

The Art Moderne style of this home, with its flat rooflines, asymmetrical facade, corner-casement and large plate-glass windows, smooth stucco walls, and unadorned roof/wall junctions was an uncommon residential style during the 1930s and 1940s. The Rufus home

is built of concrete block covered in stucco and features glass block around the front door. The uneven terrain of the property allows for ground floor terraces on each of the home's two stories. The unusual "moon gate" arch in the front yard, a traditional feature of aristocratic Asian gardens, was originally surrounded by lush plantings and a pond, and was inspired by the 10 years that the Rufuses spent in Korea.

The unorthodox architectural details and style of the Rufus house befit the interesting lives led by its original owners, W. Carl and Maude Rufus. Will Carl Rufus served as a Methodist pastor for two years in Michigan, and was a teacher of mathematics and astronomy in Korea, before being hired as acting director of the Detroit Observatory (see #206) at the University of Michigan in 1917. He became internationally known for his work on Cepheid variables and the pulsating phenomenon, and his studies of the history of astronomy. Maude (Squire) Rufus was W. Carl's college sweetheart and shared her husband's interest in Asian culture. Both played an active role in helping Asian students at the University of Michigan. Later in life Maude Rufus took up aviation, serving in the Civil Air Patrol during World War II, and in 1942 wrote a book titled *Flying Grandma, or Going Like 60*. She died in 1945 from injuries she sustained in a plane crash. W. Carl Rufus died a year later in September of 1946.

Current owners Kenneth and Elizabeth Nesbit received a Preservation Award in 2012 for their 30 years of stewardship.

358 2250 Belmont

Oscar and Minerva Eberbach House 1950

This is one of only three houses in the city designed by the acclaimed architect Walter Sanders. Walter Sanders was a founding member of the International Congress of Modern Architecture, begun in 1929 to promote the principles of modern architecture around the world (see #363). He was an instructor at Columbia University in New York when he was

invited to come to the University of Michigan as a lecturer in 1947. In 1949, he became a full professor, and served as Chair of the Architecture Department from 1954 to 1964. Along with Professor Theodore Larson (see #375), Sanders was active in the development of the unistrut system of home building, and his own home in Barton Hills is one of the few houses in the area to be built using this metal framing method. Sanders' design for the Eberbach home is a unique expression of the Mid-Century Modern style. It is more geometric and cube-like than its ground-hugging Mid-Century Modern neighbors, and features unusual screens that project from the front facade over the front windows.

The singular appearance of the house would seem to be a surprising choice for the 69-year-old Oscar Eberbach, though Ann Arbor has always attracted unorthodox and progressive people, many of whom built houses that fit their eccentric and forward-looking tastes. Eberbach was a native of Ann Arbor and the owner of Eberbach and Co., founded by his grandfather Christian Eberbach (see #325) in 1843. In 1868, Eberbach and Company began manufacturing scientific and medical equipment, and it remains one of Ann Arbor's oldest companies. The Eberbachs lived in the home until 1970.

Current owners Jane and James Kister received a Preservation Award in 2012 from the Historic District Commission for their 20 years of stewardship.

2010 Devonshire
Powell-Abbott House

359

1928

This textbook example of the Tudor Revival style stands out in an area of grand and stately houses. The multiple steeply pitched rooflines are graced with a multicolored slate roof, while false half-timbering and stucco break up a facade that is mostly built of clinker brick and randomly coursed ashlar. The chimney is built of stone, topped with fanciful curved terra-cotta. The house boasts leaded glass casement windows, some with diamond panes and others with stained glass crests in the center. Extensive and lush grounds on the large corner lot are surrounded by a brick and iron fence with stone posts capped with slate tops.

The house was built in 1928 by Chester and Margaret Powell. The Powells only lived in the house for two years and sold the house to Horatio and Florence Abbott in 1930. Horatio Abbott was owner of the Abbott Gasoline Co., which distributed oil and gasoline to ten gas stations in Ann Arbor. He was on the boards of the Farmers and Mechanics Bank and the Ann Arbor Artificial Ice Company (see #7). Abbott served in local offices, including registrar of deeds and eight years as postmaster. He was active in the Democratic Party, including a stint as state chair, was a member of the Democratic National Committee, and was an unsuccessful candidate in a number of state political races. Horatio Abbott died in 1936, and by 1939 the house was vacant. In 1942, the home became the longtime residence of Raymond and Elizabeth Spokes, who were active in the Sesquicentennial Celebration in 1974 and founders of the Ann Arbor Historical Foundation (the publisher of this book).

360 2855 Devonshire
Raymond and Anne Chase House
1968

This refreshing take on modernism was designed in 1968 by Ann Arbor architect David Osler (see #373). Showing the diversity and eclecticism of Osler's designs, the home is built around a central, flat-roofed section with large overhangs and walls of windows. A series of gable-roofed sections break from the purely Mid-Century Modern tradition of blending into the surrounding landscape, giving an air of a Vernacular Midwestern farmstead. These Post-Modern gabled portions break the home into separate zones while providing additional ceiling height and light.

The home was built for Raymond Chase, an executive at the Dundee Cement Co., and his wife Anne, who still owns the house today. The gabled sections were an attempt to align the modern home's appearance with his clients' more conservative tastes by making the home relate to the traditional sense of what a house should look like. The house backs onto a ravine and creek, and Osler made the home very private from the front, while open to the tranquil backyard.

1336 Glendaloch Circle
Walter and June Holcombe House

361

1959

Designed a few years after a trip to study church architecture in Sweden in 1956, University of Michigan Professor of Architecture Herb Johe's design for the Holcombe House was deeply influenced by Scandinavian architecture. The home is boxy, with no overhangs and tall narrow windows. The vertical wood siding is both typical of the era and influenced by the architecture of Scandinavia. The covered walkway to the garage is similar to Robert Metcalf's Dennison House (see #362). Visitors who have been inside are struck by its beauty, and the wonderful and light open spaces. The Holcombes gave Johe free rein, which is perhaps why this was Johe's favorite of the residences he designed in the city. He designed nine homes in Ann Arbor, and his own home in Barton Hills. Johe was also a noted watercolor artist. Johe's collection of Mid-Century Modern furniture is now on display at the U-M Museum of Art.

The first owner of the home, Walter Holcombe was a researcher and administrator for Parke-Davis in Ann Arbor. He and his wife June lived in the home from 1959 until 1970. Thomas Rowe, Dean of the College of Pharmacy from 1951–1975, and his wife Georgia lived in the house until 1987.

Current owner Glenn Watkins received a Preservation Award in 2012 from the Historic District Commission for his 25 years of stewardship.

362 2511 Hawthorne

David and Helen Dennison House   1954

Built in 1954, the year of his first commission (see #332), this Robert Metcalf-designed home was the residence of world-famous physics professor and researcher David Dennison and his wife Helen (Johnson).

Professor Dennison was well known and respected for his contributions to spectroscopy and quantum mechanics, first becoming known for his work on the specific temperature of

hydrogen gas in 1927, which gained him wide recognition in the field of molecular physics. That year he came to teach at his Alma Mater, the University of Michigan, where he made advances in microwave spectroscopy and particle accelerators. He served as chair of the Physics Department from 1955 through 1965. Always intellectually curious, Dennison undertook many experiments in the basement and office of this home. Dennison Physics and Astronomy Building, built in 1963 on the University of Michigan's campus, is named in his honor.

Unlike many of Metcalf's other commissions, the Dennison home features a shallow gable roof, rather than the typical flat roof. An unusually long overhang spans 37 feet, from the home's entry to the garage, protecting residents and the front of the garage from the weather. The elevated front deck is unusual among the modern houses of the era.

1251 Heather Way
William Muschenheim House

1953

Influential modern architect William Muschenheim's own home on Heather Way is another landmark of modern architecture in the city. Its low, almost wing-like appearance is striking and stands out even in a neighborhood filled with spectacular examples, such as the Metcalf House (see #356). Large trapezoidal windows on the front and back elevations fill the interior with light, and along with the blank exterior panels, highlight the home's geometric nature.

The multi-leveled interior is made possible by the home's site on a small hill, which allows the sweeping shape to remain uninterrupted, while allowing five internal levels. The home had 32 colors inside and out, a feature that the color theorist Muschenheim was known for.

Born in New York City in 1902, William Muschenheim was a well-known and respected architect when he arrived to teach at the University of Michigan in 1950. He designed many renowned modern buildings on the East Coast in the 1930s and 1940s, including renovations to the Astor Hotel, the Bath Houses on the dunes on Long Island, and the Marine Transportation building at the 1939 World's Fair. Along with Mies van der Rohe, Muschenheim was a member of the influential International Congress of Modern Architects. Muschenheim taught in the Architecture and Design Department until 1973, where he introduced new material to the curriculum, emphasizing the integration of disciplines including sociology, history, philosophy, and economics with architecture.

Current owners Karl and Kristin Shaffer won a Preservation Award in 2010 from the Historic District Commission recognizing their 10 years of care.

364 2601 Heather Way
Leonard Eaton House   1962

Though Leonard Eaton studied architectural history, he was also a student and fan of modern architecture, choosing the style for his own home completed in 1962 and designed by his colleagues in the College of Architecture, Edward Olencki (see #42) and Joseph Albano (see #43). Unassuming and somewhat plain from the street, the design allows the living areas to be screened from public view. The home was built as a series of connected

boxes that open onto inner courtyards, which bring large amounts of light and a feeling of the outdoors into the house, while achieving privacy. A large courtyard is off the main living areas, while smaller ones are off the bedrooms. The free-standing carport shares design elements with the house and features glass-free openings similar to the clerestory windows found on many modern homes of the era.

Born in Minneapolis, Leonard Eaton studied at Harvard under Arthur Schlesinger Sr. before coming to Ann Arbor to teach at the University of Michigan in 1950. A full professor of architectural history in 1963, he studied and wrote extensively about the Chicago School of Architecture and Frank Lloyd Wright. Along with his wife Ann, Eaton collected interviews and information about Frank Lloyd Wright's Palmer House (see #344), which was turned into a book. In 1977, the Eatons built another house in town that was designed by Robert Metcalf.

Current owner Carol Amster (and her late husband Herbert) has maintained this home since 1978 and was given a Preservation Award in 2012.

3020 Hunting Valley

John Jr. and Blythe Airey House

365

1962

This fine Mid-Century Modern home was built by John Airey Jr. and his wife Blythe M., who lived here from 1962 until 1988. John Airey Jr. was president of the Trilex Corporation of Wayne, Michigan, which manufactured die-cast decorative hardware, primarily for the automotive industry. The company's CIMCO division was located on South Industrial in Ann Arbor.

Set on a beautiful wooded lot, the home was designed by Ann Arbor architect David Osler (see #373). Elements of Osler's design resemble the works of Alden Dow from the period, with its flat roof and unusually heavy fascia, which is clad in copper in Osler's design. Simple in appearance from the street, the home is quite sprawling; at 3,338 square feet, it is the largest home that Osler designed. John Airey Jr. gave Osler a budget and a few requirements, including a nuclear bomb shelter, but allowed Osler relatively free rein to design the house as he pleased. The result is one of Osler's personal favorites. A porch spans most of the home's front, and is supported by five masonry columns, creating an unusual long colonnade. More typical are the lack of windows on the front facade, creating a sense of privacy from the street. Additional light was brought into the interior by eleven custom-made pyramidal skylights on the home's flat roof and a series of internal garden spaces.

366 | 2417 Londonderry
Theodore and Joanne Kabza House　　　　　　　1961

From 1961 through 1997, this striking Mid-Century Modern residence was the home of Theodore and Joanne Kabza. Following a stint in the U.S. Army Medical Corps, Theodore Kabza graduated from the University of Michigan Medical School in 1945. Kabza was a staff member at the Veterans Administration Hospital in Ann Arbor and at St. Joseph Mercy Hospital, as well as an instructor of internal medicine at the University.

For their Ann Arbor Hills home, the Kabzas hired architect Robert Pond, an apprentice of Frank Lloyd Wright at Taliesin from 1949 to 1954. Pond came to Ann Arbor to work for George Brigham (see #346). Pond's design for the Kabza House owes a huge debt to Wright's Usonian houses, with its large overhangs, clerestory windows, carport, obscured entry, and L-shaped floor plan. In contrast to its more conventional Mid-Century Modern neighbors, the house is sited at an angle on the lot. In the Wright tradition, the medium-toned brick, natural wood, and copper fascia help blend the house into the natural landscape of the lot and neighborhood.

Pond went on to work on many of Wright's later projects and later taught at Indiana University in Bloomington for many years. Though the Ann Arbor Hills neighborhood is filled with spectacular Mid-Century Modern homes, Robert Pond's Kabza House stands out in design and materials, and is a great example of Frank Lloyd Wright's massive influence.

2015 Washtenaw

367

Hoover Mansion

1917

One of Ann Arbor's only examples of a French Château-style house was designed by local architect Rupert Koch for Leander J. Hoover, founder of the Hoover Steel Ball Company. Hoover became very rich when ball bearings ceased to be imported from Germany because of World War I. Unfortunately, he died in the flu epidemic of 1918 and didn't enjoy his home very long.

The house and grounds cost $350,000 at the time, and there was a small theater and ballroom on the third floor. The 24-acre site included a greenhouse, gazebo, and extensive gardens. The house is made of smooth-cut limestone with a characteristic steep slate roof, extremely tall stone end chimneys, a classical balustrade fronting the driveway, copper gutters and trim, and dormers in the attic.

In 1922, the estate was purchased from the family by the Kappa Sigma fraternity but was vacant for most of the 1930s. It was almost razed but was rescued at the last minute by Carrol Benz and his wife in 1946. They renovated it and sold it to the Tau Delta Phi fraternity in 1950.

In 1968, it became the headquarters for Youth for Understanding, who moved out in 1978 leaving it empty again. Later that year it was opened to the public for a Designer's Showcase, where decorators helped raise money for Mott Hospital. It is now the headquarters for University Bank, which moved here in 2005.

Former IHP

368 2117 Washtenaw
Bell-Spaulding/Tuomy House
1854/1864

This clapboard house in the Italianate style with bracketed eaves at the roofline and full front porch was built for Frederick A. and Almina S. Spaulding in 1864. They led a quiet life in retirement here after arriving from upstate New York in 1863. Spaulding's children Frederick and Volney were members of the University of Michigan faculty—Frederick a doctor and Volney a botanist and founder of the University Botanical Gardens. They built their house in front of an earlier house constructed in 1854 by George W. and Jane E. Bell in the Greek Revival style.

The house is a typical Italianate, with a hipped roof on a cube-shaped structure, paired four-over-four arched windows capped by a small pediment, eared trim on the first floor, and painted grisaille glass in the double entry doors. Much of the exterior (with its antique screen door) and interior remain, including a marbleized slate fireplace, curving walnut staircase, and escutcheon on the chimney.

Known as the Tuomy House for many years, the house and 214 acres were purchased in 1874 by Patrick and Cornelius Tuomy. Cornelius lived here eleven years before marrying Julia Ann Kearney. Both were descendants of early Irish pioneers of Washtenaw County. They bred winning racehorses, sheep, and cows, and ran a successful dairy farm.

Two of their children, Kathryn and Cornelius W. ("Bill"), formed a partnership as a realty and insurance company and developed the subdivision known as Tuomy Hills. As the city grew they built the Tuomy Hills Gas Station in 1927 (see #322), which also housed their firm Tuomy and Tuomy.

When Bill Tuomy died in 1966, he willed the property to the city for a historic purpose. In 1968, an agreement was signed giving the property to the University, which left many of the original furnishings and rented it to the Historical Society of Michigan (HSM). HSM was given the house in 1983, and renovated it in 1998, for which they received many accolades. The Society moved to Lansing in 2005, and the house has been sold and returned to single-family use.

NR, SR, Former IHP

NORTH CAMPUS/ FAR EAST SIDE

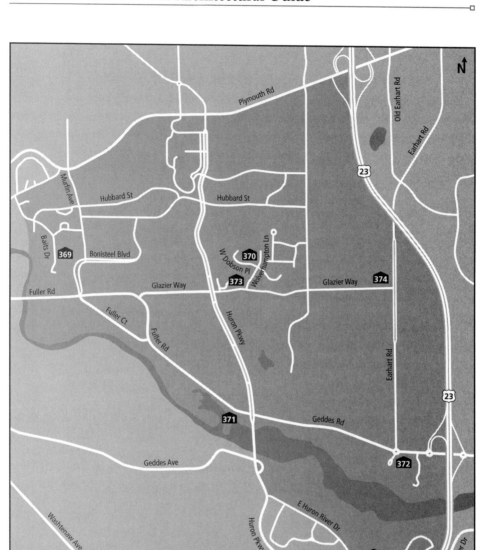

The far eastern edge of Ann Arbor remained quite rural into the 1950s and 1960s, with a number of the developments in this area staying part of Ann Arbor Township until quite recently. A few pioneer farmhouses can still be found here, including the 1836 home of Orrin White (see #371), who was the first white settler in Ann Arbor Township. In the 1910s and 1920s, large "gentleman farms" were developed in this part of town (see #370 and #372) due to the picturesque landscape and the area's proximity to the city. The rural character of the area persisted until the 1950s when the fast-growing University of Michigan developed the farmland along Plymouth Road and Fuller Road as its North Campus. The University hired the innovative architect and designer Eero Saarinen to develop a plan for the campus, and to design the E.V. Moore School of Music (see #369). Parke-Davis (later Pfizer) built a research facility at Plymouth and Green Roads, which also encouraged the development of suburban-style neighborhoods in the area during the 1960s.

Since 2008, the University of Michigan has been developing the North Campus Research Complex, spread across the 28 buildings and two million square feet of the former Pfizer Complex. The city has turned large tracts of land into areas of public recreation, including Gallup Park and the Huron Hills Golf Course.

369 1000 Baits
Earl V. Moore School of Music Building   1963

Eero Saarinen is one of the giants of Mid-Century Modern architecture. Born in Finland in 1910, Saarinen came to the United States in 1923 with his father, Eliel Saarinen, legendary architect and designer of the Cranbrook campus in Bloomfield Hills. Eero first gained recognition for his furniture with the influential "Tulip Chair," which he designed in collaboration with Cranbrook classmate Charles Eames. His most famous buildings include the General Motors Tech Center in Warren, designed in collaboration with his father, the Jefferson National Expansion Memorial (St. Louis Arch), the MIT Chapel in Cambridge, Massachusetts, and the TWA Flight Center at JFK Airport.

In 1951, Eero Saarinen designed a plan for the University of Michigan's North Campus and the School of Music Building, one of the early buildings on the new campus. He was soon diagnosed with a brain tumor, and died in Ann Arbor on September 1, 1961.

Overlooking a pond, the School of Music Building is a multi-leveled structure with flanking wings. It is clad in tan-colored brick, known as "Cranbrook buff" after similarly colored buildings that were designed by both Saarinens on the Cranbrook campus. This brick color is found on a majority of the later North Campus buildings, and was part of Saarinen's attempt to make the buildings harmonize with the natural landscape. Though many of the interior spaces are obsolete or have been outgrown, the historical value of the building is unquestioned. It is Eero Saarinen's only design in Ann Arbor. Today the building is undergoing a multi-million dollar upgrade and expansion.

3215 Dobson
Skylodge/Arnold and Gertrude Goss House

370

1923

Arnold Goss was secretary of the Buick Automobile Company when he began financing Nathaniel B. Wales' home refrigerators, which led to the founding of the Kelvinator Company in 1916. In the early 1920s, Kelvinator held a vast share of the home refrigeration market in the U.S., making Arnold Goss a very wealthy man. He bought 600 acres of land in Ann Arbor Township and built his country estate in 1923, hiring Detroit architect George DeWitt Mason to design the Georgian Revival/Arts and Crafts-style home known as "Skylodge."

The massing of the home is Georgian, with a symmetrical facade, hipped copper roof, matching stone end chimneys, and center entry sheltered by a small portico. The home features double side porches with attached "sun parlors," Arts and Crafts-style overhangs, and exposed rafter tails in the eaves. The grounds were designed by Italian landscape designer Aubrey Tealdi, who was the architect and director of Nichols Arboretum.

Gertrude Goss was an avid gardener and a member of the National Farm and Garden Association and the Ann Arbor Garden Club. Arnold Goss retired from Kelvinator in 1927 and lived the life of a gentleman farmer, raising Jersey cattle and starting the Oaklands Dairy. Despite his successes in life, Arnold Goss suffered from crippling depression and killed himself in 1938. Gertrude Goss died in 1973 at the age of 90. Today the Goss's extensive farmland has been subdivided, but the home still remains on a generous five-acre lot. In recent years, Ian and Sally Bund have restored the home and grounds, with great care taken in preserving the original details of both. They received a Preservation Award in 2002 from the Historic District Commission and donated the house and land with a permanent easement to the Michigan Historic Preservation Network.

Former IHP, MHPN

371 2940 Fuller
Orrin White House

1836

This wonderful cobblestone house is one of eleven in Washtenaw County (see #328) and was constructed in 1836 by Orrin White, who emigrated with his family in 1823 from Palmyra, New York when Michigan was still a territory. When they built their first house here along the Huron River, they were the first settlers in Ann Arbor Township. White purchased 176 acres, and slowly sold off his property until only the house remained.

The family nervously shared their space with many Indians who traveled along the Huron to Canada to collect their treaty gifts from the British. White held many political positions, including Washtenaw County commissioner (1827), sheriff (1832), associate circuit court judge (1833–37), delegate to the State Constitutional Convention, and member of the Michigan Legislature (1842).

In 1836, White's family built this house with cobblestones gathered from the area. They are set in a herringbone pattern on the front elevation while horizontal courses provide contrast at the rear and sides. The deep-set center entry is enhanced by delicately incised columns, handmade glass sidelights, and a massive lintel of oak. Wooden eaves with hex-like symbols decorate the gables. The windows are 12-over-12 on the front facade.

In the 1970s and '80s, Rob and Nan Hodges did a magnificent restoration of the house. They carefully researched the history and its original owners and received a Rehabilitation Award from the Historic District Commission in 1989.

NR, Former IHP

4090 Geddes
Earhart Manor/Concordia University

372

1936

Harry Boyd Earhart, president of the White Star Refining Company, purchased the old Botsford Farm on Geddes Road in 1917. Earhart was a wealthy man thanks to his gas stations and refineries, which he sold to the Vacuum Oil Company in 1930 (later part of Mobil Oil). Earhart and his wife Carrie (Beale) lived in the old farmhouse on the property until 1936, when this French Eclectic-style mansion was built as their retirement home.

Designed by the firm Smith, Hinchman, and Grylls (Smith Group) and built by contractors Bryant and Detweiler, the home features an unusual structure of reinforced concrete faced with hand-chiseled stone. It was one of the first private homes in the nation to have air con-

ditioning. The interior features Pewabic tiles designed for the Earharts by Pewabic's founder Mary Chase Stratton. The placement of the house and the design of the gardens were executed by the Olmsted brothers, John and Frederick Law Jr., the sons of the great landscape architect Frederick Law Olmsted. Other landscape features on the property were designed by E.A. Eichstaedt and Carrie Earhart herself, who was an avid gardener, a founder of the Ann Arbor Garden Club, and president of the Michigan Federated Garden Club.

Enjoying their retirement years, Mrs. Earhart gardened and rode horses, and Mr. Earhart practiced his golf game on his private golf course. In 1929, they founded the Earhart Foundation which funded charitable and religious causes. In 1949, they began supporting conservative economists and think-tanks, including the American Enterprise Institute and Nobel Prize-winning economists such as Milton Friedman and Gary Becker.

Following Harry Earhart's death in 1954, the property was purchased by the Lutheran Church–Missouri Synod, which founded Concordia College on the site. Concordia began as a two-year college, but has grown into Concordia University over the past forty years. In 1997, Concordia undertook a major renovation/restoration of the home, repairing original details and converting the building into the Otto G. Schmid Center. They received the Historic District Commission Project of the Year Award in 1998.

373 3081 Glazier Way
David and Connie Osler House   1961

For over fifty years, David Osler has designed many of Ann Arbor's great Mid-Century Modern buildings, including the Canoe Livery at Gallup Park, St. Clare's Episcopal Church, the John Airey Jr. House (see #365), and the Raymond and Anne Chase House (see #360). Osler grew up in Ann Arbor and in 1946, following service in the Navy, he married his high

school sweetheart, Connie Lorch. Connie was the daughter of influential University of Michigan professor and architect Emil Lorch. Osler first worked for architect Douglas Loree before opening his own practice, David Osler and Associates, in 1958. He set up shop in 1961 in an old power building (see #170).

The Oslers lived in an apartment that David had built in his parents' barn until 1961, when they built this home on his parents' farm. Osler's primary focus in his designs was practicality and usefulness over architectural form, keeping in mind the financial constraints of his clients. With a limited budget, the Oslers hired builder Dick Wagner to construct the home. The outside is a restrained cube covered in cedar shakes. The home's narrow entry leads to bedrooms a half-story down and the primary living area a half-story up. Though the home has been tweaked over the years, it remains very much the way it was in 1961, and is still the home of the Oslers. Recognized over the years for his innovative and creative designs, in 1981 David Osler was a finalist in the competition for the design of the Vietnam War Memorial.

The Oslers received a Preservation Award from the Historic District Commission in 2013, recognizing their 50 years of stewardship of this house and its "aging-in-place" modifications.

3865 Glazier Way
Lemuel and Abi Foster House

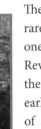

Late 1830s

The Lemuel Foster House is a rare surviving example of the one and one-half story Greek Revival farmhouses built by the thousands during the early years of the settlement of southern Michigan. The highlight of the simple, side-gabled structure is the original classical entrance, with wide pilasters, sidelight and transom windows, and original two-paneled front door. An old lithograph of the house shows a number of bump-outs, or "warts," on the east side of the house, including the small hipped roof addition that remains today. The sympathetic garage addition is believed to date from the mid-20th century.

Lemuel Foster, a pensioner from the War of 1812, came to Ann Arbor Township from Orleans County, New York in 1836. He built the house shortly after his arrival. He worked as a farmer and carpenter in Ann Arbor Township for the next 36 years and was active in the Whig Party, serving as highway commissioner in the Township for 20 years. Lemuel and Abi (Fenn) Foster's son Gustavus L. Foster, a Presbyterian minister in Jackson and Ypsilanti, gained prominence in the state for his strong anti-slavery views and eloquent sermons. Abi Foster died in 1853, followed by Lemuel in 1881. The farm remained in the Foster family well into the 20th century, with son Isaac N.S. Foster and his wife Almira inheriting, along with grandson George N. Foster. It has been in the Samborski family for decades and is well preserved.

375 | 3575 E. Huron River
C. Theodore and Myra Larson House   1953

On a beautiful lot on the banks of the Huron River, the Professor C. Theodore and Myra Larson House is the only one built within the city limits of Ann Arbor using the unistrut system. Unistrut, or strut channel construction, was developed by the Unistrut Corporation of Wayne, Michigan and the University of Michigan's Architectural Research Laboratory which was started by Professor Larson in 1948. Larson's Architectural Research Lab was the first of its kind in the world, and experimented extensively with the unistrut construction during the early 1950s. Unistrut buildings were designed to be prefabricated and were built of metal parts that could be bolted and snapped together by workers with minimal skills. The idea was that the home could be easily constructed at a minimal cost, and be expanded, shrunk, or moved with relative ease. Like Lustron homes (see #285), unistrut was not successful in residential applications, though it is still used extensively in commercial and industrial buildings.

Professor Larson's home, and that of colleague and fellow unistrut developer Walter Sanders' home in Barton Hills, are the only remaining unistrut homes in the area. Built on a crawlspace, the home stands at 1,440 square feet and is a basic rectangular unit, with a projecting carport. It has a very modern appearance, befitting its unusual construction, and features metal siding, clerestory windows, and an unusual flat roof with copper-faced angled fascia. Professor Larson remained director of the Architectural Research Lab until 1973. The home is still owned by Myra Larson, professor emerita in the School of Art and Design.

INDEX